FROM IMPRESSION TO INQUIRY

PSYCHOANALYTIC IDEAS AND APPLICATIONS SERIES

Wolfgang Loch—The Art of Interpretation: Deconstruction and New Beginning in the Psychoanalytic Process
edited and commentary by Peter Wegner

The Unconscious: Further Reflections
edited by José Carlos Calich & Helmut Hinz

Escape from Selfhood: Breaking Boundaries and Craving for Oneness
Ilany Kogan

The Conscious in Psychoanalysis
Antonio Alberto Semi

Talking about Supervision: 10 Questions, 10 Analysts = 100 Answers
edited by Laura Elliot Rubinstein

FROM IMPRESSION TO INQUIRY

A Tribute to the Work of Robert Wallerstein

edited by

Wilma Bucci, Norbert Freedman

Associate Editor

Ethan Graham

Foreword by

Cláudio Laks Eizirik

Psychoanalytic Ideas and Applications Series

Routledge
Taylor & Francis Group
LONDON AND NEW YORK

International Psychoanalytical Association

LONDON

Figures 10.2–10.5 from "The Scales of Psychological Capacities: Measuring Beyond Symptoms", *Psychotherapy Research* (2004), *14*, no. 1, and from "The Scales of Psychological Capacities: Measuring Change in Psychic Structure", *Psychotherapy Research* (2004), *15*, no. 4. By permission of Taylor & Francis (http:/ /www.informaworld.com).

First published 2007 by The International Psychoanalytical Association

2 Park Square, Milton Park, Abingdon, Oxfordshire OX14 4RN
52 Vanderbilt Avenue, New York, NY 10017

Routledge is an imprint of the Taylor & Francis Group, an informa business

First issued in hardback 2019

British Library Cataloguing in Publication Data

A C.I.P. for this book is available from the British Library

Produced for the IPA by Communicatino Crafts

ISBN: 978-1-90588-800-9 (pbk)
ISBN: 978-0-367-32461-2 (hbk)

"From Impression to Inquiry *is more than a tribute to the work of Robert Wallerstein; it is also a homage to his exceptional attitude regarding the problem of agreements, divergences, and uncertainties in psychoanalysis. His famous 'summaries' reveal a very special capacity to combine a strong tendency towards synthesis with an incredible ability to recognize and value the subtlest differences in the positions at stake. As I live in Montevideo, I have not had many opportunities to see Wallerstein, but his ideas have given me strong support at turning points in my own reflections. During the 1980s there was a discussion in Montevideo and Buenos Aires about the degree to which different psychoanalytic theories were coincident, complementary, contradictory, or incommensurable. Wallerstein's 1987 Presidential Address ('One Psychoanalysis or Many') called our attention to the common clinical ground of our hypothesis. But once we accept the existence of many theories, we require better evidence for them. He also showed how to improve the gathering and quantifying of this evidence. His monumental 1986 book* Forty-Two Lives in Treatment *demonstrated that clinical hypothesis could interact in a productive way with empirical research. In* From Impression to Inquiry *we encounter new advances in that direction, finding a wide range of contributions that go from useful detailed information—such as the properties of the Scales of Psychological Capacities—to a critical overview of past and present trends in outcome and process research. The evidence problem is not a simple one, as psychoanalytic practice has to face questions of a different nature. As Wilma Bucci tells us, building the research–practice interface is only possible if we are able to open our minds to multiple complementary perspectives and open our spirit to considerable doses of optimism."*

Ricardo Bernardi

"To a large extent, the trajectory of Robert Wallerstein's career parallels the history of psychoanalysis in the last fifty years. Working in the rolling hills of eastern Kansas in the 1950s, Wallerstein galvanized his colleagues at the Menninger Clinic, insisting that they take psychoanalytic research seriously. In an era when patients were lining up for psychoanalysis, Wallerstein refused to be complacent with the rising prestige the field was enjoying. He had the prescience to realize that the value of psychoanalysis needed to be tested by rigorous scientific methodology. His monumental Psychotherapy Research Project was the result. Wallerstein thus blazed a trail for generations of psychoanalytic researchers to

follow. As pluralism swept the field, Wallerstein was again at the vanguard of the profession, accommodating this development in his 1987 Address at the Montreal IPA Congress. He contextualized the pluralism by identifying the common ground of clinical theory that brought analysts of all persuasions together. In this superb new volume, the contributions of Bob Wallerstein are catalogued and elaborated by colleagues from around the world, all leaders in their own right. The book is a fitting capstone to Wallerstein's illustrious career and will be informative to analysts and mental health professionals of all levels of experience and training."

Glen Gabbard

"As a researcher I view Robert Wallerstein's contributions to the knowledge of the human mind as seminal. When I was a young psychoanalyst interested in research, I was amazed and very encouraged listening to a leading psychoanalyst lecturing on the subject, making it sound obvious that research was not only important for psychoanalysis, but also a legitimate part of a psychoanalyst's working day. Like all other members of the International Psychoanalytical Association, I cannot but deeply appreciate what Bob Wallerstein has done to make research an integral part of the psychoanalytic community's work, allowing me and many others to come into contact with some of the most brilliant minds in research today and to develop our own ideas. His book Forty-Two Lives in Treatment *represented for many working with the more ill patients a landmark for the understanding of how things work in psychoanalysis and psychoanalytic therapy. This and others of his works focus not only on results/outcome but also on how things work and what changes might be expected. The development of the Scales of Psychological Capacities is a landmark in this connection. A book that pays tribute to this modern psychoanalytic renaissance person is both most welcome and necessary. In this volume one can find broad presentations of Wallerstein's work as well as application of his methods and original development of his line of thinking, exemplifying the fruitful relationship between research and the consulting room."*

Sverre Varvin

CONTENTS

IV
The CAMP initiative and looking ahead

EPILOGUE
The Wallerstein summary

PSYCHOANALYTIC IDEAS AND APPLICATIONS SERIES

IPA Publications Committee

The Publications Committee of the International Psychoanalytical Association continues, with this volume, the series: "Psychoanalytic Ideas and Applications".

The aim is to focus on the scientific production of significant authors whose works are outstanding contributions to the development of the psychoanalytic field and to set out relevant ideas and themes, generated during the history of psychoanalysis, that deserve to be discussed by present psychoanalysts.

The relationship between psychoanalytic ideas and their applications has to be put forward from the perspective of theory, clinical practice, technique, and research so as to maintain their validity for contemporary psychoanalysis.

The Publication Committee's objective is to share these ideas with the psychoanalytic community and with professionals in other related disciplines, in order to expand their knowledge and generate a productive interchange between the text and the reader.

It is befitting that this volume, in honour of Robert Wallerstein, is published in this series by the IPA, to whom he gave and is giving so much. We are thankful to the editors, Wilma Bucci, Norbert Freedman, and Ethan Graham, for having brought this remarkable work to us, and to all the contributors for their labour of love. Last but not least, we are grateful to Robert Wallerstein himself for his cooperation and indefatigable attention.

Leticia Glocer Fiorini
Chair, IPA Publications Committee

ACKNOWLEDGEMENTS

This volume began as a special conference of the Collaborative Analytic Multi-site Project (CAMP) of the American Psychoanalytic Association in 2001, celebrating the vision of Robert Wallerstein in bringing together analytic researchers with diverse approaches and diverse methodologies to find their common ground. In the long path from presentations at a conference to a published volume, the editors required and received help from many people. First, we wish to express our heartfelt gratitude to the IPA Publications Committee, and its Chair Leticia Glocer Fiorini, for their interest and support of this work. We were most fortunate to have the guidance of Cesare Sacerdoti of the IPA Publications Committee and the assistance of Rhosyn Tuta and Philippa Hodges; we would like to express our appreciation for their highly professional, knowledgeable, and thoughtful contributions in shaping this volume in its final form. The volume owes much to the copy-editing of Klara King of Communication Crafts. Her clarity of expression, respect for language, and sensitivity to nuance made this a model, in our experience, for collaborative work of a copy editor with authors and editors.

Robert Wallerstein's vision in developing CAMP, now being carried forward as the Research Associates of the American Psychoanalytic Association (RAAPA), represented the formal opening of an institutional base for collaborative psychoanalytic treatment research, with a central emphasis on the integration of research and clinical work. We hope that the publication of this volume, including historical material never previously published concerning the past of psychoanalytic research, critical examination of the present, and looks to the future, will serve to encourage and inspire new efforts to carry forward Robert Wallerstein's integrative vision.

Wilma Bucci, Norbert Freedman

EDITORS AND CONTRIBUTORS

Wilma Bucci (United States) is Professor of Psychology, Derner Institute, Adelphi University; Chair, Research Associates of the American Psychoanalytic Association; Member of Faculty, Research Training Programme of the International Psychoanalytical Association; Visiting Professor in Psychoanalytic Research, University College London; Honorary Member, American Psychoanalytic Association, N.Y. Psychoanalytic Institute and Society, and Institute for Psychoanalytic Training and Research (IPTAR).

Hartvig Dahl (United States) was a graduate of the Residency Program of the Menninger Foundation, Topeka, Kansas. In 1964 he received a Public Health Service Research Scientist Award from the National Institutes of Health and joined the Research Center for Mental Health at New York University, working with Robert Holt and George Klein. In 1972 he joined the faculty of the Department of Psychiatry at the SUNY Downstate Medical Center, Brooklyn, New York, where he established his Research Unit for the Study of Recorded Psychoanalysis. He was a graduate of the San Francisco Psychoanalytic Institute and later became a member of the New York Psychoanalytic Institute and Society, where he served as Director of Research.

Kathryn N. DeWitt (United States) is currently: Senior Lecturer, Department of Psychiatry and Behavioral Sciences, Stanford University School of Medicine; previously: Assistant Professor in Residence, Department of Psychiatry, University of California, San Francisco.

Cláudio Laks Eizirik is a medical doctor, and he has a PhD in Medicine. He is a Training and Supervising analyst of the Porto Alegre Psychoanalytical Society, as well as its former President and Institute Director, and an Adjunct Professor of the Department of Psychiatry, Federal University of Rio Grande do Sul, Brazil. He was also President of FEPAL, the Latin American Psychoanalytic Federation, and a former Dean of the Medical School at the same University. Having been a vice-president and associate secretary, as well as chair of the House of Delegates, he is currently the President of the IPA. He is also member of the Editorial Board of the *International Journal of Psychoanalysis* and of several Brazilian journals. His main interests in psychoanalysis are in psychoanalytic technique, mainly studies on countertransference and neutrality; psychoanalytic training, with several papers and researches on supervision; and the relation of psychoanalysis and culture, and the psychodynamic perspective of the human life cycle. He has edited four books on these topics and has published several papers on them.

Tamara Fischmann (Germany) is a Member DPV (German Psychoanalytic Association) and Research Associate of the Sigmund Freud Institute, Frankfurt.

Peter Fonagy (London) is Freud Memorial Professor of Psychoanalysis and Director of the Sub-Department of Clinical Health Psychology at University College London. He is Chief Executive of the Anna Freud Centre, London, and Consultant to the Child and Family Program at the Menninger Department of Psychiatry at Baylor College of Medicine. He is a clinical psychologist and a training and supervising analyst in the British Psychoanalytical Society in child and adult analysis. He holds a number of important positions, which include Co-Chairing the Research Committee of the International Psychoanalytical Association and Fellowship of the British Academy.

Richard Fox (United States) is Training and Supervising Analyst and Past Director of Education, Los Angeles Psychoanalytic Society and Institute; Past President of the American Psychoanalytic Association (2000–02); a North American Representative to the Board of Directors of the International Psychoanalytical Association.

Norbert Freedman (United States) is a Past President, Director of Research and Training Analyst at the Institute for Psychoanalytic Training and Research (IPTAR New York); Faculty and Adjunct Professor at New York University, Program in Psychoanalysis and Psychotherapy; Professor Emeritus, SUNY Downstate Medical Center; formerly, Director of Psychology and Director of: Research Unit for the Study of Clinical Communication.

Ethan Graham (United States) is a doctoral candidate in psychology, Adelphi University, New York.

Dorothea Huber (Germany) is a psychoanalyst and works as assistant medical director at the Institute and outpatient clinic of Psychosomatic Medicine, Klinikum rechts der Isar, University of Munich.

Otto Kernberg (United States) is Director, Personality Disorders Institute, The New York Presbyterian Hospital, Westchester Division; Professor of Psychiatry, Joan and Sanford I. Weill Medical College of Cornell University; Training and Supervising Analyst, Columbia University Center for Psychoanalytic Training and Research

Guenther Klug (Germany) is a psychoanalyst and assistant medical director at the Municipal Hospital of Munich–Harlaching, Department for Psychosomatic Diseases and Psychotherapy.

George Klumpner (United States) is a member of the Chicago Institute for Psychoanalysis.

Thomas Klumpner (United States) is a freshman in the MD programme at Northwestern Medical School, Chicago.

Marianne Leuzinger-Bohleber (Germany) is Professor of Psychoanalytical Psychology, University of Kassel; Director, Sigmund Freud Institute; Training Analyst, DPV (German Psychoanalytic Association) and Swiss Psychoanalytic Society; and Chairman, Committee for Conceptual Research IPA.

Lester Luborsky (United States) trained as a psychoanalyst at the Menninger Foundation, where he engaged in the Psychotherapy Research Project, and he has been Professor (now Emeritus) of Psychology in Psychiatry at the University of Pennsylvania for 40 years. He is the author of nine books and over 400 hundred articles and chapters. He has been the recipient of numerous professional awards including the Gold Medal Award for Lifetime Achievement in the Applications of Psychology from the American Psychological Association and the Sigourney Award for Research in Psychoanalysis from the American Psychoanalytic Association. He was honoured by the Society for Psychotherapy Research for his contributions to psychotherapy research.

Bernard Maskit (United States) is Leading Professor of Mathematics, Stony Brook University.

Andres Roussos (Argentina) is a research member, Consejo Nacional de Investigaciones Científicas y Técnicas CONICET. Adjunct Professor, Universidad de Belgrano and Universidad de Buenos Aires, Buenos Aires, Argentina. Adjunct Professor, Derner Institute, Adelphi University, Garden City, N.Y.

Robert Wallerstein (United States) is Emeritus Professor and former Chair, Department of Psychiatry, University of California San Francisco School of Medicine; Emeritus Training and Supervising Analyst, San Francisco Psychoanalytic Institute; Past President (1971–72), American Psychoanalytic Association; Past President (1985–89), International Psychoanalytical Association.

Daniel Widlöcher (France) is a Past President of the IPA, past professor of psychiatry at the University Pierre and Marie Curie, and Head of the Psychiatric Department at the Salpêtrière Hospital, where he is head of the centre for psychoanalytic and psychotherapy training. He was also director of a research unit in pharmacology and psychopathology in the National Institute of Medical Research. He trained in the French Psychoanalytical Society and was in private practice in psychoanalysis. He founded, with Lavie and Laplanche, the French Psychoanalytical Association and Institute, in which he plays an active role as full member and training analyst.

FOREWORD

Cláudio Laks Eizirik

While reading the enlightening essays elegantly put together by Norbert Freedman and Wilma Bucci to celebrate Robert Wallerstein's great achievements, the title of an English play, by Robert Bolt, came to my mind: *A Man for All Seasons*. The play, which was first performed in London in July 1960, is based on the true story of Sir Thomas More, the sixteenth-century chancellor of England who refused to endorse or denounce the King's wish to divorce his ageing wife, who could not bear him a son, so that he would be able to marry his mistress. Thomas More is portrayed in the play as a man of principle, loved by the common people and by his family, but envied by rivals such as Thomas Cromwell.

Bob Wallerstein is, indeed, a man for all seasons. *From Impression to Inquiry*, a new title in the IPA Publications Committee's "Psychoanalytic Ideas and Applications Series", shows very clearly the many dimensions along which Bob contributed to the progress of psychoanalysis and to the development of the IPA. It is also a new important title for which Leticia Glocer Fiorini and her colleagues should be commended.

The main focus of the book is on Bob's fundamental role in putting research into the mainstream of the psychoanalytic movement and his continuous and successful efforts to build a structure into the

IPA that proved able and effective in stimulating new researchers as well as selecting, funding, and monitoring relevant projects. It was not an easy task, for even today there are still colleagues who have resistances against research or even criticize the amount of money the IPA has spent in recent years on this subject. However, thanks to the strenuous efforts of Bob—and to other analysts with a wide vision of what is relevant to keep psychoanalysis in touch with the wider world and with the universities and producing new knowledge—research is today a full part of our association's life, as we observe more and more panels, conferences, and publications showing the importance of research and its relevance to our clinical practice.

But in addition to this, Bob has had a decisive role in many other areas: as a leader, as a negotiator in the traumatic lawsuit against APsaA, as an author of many papers and books, and as a man able to grasp some of the main challenges to psychoanalysis—for instance, through his still controversial proposition of a common ground and his scholarly studies on what this would mean and include.

Like many other colleagues from all over the international psychoanalytic community, I first met Bob Wallerstein in the early 1970s, when I was a resident in psychiatry and he visited Porto Alegre to lecture and supervise.

Some three decades later, with his prodigious memory Bob is still able to recall people, situations, and facts of that stimulating visit, which opened so many new doors and new interests to me and my colleagues.

In the following years Bob was a permanent and inspiring reference, with his many papers and books, among which *Forty-two Lives in Treatment* remains as a monument to psychoanalytic research in its empirical, clinical, and conceptual versions, as we have structured them today.

From one International Congress to another, from a growing personal acquaintance, and from several meetings with him and his lovely wife Judy, herself also a distinguished analyst and researcher, I was able to discover that our celebrated author is also a warm, holding, stimulating, and kind person.

I also had the privilege of closer contact with Bob in recent years, while he chaired the IPA's Research Advisory Board (RAB)—something he has been doing since its creation in 1997 and from which he asked to be released in July 2007. In the RAB, Bob was again able to display his superb ability to structure and organize this new committee, which selects and monitors new research projects funded by the IPA.

The organization of *From Impression to Inquiry* by Norbert Freedman and Wilma Bucci seems to be inspired by Bob's rational, methodical, and comprehensive way of approaching problems, be they of a theoretical, clinical, research, or institutional nature. The book highlights the main aspects of his career and the development of research in the psychoanalytic establishment, then describes Bob's progress from Topeka onwards, continues with more specific research subjects such as outcome measures for structural change and the CAMP initiative, and concludes with his own vision of CAMP and the future of psychoanalytic therapy research. A comprehensive scientific bibliography is extremely useful to show his impressive achievements in so many dimensions of psychoanalysis. All the essays are written by some of the most important psychoanalytic researchers.

Among his many contributions to psychoanalysis and to our international association, Bob was President of the IPA from 1985 to 1989, but in addition before and after that period he has served on many committees. He has been a constant, solid, and inspirational presence, to which his successors could and can always turn in moments of difficulty, when his vision, wisdom, and ability to face every new challenge with balance and objectivity have always been and are today of great value. This availability—and his tireless passion for psychoanalysis, about which we can learn by reading *From Impression to Inquiry*—were certainly among the reasons that led the IPA's then Executive Council to elect him as an IPA Honorary Vice-President.

In my current position I feel proud of occupying a place that was once Bob Wallerstein's.

As was the case with Sir Thomas More, it is just natural that this volume so fairly celebrates and shows the many reasons that make Robert Wallerstein "a man for all seasons".

19 April 2007

FROM IMPRESSION TO INQUIRY

Introduction: Robert Wallerstein's vision and the evolution of psychoanalytic research— the one and the many

Norbert Freedman & Wilma Bucci

Robert Wallerstein has given shape to the psychoanalytic community at home and abroad, through actions, through the written word, and through the range of his ideas. The scope of his enduring contribution is indicated—but only partially—in the Scientific Bibliography that appears at the end of this volume. His impact is unique, extending from clinical, empirical, and theoretical contributions to the restructuring of our international psychoanalytic world. While it is hard to find a single theme that does justice to the scope of Bob Wallerstein's statement, "the one and the many", which evokes William James's historical work (James, 1907), may be seen as a *leitmotif* that informs his career.

"One Psychoanalysis or Many?" was, of course, the theme and title of Wallerstein's historic Montreal Congress address in 1987 (Wallerstein, 1988b). As he said then:

> My current vision of psychoanalysis then is of a unitary clinical theory that is empirically testable—a theory which binds and unifies us as psychoanalysts—and of a pluralistic general theory, the explanatory symbols, i.e. the metaphors, which embody our intellectual commitments and values and to which we differentially adhere. [p. 17]

This was an epoch-making address, evoking the image of a psychoanalytic core in an era and a context of increasing diversity. With the 1987 Congress paper, Wallerstein challenged the worldwide psychoanalytic community to find its common ground, common heritage, and shared clinical task. This theme also finds elaboration in the 1992 volume *The Common Ground of Psychoanalysis* edited by Wallerstein; and in his 1995 volume on *The Talking Cures* (Wallerstein, 1995); it is through our commitment to spoken language, emerging in intimate dialogue, that we find the shared substrate of much of psychoanalytic knowledge.

The theme of common ground was also implicit in the arena of psychoanalytic politics in that era, becoming manifest in the historical moment of the 1989 Rome Congress. Bob Wallerstein, as the leader of the International Psychoanalytical Association (IPA), had been instrumental during the peak of the controversy surrounding the lawsuit concerning the full opening of the American Psychoanalytic Association (APsaA) to non-medical candidates, and he played a major role in bringing together those psychoanalysts who had been barred from membership in the IPA. In an unforgettable ceremony in Rome, those colleagues who had previously been excluded underscored the theme of unity. Wallerstein deserves much appreciation for this organizational achievement—not only from colleagues who had previously been excluded, but also from organized psychoanalysis in general, which has been vitalized in many ways by this expansion. His perspective on this historic policy of inclusion and its broader significance is expressed in his statement in the IPA Newsletter in 1998:

> To me, the central question at issue was whether psychoanalysis is simply a branch of the medical healing arts, a subspecialty of psychiatry; or is it rather a fully independent discipline with an important interface, to be sure, with biological and medical science, but with equally strong interfaces with academic and clinical psychology, with the full range of the behavioral and social sciences, and also with philosophy, linguistics, law, and other relevant domains of human thought?
>
> . . . What is germane here is that with the settlement of the lawsuit and the opening of the American Association to non-medical candidates on a fully equal basis, bringing the American into line with the practice in the rest of the world, there has been a new invigoration of the psychoanalytic scene, certainly in the United

> States, with interpenetrating discourse between individuals and between psychoanalytic perspectives that had theretofore been arbitrarily separated, and this has indeed added to the vitality of (at least the American) psychoanalytic arena, again counter to the perception of some, of decline. And this now worldwide agreement on the independence of psychoanalysis as a discipline, no longer to be conceived anywhere as but a branch of another discipline, is itself a factor conceptually in our (at least, my) renewed confidence in an established present and future.

The pluralism inherent in Bob Wallerstein's image of the one and the many is as forceful as the theme of unity. A striking example of his capacity to facilitate connections without losing the vitality of diversity is his description of his work as the first Chair of the newly formed Committee on Scientific Activities (CSA) of the American Psychoanalytic Association:

> I sat at the head of a long table flanked by Kohut and Gill on either side, and the incisive, and at times disputatious, interchanges between the two of them face-to-face have been to me among the most rewarding discourses on the nature and the parameters of psychoanalytic research and scientific activity that I have ever been privileged to be party to. [Wallerstein, chapter 4, this volume]

(One might wish to have been a fly on the wall at these meetings; we also suggest that Bob may have honed his well-known and widely admired skills for running a meeting smoothly, including keeping speakers within their assigned times, during his stint at this long table.)

The theme of unity and diversity was nowhere more evident than in Wallerstein's role in establishing a central position for psychoanalytic research within both the IPA and the APsaA. As emphasized in his 1987 address and throughout his career, and as underscored in this volume by Widlöcher (chapter 1, this volume), Wallerstein's core commitment has been to psychoanalytic knowledge rooted in empirical documentation; there is of course widespread controversy concerning this position that continues today. The memorable and controversial discussion between Bob Wallerstein (1996) and André Green (1996a, 1996b) was highlighted by the metaphor "The proof of the pudding will be in the eating". In contrast to Green's mistrust of the research "pudding", many of Wallerstein's research endeavours over several decades have in fact facilitated the capacity of the psychoanalytic community to digest and accommodate an empirical and investigative approach. As the field has developed, researchers have come to recognize that the "proof" that we seek rests on a conceptual foundation but also requires innovative technology and a shared database, including an archive of recorded treatments.

In an early effort, during his psychiatric residency at the Menninger Clinic (as reported in chapter 4), Bob turned the ward for chronic alcoholic patients into a research unit, and made early discoveries both concerning the significance of the interaction of treatment assignment with personality type, and also concerning the effects of the so-called control-group assignment. As outlined by Kernberg (chapter 5), both of these discoveries were later applied and extended in the Psychotherapy Research Project (PRP) of the Menninger Foundation.

Wallerstein's monumental volume, *Forty-Two Lives in Treatment: A Study of Psychoanalysis and Psychotherapy* (1986), is rooted in the PRP project but transcends it in its openness to clinical description, its willingness to tolerate unexpected findings, and a theoretical stance that is couched in a language open to the broader mental health community, outside psychoanalysis. While there is an appreciation in that book of the rationale that governs the analytic frame, there also emerges the recognition of its pitfalls. *Forty-Two Lives* remains a stellar example of clinical psychoanalytic research that is not simply confirmatory. It is a model for the use of empirical findings to inform and influence clinical practice and a significant resource for the teaching of psychoanalytic therapy.

The vision of psychoanalytic knowledge as an expanded horizon of inquiry is well represented in Wallerstein's depiction of the generations of psychoanalytic research (outlined by Bucci, chapter 13). The evolution may be seen through three generations of outcome research, asking the question: "*What*" change has taken place? using increasingly sophisticated methods and tools of inquiry, then entering the fourth generation of psychoanalytic treatment research, focusing on treatment process and asking the question: *How* does change come about? The studies in this fourth generation are dependent on the availability of verbatim session recordings and involve the development of reliable and valid measures of psychoanalytic concepts applied to session material by individual researchers.

As highlighted by Fox (chapter 2), many active psychoanalytic researchers representing projects in the United States and abroad were brought together by Bob Wallerstein through the new organization of the Collaborative Analytic Multi-site Program (CAMP). What had begun with an unexpected offer of funding that failed to materialize then evolved creatively, as described by Wallerstein (chapter 4), into a milestone of organized psychoanalytic process research on the national level. In the concept of CAMP—"collaborative", "analytic", and "multi-site", we find an expression of Wallerstein's vision of the one and the many and the foundation of the new generations of psychoanalytic process research. It was the goal of CAMP to bring together psychoanalytic therapy researchers, representing many perspectives, to apply their research measures to a shared archival set of recorded treatments; to assess convergences and divergences; and to arrive at an array of measures that will provide a comprehensive view of the psychoanalytic process, ultimately also linked to outcome. Moreover, outcome should also be defined along lines of psychoanalytic goals, not symptoms and behaviours only. As indicated in this volume by Dahl (chapter 6), Luborsky (chapter 7), and Klumpner (chapter 11), the members of CAMP shared this vision, expressed in their own unique ways.

We may see the development of the Scales of Psychological Capacities (SPC) as representing Bob's own scientific affirmation of the fourth generation of analytic research, and also representing his own recipe for integrating the conceptual and empirical research approaches. The concept of structure contains within it many of the claims inherent in long-term psychoanalytic treatment, and it is also a notion that has deep roots in Bob's Topeka days. We can note a direct line from Menninger and Rapaport, to *Forty-Two Lives,* to the development of the SPC. The Scales speak both the theoretical language of contemporary concepts of the ego and also their embedding in clinical practice. In this project, we can note Bob Wallerstein's intellectual roots, including Rapaport's ideas of structure as indicating a slow rate of change, but now endowed with a new reflective flexibility. The line of thought in the development of the measure is elaborated in the present volume by DeWitt (chapter 8), Leuzinger-Bohleber and Fischmann (chapter 9), and Huber and Klug (chapter 10). As DeWitt, a major collaborator with Wallerstein in the development of the SPC, notes (chapter 8), structure is a multifactorial and elastic clinical concept that has undergone change over the decades; the diversity of the concept is seen both in the components of the scale and its potential use in a range of diagnostic groups and therapeutic approaches, including long- and short-term psychodynamic treatments. The SPC have been developed into a reliable and valid instrument that is now part of the repertoire of treatment evaluation, as discussed here by Leuzinger-Bohleber and Fischmann (chapter 9) and Huber and Klug (chapter 10).

Current directions: the one and the many in psychoanalytic research today

We have briefly outlined the scope of Robert Wallerstein's contributions: opening the field of empirical psychoanalytic research, situating it institutionally, and addressing and attempting to resolve issues of integration of theoretical, clinical, organizational and research perspectives. In all these areas, as in any generative endeavour, he has produced, not a completed product, but a point of view and a body of work that invites criticism, challenge, and change. That is what we see as his ongoing legacy: to have developed the field of psychoanalytic research as an open and inclusive endeavour, with scope for continuous development and growth. In all the major areas in which Bob has made contributions, he has also opened the door to the introduction of alternative perspectives, going perhaps in somewhat different and new directions.

In what follows we shall touch upon just a few of many salient challenges that Wallerstein has begun to address and that face us now—as members of CAMP, or its institutional descendant in the Research Associates of the American Psychoanalytic Association (RAAPA), or more generally as members of the national and international psychoanalytic research community.

The archival base

While CAMP enabled psychotherapy researchers to break new ground in collaborative research, the CAMP data were limited to recorded treatments that had been conducted several decades earlier, largely without auxiliary material concerning the patient and therapist, and with essentially no evidence concerning treatment outcome. The evaluation of outcome for archival treatments was addressed to some degree in Luborsky's project (chapter 7); the modern understanding of psychoanalytic treatment research requires further systematic broadening of the evidential base.

To address the goals of the new generation of process research, there is an urgent need for acquisition of a fresh database of recorded psychoanalyses incorporating multiple clinical and empirical perspectives, including the subjective experience of the treating analysts, the evaluations by clinical consultants examining the recorded material, and also potentially including the patient's subjective experience as well, along with verbatim transcripts to which objective measures may be applied. Such an expanded data set will require a considerable outlay of money, talent, and time, not so readily available in our field, and will also raise new concerns regarding the sharing of data in collaborative research.

There is also urgent need for studies incorporating outcome assessment and including variations in treatment approaches and length of therapy. This may be difficult in the United States (in view of managed care requirements), but it has been possible in Europe, as seen, for example, in the studies of the Stockholm Institute (Sandell et al., 2000) and the long-term study of the German Society (Leuzinger-Bohleber and Fischmann, chapter 9). Could we envisage the translation of criterion sessions into English for comparative study?

Modern collaborative research will also include new empirical and clinical measures, better adapted to treatments of today, and will require new technical methods for storing and protecting sensitive clinical material and monitoring accessibility, as discussed by Roussos, Bucci, and Maskit (chapter 12) and Klumpner (chapter 11). Some of these goals for the new generation of psychoanalytic treatment research have been foreseen by Wallerstein, some of these issues have been partially resolved; as in any living field new questions, and new solutions, will continually emerge.

Diversity of epistemology in psychoanalytic research

The work of process researchers has relied heavily on methods of observations that have their roots either in clinical psychoanalytic description or in psychology. New methods and new findings derived from disciplines outside psychoanalysis, in fields such as cognitive psychology, neuroscience, developmental psychology, psycholinguistics, and computer science, have now refocused the guiding assumptions and concepts of psychoanalytic research—revisiting, questioning, and extending the need for a psychological foundation for psychoanalysis that was argued by Rapaport (1959), Gill (1976), and their colleagues. On the one hand, psychoanalysis has much to offer other scientific disciplines such as those mentioned here, and these contributions have not been widely recognized—if at all—in these fields; on the other hand, psychoanalysis has much to gain from broadening its interface with disciplines outside its scientific boundaries.

A different strategy of analytic inquiry is suggested by the approach of *conceptual psychoanalytic research*, introduced by Sandler, Dreher, and Drews (1991) and furthered by Dreher (2000). According to this approach, which is also consistent with recommendations from the House of Delegates of the IPA during the work of the Committee on Psychoanalytic Specificity in 1996, all analytic inquiry begins with a focus on crucial analytic concepts, their history, their evolution over time, their clinical evidence, and then their confirmation through empirical methods.

At least two versions of conceptual research have been put forth, one compatible and the second incompatible with the commitment to empirical and consensual validation. A version of the incompatible view was voiced by André Green (1996a, 1996b) in his discussion with Wallerstein (1996), mentioned above. According to Green, the "truth value" of a concept inheres in the intuitive grasp of meaning derived from the analyst's awareness of the intersubjective dialogue, buttressed by his/her awareness of the concept in question rooted in the history of analytic ideas.

The version of conceptual research offered by Wallerstein, as indicated by Leuzinger-Bohleber and Fischmann (chapter 9) and as embodied in the evolution of the SPC, is a different brand. The development of the SPC involved a sequence of crucial steps including identification of the historical roots of the concepts, their evaluation by a pool of sophisticated clinical observers, and preliminary sketches of the scales, followed then by the assessment of their psychometric properties of reliability and validity, and further interactive development. While the process incorporates conceptual and qualitative phases, calling on the subjective understanding of the participating clinicians, it also moves from this to development of an instrument that may be applied for objective assessment in empirical research. This incorporates the subjective and intuitive perspective privileged by Green, but adds the further dimensions of interaction with a range of alternate perspectives, including objective measures, applied to the same material.

Diversity of theoretical concepts

All psychoanalytic research aims to enhance the legitimacy of our discipline. Outcome research, including effectiveness and efficacy studies, speaks to public health concerns. Process research seeks to examine what goes on in the room between analyst and patient, and what goes on within each participant. Conceptual research speaks to the needs of the psychoanalytic community in affirming the "truth value" of guiding ideas. All of these steps towards legitimacy have been advanced in Bob Wallerstein's work.

We may also talk briefly here about a vision of psychoanalytic research that looks beyond the confines of the guiding psychoanalytic concepts—questioning rather than "affirming" or "providing evidence for" them. We may see this in the diverse definitions of concepts in different theoretical orientations, leaving us to some extent without theoretical common ground. This issue was addressed by Sandler, Wallerstein, and others primarily by embedding the definitions of concepts in the experience-near perception and understanding of the clinician.

In the spirit of Wallerstein's own generative, open, and questioning approach, we may ask whether even the experience-near clinical formulations that are represented in the SPC make implicit theoretical assumptions that need to be questioned.

Huber and Klug (chapter 10) open—but refrain from endorsing—the potential of a "structural change of psychoanalysis itself". Ultimately, it seems possible that new information gathered through innovative methods of evaluation, and the infusion of ideas from neighbouring disciplines, may feed back to restructure aspects of the guiding psychoanalytic ideas themselves.

Effective psychoanalytic work is perhaps best characterized, not so much by change in specific symptoms and behaviours, nor even by changes in capacity for love and work, but by the development of a capacity for continuing self-examination. It is this function, valuing openness to discovery and change, as embodied in the process of self-exploration, that seems to be a unique aspect of psychoanalytic treatment, differentiating it from other treatment forms. Bob Wallerstein's many specific contributions have been briefly mentioned in this introduction and are discussed in greater detail in the chapters that follow. Along with these, however, his enduring contributions are also seen in the spirit of generativity, exploration, and inclusiveness that characterize his career—leading us to view psychoanalytic research and theory as a work in progress and opening the field to new viewpoints and new directions; it is this spirit that we seek to retain as we continue this work.

The themes of Wallerstein's career are addressed in different ways by each of the contributors to this volume. We will not attempt to summarize or synthesize these contributions here. No introduction to his work and its unifying principles would be adequate, however, without at least a mention of the fabled phenomenon of the "Wallerstein summary". As Peter Fonagy mentions (chapter 3), those of us who attended the annual IPA Research Conferences in London and New Orleans have had the experience of observing Bob's capacity to digest, filter, and organize the papers presented at a long conference and to produce an instant summary, at the close of the meeting, that unified them in an overall vision while consistently reflecting what the contributors were trying to say. We have asked Bob to contribute the last words for our volume here.

1

Robert Wallerstein's career and the development of research in the psychoanalytic establishment

1

In honour of Robert Wallerstein

Daniel Widlöcher

Empirical research is now part of the International Psychoanalytical Association's fundamental objectives, and it was during Robert Wallerstein's presidency that the very principle of this objective was established. It is surprising that this principle was recognized so late, as we all know that the necessity of developing research, which is scientifically founded on the method and the effects of psychoanalytic treatment, has always been recognized. Everyone knows that the first work in this area goes back to the 1920s. It is strange to note that for several years the IPA developed its creativity and its spirit of research in the widening of clinical practice and its theoretical model in metapsychology. Without doubt the psychoanalytic cause needed to be defended in the area of this clinical practice.

This did not prevent empirical research on this practice and its effects being developed and continued, but this happened outside the IPA, with Robert Wallerstein, at the Menninger Foundation, playing an important role in the development of this research. It was natural, therefore, that when he became President of the IPA, Wallerstein proposed to introduce the latter within the area of empirical research and not to leave this outside in the area of universities, public and private institutions, and treatment centres.

As soon as preparation for the Montreal Congress had begun, the Programme Committee, under the direction of Otto Kernberg, decided to include research in the Congress programme. Progressively, with the help of the Association's treasurers, Steve Firestein and Peter Fonagy, and with the support of Executive Council, the appropriate structures were implemented for consequent development by the Councils presided over by Joe Sandler, Horacio Etchegoyen, and Otto Kernberg.

I would add that this interest in the integration of research was not foreign to Robert Wallerstein's concern for a better definition of the "common ground" of our practice, independent of various theories, and a major theme for reflection in his contributions at Congresses during his presidency.

So for a decade we have now had a Committee for Research chaired by Peter Fonagy, which uses a significant part of our budget for the development of research programmes and the management of summer schools that help to train young analysts in research. A pre-Congress is dedicated to results derived from this programme, and an Expert Committee, chaired by Robert Wallerstein, has the task of evaluating the quality of these research projects.

All this has not been achieved without some resistance, and we can recall debates on theory that have, over recent years, fed the controversy—not least Wallerstein's well-known debate, mainly with André Green. The idea that psychoanalysis is an enterprise that is scientific in nature stems, however, from our epistemological credo. It enters into the definition that Freud gave to psychoanalysis. It is true that, at the time, science and practice were linked. Medical science was based to a great extent on clinical observation, and Freud, faithful to his calling as a research investigator, found nothing shocking in moving from biological experimentation to the psychological observation of patients.

Without necessarily impugning the legitimacy of the psychoanalytic approach, contemporary culture is more interested in its future than in its past. Many would agree that it was a great discovery of the mind, but there is also a tendency to doubt whether it continues to live up to its early promise. Should the task of deepening the area of knowledge in which it had the merit of first breaking ground not be left to other methods, to other sciences? This is what is at stake in the current debate.

Some psychoanalysts prefer to turn a deaf ear to this challenge. They find that the discovery that Freud and his successors have transmitted to them is sufficient, and they content themselves with being able to bear witness to it in each of the individual situations that they are called upon to treat. At the opposite extreme, others no longer have confidence in clinical experience and believe that the methods of natural science must be recruited imperatively in order to broaden and consolidate the discoveries of psychoanalysis. A polemic has ensued. It is important to draw a distinction between a clinical approach that takes into account individual clinical experiences and their plurality—the usual clinical debate in which psychoanalytic practice is the instrument for research from a more "scientific" approach that takes psychoanalysis itself, its methodology, its process, its issues, and its discoveries as an object of research.

It was for this reason that it was decided to develop, alongside empirical research, clinical and conceptual research as part of the competence of our Research Committee.

We need, in this new domain, to ensure the quality of the projects that are submitted for grants. The standard methodological requirement, inspired by Robert Wallerstein's thinking and policy, is that these projects fulfil four requirements that apply to all research:

1. appropriateness of method to object: in which way planned and clinical research is the best method to respond to the question raised;
2. possible falsification of hypotheses;
3. reliability of expert opinions;
4. concern for methodological criticism.

By fulfilling these four criteria, the clinical and conceptual method will no doubt join the research known as empirical and will, I feel, fulfil the hopes of Robert Wallerstein.

2

Tribute to Bob Wallerstein

Richard P. Fox

Robert Wallerstein's extraordinary contributions to the American Psychoanalytic Association (APsaA) began early in his analytic career. Shortly after completing his psychoanalytic training, he helped initiate and develop a special category for psychoanalytic training for non-clinical research candidates. Up to this time, analytic training and subsequent memberships in the APsaA had been the sole province of physician–clinicians. This extension of training was the first chink in the armour of medical orthodoxy that had restricted psychoanalysis in terms of its scope and perspective. The programme grew in size and range to include other academics as well as researchers and became institutionalized in the form of the Committee on Research and Special Training—or CORST, as it has come to be known. The CORST programme became one of our greatest assets, and our CORST candidates became valued contributors to psychoanalysis as well as to their own disciplines. As a result, the programme has greatly expanded the breadth of psychoanalysis and opened the door to making psychoanalysis truly multidisciplinary in the United States.

Bob Wallerstein paid his dues with his work on committees and task forces before becoming President of the Association in 1971. I can testify personally to the challenges facing the President of a psychoanalytic association. Analysts can be a taxing group to lead. Contentious issues are not only debated but also passionately fought over. During Wallerstein's tenure, psychoanalysis in the United States was in turmoil as newer ideas and theories, including object relations and self psychology, were being promoted, and these raised institutional challenges to what had been the unofficial theoretical paradigm, ego psychology. Psychoanalysts take their theories and politics seriously, and debates become intense and personal. At the same time, disputes about membership and local autonomy that were to plague the APsaA for years also were heating up. Although these disagreements competed for Bob's attention, they did not derail his personal agenda to promote science and research within the APsaA.

An important beginning was the establishment of the Committee on Scientific Activities—or "CSA", as it has come to be known. This committee established a home for science in the APsaA and promoted this neglected aspect of our discipline. An important next step was the creation of the Fund for Psychoanalytic Research. An ongoing impediment to the development of psychoanalytic research is the lack of funding, and although the Fund was never able to fully finance major research projects, it has been able to launch a number of research projects and younger researchers through much needed seed grants.

Even as he moved onto the international stage, Wallerstein continued his tireless efforts on behalf of research in the APsaA. He organized the Collaborative Analytic Multi-site Program—or "CAMP"—which has continued to provide a forum for researchers, both members and non-members. Most recently, building on the CAMP tradition, we have developed a new category of affiliation, the Research Associates of the American Psychoanalytic Association. We hope this new group, abbreviated RAAPA, will extend Wallerstein's legacy within the Association.

Many of Wallerstein's contributions to the APsaA have been institutionalized within the Association: CORST, CSA, the Fund for Psychoanalytic Research, CAMP, and RAAPA, and he has contributed not only his organizational and leadership skills, but also his intellect and his soul. His greatest gifts to us are the inspiration and model he has provided to psychoanalysts, young and old, clinicians and researchers, administrators and members.

3

An appreciation of Dr Wallerstein's contributions to psychoanalytic research

Peter Fonagy

Psychoanalysis has produced many heroes for all of us over its hundred-year history. My heroes fall broadly into two groups: heroes of theory who have successfully battled the almost unimaginable complexities of a rapidly proliferating body of ideas—I would count Robert Wallerstein's close friend and collaborator, Joseph Sandler, among these. The second group of heroes are clinicians. These are often less well known individuals who guide us, in supervision or simply by personal example, through the morass of the human understanding we need to work with our psychoanalytic patients. My personal heroine, also well known to Bob, is Ilse Hellmann, a psychoanalyst who came over from Vienna to London with the Freud family. Robert Wallerstein qualifies for many in both of these two groups, but for me he is a special hero of a unique third category: he is the hero of psychoanalytic research. I don't believe that I am exaggerating when I assert that more than any other psychoanalyst in the world, Robert Wallerstein has legitimized research in the eyes of the average clinician.

During much of his career, throughout which Bob had a very deep commitment to psychoanalytic research, the antagonism to empirical research from psychoanalysts of all theoretical persuasions was crushingly powerful. This was, if possible, even more marked on the international scene than in the United States, where the research tradition was treated as a relatively legitimate interest. Of course, as President of the IPA following Adam Limentani, Wallerstein had the opportunity to bring change to the international organization. He established research half-days at international congresses. This was considered quite revolutionary, and it has to be said that the first of these sessions was not well attended. However, gradually the venture gathered momentum. At the Barcelona Congress, for example, there were over 200 people in the research session, and in Santiago there was standing room only. Of course, it took courage to bring such change to the IPA, but courage is something that Bob has in great abundance.

The Research Committee of the IPA was also Wallerstein's intellectual progeny. Although first established under his successor's, Joe Sandler's, presidency, the most senior researcher in the IPA was appropriately the founding Chair. He established the March Research Conference in London. The first Conference, organized by Otto Kernberg in 1991, was an enormous success, its high point Wallerstein's end-of-conference summary of the meeting, where all attendees—both those presenting and those listening—learned what had been said. I have witnessed Wallerstein's capacity for integration in a number of different contexts, but his end-of-conference summaries at all the London research meetings were peerless. Not only was he able to weave together the diverse themes of the papers into a single framework that had intellectual coherence, but he brought into this latticework all the discussants' contributions and even many of the significant contributions from the floor, together with the names and affiliations of the contributors. I happen to know that many who attended the conference felt their attendance justified by earning an honourable mention in the Wallerstein summary. Unfortunately, these summaries have not been preserved and so can never receive the acclaim that they deserve, but for those who heard them, Wallerstein's summaries gave powerful evidence of his unique mastery of psychoanalytic and research issues across a wide range of specializations.

The committee never received strong financial support, and in recruiting members for the committee, Wallerstein made it clear that those serving on it were there because of an emotional and intellectual commitment and were all expected to make a financial sacrifice. There were no reimbursements for attending the committee meetings for him or for other members of the group. His leadership ensured that, notwithstanding the financial obstacles, all those who were privileged to have been asked felt honoured to serve under him. Although no longer Chair of the Committee, Wallerstein continued to serve as one of its most active members throughout Etchegoyen's administration.

Wallerstein's most important contribution to international psychoanalytic research came during Kernberg's presidency of the IPA. The Kernberg–Tyson administration was elected with a promise of financial support for systematic psychoanalytic enquiry. The leadership committed over $200,000 per year to kick-start research in psychoanalysis. Psychoanalysts not always being trusting of each other where money is concerned, the administration had to find a person whose impartiality and integrity when dispersing these funds would never be doubted. There was only one person for the job: Robert Wallerstein. Having worked very closely with him on this task, I have no doubt that the administration made the right decision to appoint him Chair of the Research Advisory Board. It required his unrivalled contacts across the world to assemble the most prestigious group of psychoanalytic researchers to serve as peer reviewers for applications. It then required someone of his breadth and capacity for integration to be able to review each and every one of the applications for funding that the IPA received. It required his attention to detail to organize the system of ranking, prioritization, and feedback. In the first round there were 86 applications. In subsequent years this number has decreased, but the quality of applications has improved. It is a great testament to Wallerstein's fair-mindedness and organizational skills that throughout the time money has been made available from the IPA for research, no complaint—formal or informal—has, to my knowledge, been made about the procedures he established.

Was this commitment necessary? A 1999 survey of 150 psychoanalysts who expressed interest in research revealed that less than 5% had funding from national research bodies, foundations, or international groups. Most funding came from local psychoanalytic associations or from small family foundations. Many had given up applying or learned to disguise psychoanalytic aspects of their projects. One analyst commented: "I have realized that as soon as there is a mention of psychoanalysis, the application is automatically thrown in the trash can. I no longer even list my psychoanalytic affiliation on my curriculum vitae." Two calls for proposals are reviewed by Wallerstein each year. There have been approximately 300 applications reviewed by him, and some 100 awards have been made. The average award is about $7,000. Most of the awards go to North America, which has the most advanced research culture, and the smallest number go to Latin America. A wide variety of research has been funded, topics covering Freud scholarship, psychoanalytic legal studies, history, and, of course, developmental, process, and outcome research. A great achievement was an award for conceptual research to André Green, for a collaborative project with Otto Kernberg on borderline personality disorder. But the bulk of the money has gone to empirical research.

Bob Wallerstein represents psychoanalytic research for many psychoanalysts around the world. His tireless commitment to enhancing the quality of systematic psychoanalytic enquiry has had a great impact on the context of psychoanalytic practice. His influence on the professional culture of psychoanalysis has been enormous. Wallerstein stands for the systematic study of issues of concern to psychoanalysts, and the integration of advances from other disciplines into psychoanalytic clinical work. The criteria that he applies on the RAB are those he has applied to his own work throughout a remarkably productive research career: sound methodology, serious scholarship, and unwavering commitment.

4

My life as a psychoanalytic therapy researcher and in CAMP

Robert S. Wallerstein

To begin at the beginning: I was born in Berlin, Germany, in 1921. My father was then completing his medical residency training at the Charité Krankenhaus, the main teaching hospital of his medical school, Kaiser Wilhelm University. At that time, in the immediate aftermath of the First World War, Germany was ravaged by the most disastrous inflation any nation had ever experienced, and when I was a year old, my father, his modest savings completely exhausted, answered a newspaper advertisement and was offered, and accepted, a position in New York City as assistant and office mate to an established and very successful New York internist and gastro-enterologist. A year later, in 1923, when I was two, he had saved enough to send for my mother and me to join him.

I thus grew up in a medical family in New York City, and I took it for granted that I would follow the medical career that was my family's expectation. As a schoolboy, in those pre-television days, I read voraciously, making long journeys to the nearest public library every week and coming away each time with more than one book. Two books, both about medicine—*Arrowsmith*, by Sinclair Lewis, and *Microbe Hunters*, by Paul de Kruif—were extraordinarily influential, both for me and for others of my cohort of friends as well. These two stirring tales fired me up with a vision of a dedicated medical research career, and I sustained the ambition that after the completion of basic medical training I would turn to tropical medicine—an exotic-enough fantasy—to seek specialized training in that arena—which, as I came later to find out, would be with a Professor Clarence Faust at the Tulane University School of Medicine, the widely acknowledged American leader in that esoteric field—and then be off to India to conquer malaria and other assorted tropical ills.

As it happened, I went to Columbia College in New York and then, in September 1941, entered the freshman class at Columbia University's medical school, the College of Physicians and Surgeons (P&S). Barely three months later came the attack on Pearl Harbor. To prevent medical students, whom the Armed Forces sorely needed as doctors-to-be, from dropping out to enlist as army privates—as a few did in the first frantic days after the attack—we were all put into uniform and assigned to completing medical school. The latter was condensed to three years by running four nine-month years consecutively without any holidays, followed by a basic internship before medical military service.

During this time everything proceeded on course for me. After medical school, a nine-month internship, and another nine-month assistant residency in internal medicine, I was duly taken into the army—now in the immediate aftermath of the war—and served for two years as a medical officer at a General Hospital, operating an infectious disease ward and an electrocardiography lab for army troops. Upon my release from the army I returned to a promised senior medical residency at Mount Sinai Hospital in New York, where I had served my internship and assistant medical residency, and I began to cast about for future career directions, practice or academic, clinical and/or research. I applied for and was awarded a two-year fellowship period, to start on 1 January 1949, in a physical chemistry mentorship in the famed blood fractionation laboratory of Edwin Cohn at Harvard, a fellowship sponsored by the then new National Institutes of Health, preparatory to a presumed academic medical career.

But it was at this point that I made my fateful turn to psychiatry and psychoanalysis. The reasons were not at all that clear to me. I reasoned consciously that in contrast to medicine, where I saw clinical practice and research activity as two separate and dichotomized arenas that could only uneasily be combined, psychiatry—and psychoanalysis—stood out as a discipline where the clinical activity and the research activity operated within the same context. I did not yet know, at that time, about Freud's dictum that in psychoanalysis the road to cure and the road to knowledge were the same. Also by that time my wife, Judy, was a graduate psychiatric social worker, and one of the few volumes that graced our bookshelf was Otto Fenichel's *The Psychoanalytic Theory of Neurosis.* Besides, I thought that my motivations in all of this would become clearer to me in the analysis that I was looking forward to—I am not sure that that actually happened.

So I backed out of the proffered Fellowship programme at Harvard and in order to search for yet another three-year residency stint, this time in psychiatry. I contacted a very close friend from my internship days, David Rubinfine, who was a psychiatric resident at the Menninger School of Psychiatry in Topeka, Kansas, at the time an already nationally renowned training centre, in that small town on the prairie, for 100 psychiatric residents out of a total of only 800 in the whole country—one out of every eight psychiatrists being trained in the nation. Dave wrote back that it was great, that I should come. So I applied, and to the consternation of my chief in medicine at Mount Sinai, Dr I. Snapper, who had me marked out for a scholarly career in academic medicine, I was accepted at Menninger's for a residency to start 1 July 1949.

To fill in the six-month gap between the termination of my medical residency at Mount Sinai and the start of my psychiatric residency at the Winter VA Hospital in Topeka, Kansas, the site of the Menninger School of Psychiatry programme, I asked for and was awarded a six-month stay on the newly created Psychosomatic Service at Mount Sinai (created while I was away on army service), under the chiefship of M. Ralph Kaufman. The service was an inpatient unit, serving as a combined medical and psychotherapeutic treatment centre (with both medical and psychiatric residents) for patients with severe medical disorders felt to have major psychological components and referred from the hospital's medical and surgical wards. These included patients with brittle and uncontrolled diabetes, intractable peptic ulcers, ulcerative colitis with daily spiking temperatures and ongoing bloody diarrhoea, status asthmaticus, recurrent thyrotoxic storms, and so on—a truly very ill population.

In addition to careful concomitant medical management, these patients had daily psychotherapy sessions. This was the heyday of the unbridled promises of the newly emerged field of psychosomatic medicine, fuelled by the early contributions of Flanders Dunbar in New York, of Felix Deutsch in Boston, and of Franz Alexander, Thomas French, and their numerous Chicago colleagues. The supervisor of the intensive psychotherapy into which I was precipitously thrown—four very ill patients whom I was to see in therapeutic sessions, each of them five days a week, from Day 1—was Sydney Margolin, already an established psychosomatic researcher. Sydney was psychoanalysing a young ward patient, Doris, who had swallowed lye in a catastrophic suicide attempt and had ended up with a fully stenosed oesophagus and a surgically created gastric fistula in order to be fed, while preparing for a planned attempt at surgical repair, the creation of an artificial replacement oesophagus. In return for free psychoanalytic treatment, Doris had agreed to twice-weekly experimental sessions in a physiology lab where various gastric functions, such as motility, acidity, degree of vascular engorgement, could all be directly measured, both in the resting state and after the administration of various drugs that affect gastric function, such as histamine. All of the variously co-varying gastric functions could then be correlated in combined weekly conferences with the indications of the underlying and inferred unconscious psychic processes emerging in the psychoanalytic sessions. This work was later described in an article by Margolin in the *Psychoanalytic Quarterly*.

This was my first encounter with psychoanalytic research, and it was indeed a heady brew. Also during that period Charles Fisher—then, like Margolin, a young attending psychiatrist at Mount Sinai Hospital—was conducting his early sleep–dream experiments in a constituted sleep–dream lab, created in the wake of Kleitman's initial descriptions of electrophysiologically studied REM states during sleep. This work was to be reported by Fisher in a sequence of articles in the newly established official *Journal of the American Psychoanalytic Association*.

When after six months I left the Mount Sinai psychosomatic service for Topeka, I was already envisioning the outlines of psychiatric–psychoanalytic research possibilities. When Judy and I drove into Topeka, Kansas, at the end of June 1949 with all our worldly belongings—our clothes, a few records, a few books—all packed into the car, we were heartened in the blistering Kansas summertime heat to see a huge billboard on the main highway leading into town, emblazoned by the Chamber of Commerce with the message: "Welcome to Topeka, Kansas, the Psychiatric Capital of the World."

A first research opportunity arose during my psychiatric residency years when I was assigned to a ward for chronic alcoholic patients: actually a revolving door where these young alcoholic war veterans were well-behaved and seemed to do very well while hospitalized (in an open setting), with available psychotherapy sessions and regular AA meetings that they attended in town, but who quite regularly returned inebriated—and sometimes with delirium tremens—shortly after their hospital discharge, picked up by the police in bars or on the street. With a group of colleagues, I conceived the idea of turning the ward into a research unit, where all the patients would be randomly assigned, sequentially, to one of four different treatment groups: in addition to the usual ward regimen, which for all the groups included available psychotherapy, one group would receive antabuse (the newly introduced "chemical wall", available at the time only for experimental protocols in programmes such as ours); the second group would be given, as its special modality, the then standard sanatorium treatment of aversive conditioned-reflex therapy; the third group would receive intensive group hypnotherapy sessions; and the fourth group, conceived originally as the control group, would be given only the standard hospital regimen; but in the absence of the special programmes of the other three groups, this latter group rapidly turned itself into a much more intensive psychotherapy group than any of the others.

Treatment protocols for all the groups were carefully worked out. Hospital stays with these various treatments were to be limited to one month, in contrast to the previous open-ended policy; monthly follow-ups at the hospital were built in, with the extra coercive pressure—for the antabuse group, at least—of being given only a one month's drug supply at each follow-up visit. At the time, antabuse was not yet available just on a physician's prescription. The project intent was not only to see which of these several treatment modalities was more effective in dealing with this population of severe and seemingly endlessly recidivist alcoholic patients but, even more, to ascertain which kinds of alcoholic patients, in terms of their character organizations, could fit best with the psychological meanings and the psychological requirements of each of the treatment offerings. For example, would more masochistic patients fare differentially better with the punitive aspects of conditioned-reflex aversive treatment, with its succession of induced severe nausea and vomiting training sessions, and so on?

This Alcoholism Research Project (ARP) was carried through to its planned conclusion over a two-year period. True to our expectations, the antabuse group, with its enforced continued period of sobriety before drinking could be safely resumed, did better than the others, with, overall, more sustained remission periods; but to our happy surprise our other expectation, or rather hope, was also borne out, that in terms of different character structures and psychological propensities, patients seemed to do differentially better (within our overall not large sample) if their personality dispositions fitted better our presumed understandings of the symbolic meanings to them of their treatment modality. This eventuated in my first (edited) book, *Hospital Treatment of Alcoholism,* published in 1957, with chapters on the working of each of the treatment modalities by the individual responsible for that segment.

We planned at the time to establish a successor project, identical in all respects, except that randomized assignment to each of the treatment groups successively would be replaced by directed assignment to the treatment modality that, on the basis of an initial full psychodynamic evaluation of each patient, would presumably fit best with the requirements of his psychological structure. In this second planned study we would expect an improvement in the sustained remission rate in all four of the proffered treatment modalities. Unfortunately this second project was never undertaken, because at that point I was offered a position—based largely on my work as principal investigator in the Alcoholism Project—in the research department of the Menninger Clinic. I therefore left the position as Chief of the Psychosomatic Section at the Winter VA Hospital, which I had been offered several years earlier after completing my residency, on the basis of my combined completed residency training in both internal medicine and psychiatry.

My position in the research department at the Menninger Clinic, with the unexpected title of Assistant Director of Research (at age 33!), was offered to me by Gardner Murphy, newly arrived in Topeka as Director of Research after a distinguished academic and teaching career at Columbia, and then as chair of the department of psychology at City College in New York. It was on the strong recommendation of a friend and colleague in Topeka, George Klein, who knew of my work in the Alcoholism Project, and it fitted with Gardner's strong wish to recruit a psychiatrist to the research department—then populated exclusively by an (illustrious) array of clinical psychologists—in order to have a better link with the main clinical treatment enterprise at Menninger, and also to replace the role that Merton Gill had had within the research department when David Rapaport, Gardner's main predecessor, had been the research department head.

In my new position half my time was spent in research and half in clinical work (therapy), and I was well embarked on my own psychoanalytic training (which spanned the years from 1952 to 1958), acceptance for which had induced us to stay on in staff positions in Topeka after the completion of my psychiatric residency training. Although, together with a group of colleagues, including a radiologist at a local general hospital, I created a study of the relationship of aberrant psychological functioning to the presence of demonstrated "hot spots" of exaggerated thyroid functioning within the context of an overall normal—or euthyroid—state, which did eventuate in some psychosomatic publications, my main charge, as given to me by Gardner Murphy, was to create a research programme that would involve the large clinical community at the Menninger Clinic, inserting research as much as possible into the heart of the clinical treatment enterprise.

Thus began what became over time my signature activity within the world of psychoanalytic research: the Psychotherapy Research Project (PRP) of the Menninger Foundation. It was the happy coming-together, under Gardner Murphy's benevolent oversight, of a group of us with a variety of converging interests and backgrounds: myself as principal investigator; Lewis Robbins, Director of Adult Psychiatry at the Menninger Clinic, as co-investigator and closest collaborator, who brought the entire adult clinical operations at Menninger within the research orbit; Helen Sargent, an extraordinarily gifted Rogerian-trained clinical psychologist, who elaborated the epistemological and methodological underpinnings of the programme; Lester Luborsky, who had already worked out, for psychotherapy research use, the Health–Sickness Rating Scale (HSRS), the progenitor of the now widely used GAF (Global Assessment of Functioning); and two gifted clinical psychologists, Gerald Ehrenreich, one of the heirs at Menninger to the deployment of the David Rapaport-created projective psychological test battery, and Martin Mayman, who was developing his own object-relational test of early memories.

I will not develop here any of the details of this 30-year-long research study of the treatment and subsequent life careers of our cohort of 42 patients, half in formal psychoanalysis and half in a range of expressive and supportive psychoanalytic psychotherapies. This work, by a group of, by the end, some 20 participating researchers—ranging from full-time involvement like that of Helen Sargent, or half-time, like that of Lew Robbins and myself, down to but six hours per week from many of the participating clinicians—produced over those three decades some 70 articles and 6 books. The final and culminating clinical accounting was my own: *Forty-Two Lives in Treatment: A Study of Psychoanalysis and Psychotherapy* (Wallerstein, 1986), which included follow-up data on the 17 of the 34 from the original cohort known to be still alive, who were reached at the 30-year mark. (Actually, we had had 100% follow-up at the originally designated 3-year post-treatment point—itself unprecedented in this kind of research.)

Of course, we operated within uniquely favourable, never-to-be-repeated circumstances. We started the project in the early 1950s, when ample funding was readily available for psychosocial research. At that time, if you had a good research idea and wrote it up reasonably well in terms of the then state of the art, you could expect to obtain adequate funding: a far contrast to the present-day de-emphasis of, and great paucity of, available funding for psychoanalytically conceived research. But in the early 1950s I was able to put together a million dollars (in 1954 dollars) from a variety of sources—the Foundations' Fund for Research in Psychiatry (FFRP), the Ford Foundation (during its one short window of opportunity for funding for this kind of mental health research), the National Institute of Mental Health—all along with regularly allocated support from the Menninger Foundation itself.

In connection with this, a digression about Merton Gill: We met when he arrived as one of the three designated site visitors to review our very first grant application, that to FFRP. His was the most intense, most incisive, and, at times, most acerbic questioning. He took everything in, but we were completely unable to read his take on the project. Nevertheless, in due course we received an enthusiastic favourable recommendation and the award of the full requested amount. Thus began what was to become a lifelong close professional comradeship. We never worked together, though we often dreamed of it and on one occasion came close to arranging it, but we corresponded endlessly, often at length, about our many agreements and, at times, our real disagreements. One exchange of such detailed correspondence about our differing takes on the evolving relationship of psychoanalytic psychotherapy to its parent, psychoanalysis proper, was published in four letters in the *International Journal of Psychoanalysis* in 1991.

In his fierce dedication to his scholarly activity, and the clarity and incisiveness of thought that he brought to it, Merton Gill was, for me, always an inspiring model—the individual I most regarded as mentor to my own research career. And conscience, too. When I left Topeka—to get ahead of my story for a moment—to move to the San Francisco area in 1966 to become Chief of Psychiatry at the Mount Zion Hospital there, leaving Otto Kernberg to carry the data-gathering work of PRP to its conclusion but committed, myself, to ultimately writing up my own final clinical accounting of the work of the project, I took none of the research monies with me—monies that could have helped to finance the time and effort that this would take. It was Merton who said, "If anyone else told me that this is what they had done, I would never believe that they would—or could—follow through, but with you, I'll believe it." It was this total faith of Merton's that obliged me to fulfil my commitment against all intervening pressures, which led, years later, to my massive book, *Forty-Two Lives in Treatment,* for which, at publication time, Merton gave me the book title, to replace my own much more mundane, tentative one. And Judy and I had the privilege of spending two brief vacation encounters, each of a day or two, with Merton and his wife, Ilse Judas, once in Italy and another time in England—and there we experienced the other side of Merton: warm, funny, and very sentimental.

I was in Chicago and last visited Merton, then seriously ill, just two weeks before his death. In my usual more optimistic mood than his ever was, I tried to comfort and cheer him with thoughts of carrying on, and about his continuing scientific interests and incomplete work plans. I returned to Chicago to speak at his memorial service shortly thereafter and was subsequently asked to write his official obituary for the *International Journal of Psychoanalysis.* In tribute to Merton, I can state that it is his spirit that I have used as guide and support through all the rest of the tale that I am recounting here, both during and after his lifetime.

But to get back to my own story of the unique, and never-to-be-replicated, research opportunity prevailing in the 1950s, and particularly in the Menninger Clinic. Within its full-time salaried staff, time could be allocated for research activity, just as for clinical activity with inpatients and outpatients, or educational activity within the Menninger School of Psychiatry or the Topeka Institute of Psychoanalysis, all without any direct effect on what one earned in terms of salary. And, equally important, the research programme could be endorsed as an official activity within the Menninger Clinic, giving us therefore unencumbered access to the study of the entire patient population (except where the clinical exigencies of the particular patient might decree otherwise), with the required cooperation, then, in the research inquiry, of the patient's therapist and any other involved clinical personnel, the supervisor of the therapy if there was one, the hospital doctor, again, if there was one, and so on.

In terms of the changing *Zeitgeist* over time, our project was developed during a period of still great clinical suspicion of any intrusion into ordinary and natural clinical operations—for example, audio-recording of treatment sessions, which now, a half-century later, has become such a commonplace in many types of analytic therapy research; on the other hand, it was a time when the informed-consent doctrine, with its requirement that research participants give fully informed consent before they can be enlisted for research study, had not yet evolved. At the time, the only constraint upon research activity was the original Hippocratic injunction to do no harm, so that each of us conducting clinical research needed to ensure, to the best of our consciences, that we would not knowingly do anything that might be hurtful to the research subject's overall clinical care and that we would, of course, safeguard completely the privacy and confidentiality of our patients' intimate discourse.

Within this context, we constructed a study of the processes and the outcomes of psychoanalyses and psychoanalytic psychotherapies as they "naturally occur", not impacted on by any research alteration, like recording, and without even the therapist or the patient knowing that they were under research scrutiny until the termination of the therapy. None of that can any longer be done in that way. The many articles and monographs that emerged from this project over its 30-year span report on the way we constructed our research inquiry and carried it out in a detailed study over the treatment and the planned follow-up of the 42 patients in our cohort. The study included specific predictions about therapeutic courses and outcomes that could later be tested for confirmation or refutation, thus ultimately strengthening or weakening the assumptions in our hierarchically organized psychoanalytic theory of therapy and producing, hopefully, an altered and empirically better founded theory of therapy, and we introduced varieties of control of our observational database without control groups, or randomization, or any of the other usual methods of control.

It was this research programme—our Psychotherapy Research Project of the Menninger Foundation—that launched and made my psychoanalytic therapy research career and led, through a sequence of circumstances, ultimately to the creation of CAMP, our own collective present-day multidimensional and multi-site programme. In 1958, I was invited to join the Committee on Research of GAP—the Group for the Advancement of Psychiatry—a maverick Young Turk organization of psychodynamically oriented psychiatrists, created by Will Menninger in the immediate aftermath of the Second World War as a pressure group, to rejuvenate and bring into modern times the until then rigid and by then outdated hierarchic establishment governing American psychiatry. Along with colleagues like Alfred Stanton and David Hamburg, I stayed with the GAP Committee for eight years, the final six as its chair, and during my tenure there we produced two reports: in 1959, "Some Observations on Controls in Psychiatric Research", and in 1966, "Psychiatric Research and the Assessment of Change".

In that same year, 1958, together with Lew Robbins, I was invited to participate in—and to make a presentation from our Menninger project in—the first of three conferences on psychotherapy research under the auspices of the American Psychological Association (APsyA). At that first conference on psychotherapy research, eight groups were invited (among them Carl Rogers), but only one other group was psychoanalytic in conception: that of Merton Gill and Timothy Leary at the Oakland, California, Kaiser Hospital. At the second conference, in 1961, Richard Siegal, Irwin Rosen, and Lester Luborsky participated from our Menninger programme. I again participated in the third conference in 1966, with an optimistically titled "semi-final" report from our Menninger research programme. It is out of this sequence of three conferences that the Society for Psychotherapy Research (SPR) evolved, to become, over time, one of the most active ongoing annual gatherings of worldwide psychotherapy researchers of all theoretical persuasions, psychoanalytic researchers included.

As I was becoming a member of the APsaA in 1960 (after the then mandatory two-year interval following graduation from an affiliated Institute), I was invited—on the basis of my research activities—to join the Committee on Training for Research (CTR), created in 1958 and still ongoing, and in recent years renamed Committee on Research and Special Training (CORST). The CTR had been set up to monitor the approval process for full clinical psychoanalytic training for academic scholars and researchers—mostly psychologists—who would undertake to utilize the training, and the continuing psychoanalytic work that they would be authorized to do upon graduation, in the service of psychoanalytic research, and thus to enhance psychoanalytically the research careers to which they were already committed. This was the start, albeit on a very restricted and limited basis, of the clinical psychoanalytic training of non-physicians under the auspices of the American Psychoanalytic Association and was, on that account, looked upon with great suspicion by many of its members, long committed to the proposition that as a healing art, psychoanalysis was a subspeciality of psychiatry and should therefore be limited to psychiatric physicians. When I became chair of this committee in 1966, I became responsible for presenting its reports, policy proposals, and individual waiver applications for individual non-physician aspirants who had met its standards to the biannual meetings of the Board on Professional Standards (BOPS) of the APsaA, the supreme governing body over national training standards for all its nationwide affiliated Institutes. In that context, I was perceived as the champion of non-medical psychoanalytic researchers and of formal psychoanalytic research within the APsaA, all of which led me into a position of central recognition and perhaps contributed to my election, in 1970, to the position of President-Elect of the APsaA (to then automatically become President for a one-year term starting the following year). As a result, in 1970, after a ten-year stay on the CTR, I resigned my position there.

My policy statements and recommendations from the CTR over the span of my chairmanship had not always been in accord with majority sentiment on the BOPS, who were suspicious to some extent of the formal psychoanalytic research enterprise and to a greater extent of the clinical training of non-physicians, but my views and my initiatives had always been attended to carefully, because as the chair of this important committee of BOPS, I was always speaking from within the centre of the "establishment" and on behalf of research, in the abstract, a perceived social good—a position that I have always been fortunate enough to enjoy within the APsaA and the IPA and could then use to promote my own policy commitments, in which the support of psychoanalytic research was always central.

And it was during that same period in the 1960s that I was invited to participate as a member of the APsaA's ad hoc Central Fact-Gathering Committee. This group of established psychoanalytic researchers, chaired by David Hamburg, was charged with organizing and summarizing the data gathered and studied by the Association over the decade of the 1950s about psychoanalytic patients and the adjudged outcomes of their therapy. The latter was provided by 800 participants giving 10,000 Initial Reports and some 3,000 Final Reports, all to no formulated conclusion. The overall findings of this review committee on this "survey of psychoanalytic practice" were published in the *Journal of the American Psychoanalytic Association* in 1967 (Hamburg et al., 1967), as the very largest sample ever in the array of psychotherapy research projects that I have elsewhere designated as "first-generation" psychotherapy research.

Also, during this same decade of the 1960s, on the basis of my being then known as an established and recognized psychotherapy researcher—based again on the ongoing activities of our Menninger project and the stream of publications emanating from it and on the basis also of having been the recipient of National Institute of Mental Health (NIMH) grant support for that project—I was cajoled into "taking my turn" as a member of the NIMH Research Scientist Career Development Award Committee, the body that passed on applications by research scientists across the whole array of social and behavioural sciences for financial support for the overall activities of the researcher—not for just specific projects—ranging, at the different experience levels, from five years, to (at that time) lifetime support. Participating in several site visits a year and reviewing, in three or four several-day yearly meetings at NIMH headquarters in Bethesda, Maryland—where approximately 80 applications were processed annually—gave me an unparalleled overview of cutting-edge research activities across the whole kaleidoscopic array of involved disciplines and research arenas. I served on that committee from 1966 to 1970 and was its chair from 1968 to 1970.

In 1969 an ad hoc committee, chaired by Heinz Kohut, inquired into the state of "scientific activities" within the APsaA. It reported pessimistically that there was a progressive drying up of creative scientific activity within organized psychoanalysis and that the very organization of our institutional structures, devised to promote the educational and professional activities of the APsaA, exerted a stultifying effect upon innovative work and original thinking. Several organizational remedies were proposed by the committee to reverse this parlous (and ultimately perilous) state of affairs, and the APsaA adopted the committee's "intermediate proposal": to create a standing Committee on Scientific Activities (CSA), designed to promote such activities in the broadest possible way. The full report of the ad hoc Committee was published by Kohut in the *Journal of the American Psychoanalytic Association* in 1970. Kohut declined to accept the chairmanship of this new standing committee and suggested that I should take it. I agreed to accept it, provided that both Kohut and Merton Gill agreed to serve on it, which both happily did. I held that chairmanship for the first five years of the Committee's existence (1972–77) and remained on it until 1998. At the initial meetings of the CSA, I sat at the head of a long table, flanked by Kohut and Gill on either side; the incisive, and at times disputatious, interchanges between the two of them face to face have been, for me, among the most rewarding discourses on the nature and the parameters of psychoanalytic research and scientific activity that I have ever been privileged to be party to.

A major spin-off from CSA was the creation, in 1976, of the APsaA's Fund for Psychoanalytic Research (FPR), a fund financed in its first years by voluntary contributions from members of the APsaA but now built into the ongoing dues structure. This was, for the first time, a fund created specifically to support psychoanalytic research—albeit in only modest amounts—and application was not limited to members of the APsaA. The FPR functioned like an NIMH review committee and in its early years consisted mainly of members of the APsaA who had served on NIMH review committees. About a dozen applications were received annually, and about half were found sufficiently meritorious and were funded. Some of these financed pilot programmes that could, on the basis of that work, be parlayed up later to more substantial funding from governmental or foundation sources. I was the chair of that committee for its first five years (1976–81) and was thus party to the review of approximately 60 proposals.

As a side note to all of this, and again based on my established position as a psychoanalytic therapy researcher, I was offered two Fellowship years at the Center for Advanced Study in the Behavioral Sciences at Stanford, California. During the first of these sabbatical years (1964–65) I wrote up, at the rate of one per week, the full case reports—based on all the accumulated material in their research case files—of the treatment courses and the subsequent life courses of our 42 patients in PRP up to that point. These full case descriptions run to 50–70 typed pages each. During the second year (1981–82), I used these reports, supplemented by the additional follow-up information that could be obtained on half of the still living patients' cohort (17 of the 34 from the original 42) to fashion my overall clinical accounting of that project, *Forty-Two Lives in Treatment* (published in 1986).

When I became President of the International Psychoanalytical Association for two consecutive two-year terms (1985–89), one of my first initiatives was to introduce two formal half-day sessions, one on conceptual, and one on empirical psychoanalytic research, into the programmes of the biannual week-long International Congresses—a first for that organization. Under subsequent presidents—especially Joseph Sandler and Otto Kernberg—these research initiatives within the IPA have been carried much further: an annual research conference, held annually in March in London (since his death named the Joseph Sandler Research Conference), brings together empirical researchers from every region of psychoanalytic activity, together with very senior clinical discussants of the relevance of the presented work to clinical practice; a 10-day research "summer school" held annually in July, also in London, and attended through competitive application, brings neophyte and would-be psychoanalytic researchers together with a seasoned worldwide research faculty to help the students formulate their research ideas into scientifically meritorious grant-application form; and—most recently—a Research Advisory Board (RAB) of the IPA, with an allocated budget from the IPA's dues income and with a 25-member international review board, knowledgeable in psychoanalytic research, which reviews some 40–50 applications from around the world each year (receiving them semi-annually) and funds about half of them, though, of course, like the APsaA's fund, very modestly. The RAB was created in 1997 at the inception of Otto Kernberg's presidency of the IPA, and he asked me to be its first chair; Daniel Widlöcher, his successor as IPA President, asked me to continue in that role.

It was all of this—my entire psychoanalytic research career to that point—that prompted Homer Curtis, then President of the APsaA, to turn to me in 1989 when CAMP, the Collaborative Analytic Multisite Program of the APsaA, was brought into being. The circumstances were as follows. A member of the APsaA in the Washington, DC, area had contacted Homer to inform him that he had treated a very wealthy patient who, shortly after his discharge in a state well enough to resume his business functioning, had created a Foundation that, among other interests, would wish to support psychoanalytic therapy research, if organized officially under the auspices of the APsaA, and had designated his therapist as the president of this new Foundation, with others of his business associates as the other members of its Board of Directors.

Having received this inquiry, Homer called me, and asked whether I would undertake to organize such a collective psychoanalytic therapy research programme under the auspices of the APsaA. I inquired about how much money might be available for this large project. Homer assured me that he had thought "big" and had indicated that it could require US$50,000–100,000 annually, and he had been informed in return that that would indeed be feasible. I said to Homer that he had thought "small": the kind of programme being envisaged would require a minimum of a half-million dollars a year, guaranteed for five years, which, with annual cost-of-living increases and salary increments for those involved, would add up to about three million dollars over the five-year span.

Within a few days, Homer came back to me with the news that the Foundation would be receptive to a consortium application under the auspices of the APsaA for an amount of up to the three million dollars over five years. At that point I undertook to organize what was to come to be called CAMP, and I invited all the psychoanalytic therapy researchers whom I knew around the country to an all-day organizational meeting at the December meeting of the APsaA in New York that year. In total about 30 people came, representing 16 working groups—just about everyone whom I had contacted.

Up to that point, each of the research groups—whether process, outcome, or combined process–outcome—had been working with its own instruments and measures, created within its own conceptual framework, and applied to whatever database—almost always audio-recorded therapy sessions—it had available, with some having many recorded (and in some instances even transcribed) consecutive psychoanalytic hours. Because of this diversity of idiosyncratic organizing concepts—FRAMES, Core Conflictual Relationship Theme (CCRT), Referential Activity, (RA), etc.—with each group operating with its individually available database, comparative assessment of findings across these groups was distressingly difficult. It was hard even to know whether similar words (and concepts) used by different groups meant the same or different things, or whether different words (and concepts) being used essentially encompassed the same meanings.

The research plan envisaged to deal with this issue that arose from that first meeting was the following: to create a shared database of audiotaped and transcribed therapy and analytic hours (transcribed to the rigorous Mergenthaler–Stinson standards, agreed to by all). Each of the 16 collaborating groups would then apply its own concepts and instruments to these same therapeutic sessions, and the groups would meet over a period of a minimum of two days, once or, preferably, twice each year, to contrast and compare their findings with regard to the same sessions. Additionally, in the interest of the outcome (not the process) measures, newly recruited patients entering analytic treatments who would agree to take part in the research study would have the participating outcome measures applied during the initial evaluative interviews, again at treatment termination, whenever that might be, and hopefully after that—if all this collaborative work were to go on for so long—at specified follow-up points, perhaps at one-year and then at five-year intervals.

It was an ambitious, far-ranging plan indeed, but one that would, if it could be carried out, put the whole field of process and outcome studies of psychoanalytic treatments a full quantum leap ahead. It would assess comparatively the convergences (or the divergences) of the various research instruments and measures involved; it would link outcome results (*what* changes had taken place in the therapies under study, in both their reach and their limitations) with process results (*how* those changes had come about or been brought about): it would be, finally, the full realization of the P–T–O principle enunciated by Hans Strupp, Schacht, and Henry (1988) that there should be full congruence, in language and in substance, between the patient's problems, the treatment of those problems, and the outcomes achieved.

All this would, of course, be costly in time and money in execution. Within the half-million dollars that I had agreed to as a possibly realizable budget, each of the 16 collaborating groups would receive only $25,000 a year, which already added up to a total of $400,000. In today's world, that is a modest sum for a serious analytic therapy research project, but to most, who had all along been operating on the proverbial shoestring, it would be a guaranteed addition that would make them collectively feel that the work envisaged would indeed be feasible. Only $100,000 would be left for the central organization, which would include a salaried full-time project director (in the San Francisco Bay Area, and under my supervision) plus the money needed to cover the expenses of the annual (or biannual) meetings of the collaborating groups.

This plan as a whole was agreed to enthusiastically at that first all-day meeting, and the group name, CAMP, was devised. I undertook to write the grant application, incorporating into it the statements of each of the participating groups covering exactly what they would do year by year. The five-year grant proposal was then duly submitted with its budget, including the annual increases, coming to a total that was very close to the agreed-upon three-million-dollar cap.

Unhappily, this first grant application for CAMP was turned down, with almost no explanation concerning its presumed deficiencies. I was in close contact with the President of the Foundation, and he agreed—with, in my view, some reluctance—to attend the next scheduled meeting of CAMP to discuss these issues with the membership, so that we could try to revise the application in response to whatever problems emerged in that discussion, and then resubmit.

The agreed-upon meeting took place. Its atmosphere was charged, and the Foundation President appeared uneasy. Merton Gill, one of the most articulate and forceful of the group members, was particularly incisive in pressing for clarification of what the precise scientific shortcomings of the application were presumed to be, but no serious issues seemed to be raised in response for the group's consideration. At the end, it was agreed that we could resubmit the application with whatever revisions I would incorporate, based on this long and intense discussion. But the application was again rejected, and with even less—in fact, hardly any—explanation, and the Foundation President avoided all further contact with me or with any other CAMP member. Diligent search by the APsaA failed to reveal any jurisdiction within which this new foundation had been incorporated.

Unhappily we realized that these initial hopes for funding had ended in disappointment.

But CAMP had now existed over several meetings. The members had come to know each other as working colleagues and to know the scope of each other's scientific work, and small collaborative projects had been undertaken, essentially combining the instruments from two or more of the CAMP subgroups in conjoined research programmes. Regular presentations were being made at the semiannual CAMP meetings from work in progress at various participating groups, in accord with an agenda that I prepared for each meeting, depending on my ongoing correspondence with the membership. After almost a decade, the frequency of meetings was dropped to once a year, during the December meeting of the APsaA in New York; the annual May meeting, which had rotated around the country, was discontinued. The composition of CAMP has varied somewhat over time: some groups stopped coming regularly and at least two dropped out, but others joined, especially from Europe, from Sweden, Holland, and Norway, and with the group from Ulm, Germany (Erhard Mergenthaler and Horst Kächele) becoming unfailing participants and collaborators with a number of the American groups.

In other words, CAMP was now a thriving, going concern, a yearly all-day gathering of psychoanalytic therapy researchers from around the world, reporting on new and innovative work by both established and neophyte therapy researchers and instigating collaborative activities among as many as four of the CAMP subgroups working on a shared database. Over the years of its operations, CAMP has also explored the possibilities for securing the large funds originally envisaged to carry out the full collaborative study, this time from NIMH, and has also spun off an archive of audiotaped (and, to a small extent, transcribed) therapeutic sessions from both psychoanalytic psychotherapies and full psychoanalyses.

The contacts with NIMH were initiated during a period in the early 1990s, when we were led to believe that such a grant as we had originally sought might be entertained by its psychosocial grant division. Several discussion visits were made to Bethesda by a group of CAMP representatives to meet with various members of the NIMH hierarchy. This expense was defrayed out of a total of $25,000 awarded to CAMP by the APsaA to prepare a proper NIMH application, should we conclude that this could be a worthwhile effort. But after—eventually—discouraging advice from NIMH about the likelihood of success of an application for this kind of research, this full grant application process was never undertaken. The money made available to us was mostly used to cover the secretarial costs of properly transcribing such various segments of sessions from the databases held by our constituent members as it was agreed would best serve the research needs of the CAMP majority.

For the archive—named the Psychoanalytic Research Consortium (PRC)—with Sherwood (Woody) Waldron, Jr, as its President, the original impetus came from Merton Gill. He was at the time the most senior member of CAMP and, as I have already described, a very close comrade over my entire professional lifetime. By then seriously ill with heart disease, he was considering the best possible disposition of his lifetime of accumulated research records. He did not want them to be destroyed or to disappear with his demise, but he also certainly did not want them to fall into hands that would just store and neglect them, or, even more distressingly, allow them to fall into improper use that could violate the guarantees of confidentiality under which he had secured them. What Merton did want was to have his records properly secured and maintained, "sanitized" so as to blot out identifying data (names, places, often dates, etc.), and then made available, under appropriate safeguards for their use, to qualified psychoanalytic therapy researchers. We agreed to create such an archive, which became the PRC, the research material to be stored in climate-controlled storage space that the Menninger Foundation maintained in an abandoned salt mine in central Kansas, under the direct supervision of the psychoanalytically trained chief librarian at the Menninger, Alice Brand Bartlett, who had from the beginning been one of the officers of PRC. Then, of course, we would await sufficient funding—which was then to be regularly sought—to catalogue the material, "sanitize" all of it, transcribe the tapes, and so on, so that it could all be made available for study by the psychoanalytic therapy research world.

All of this was done; Merton's research files (23 boxes in all) were made available by his widow, our psychoanalytic colleague, Ilse Judas, and shipped at my direction to the Menninger Foundation. With the recent—at that time completely unanticipated—collapse of Menninger on its home site and the decision made to move its operations to another venue under the auspices of a major medical-school department of psychiatry, Gill's research records have now been shipped to Woody Waldron, as the still ongoing President of PRC, and were stored by him (at least temporarily) in his apartment building in New York City.

The intent in creating PRC, beyond providing a proper continuously usable and useful home for Merton Gill's accumulated research records and research patient data, was to serve also as a nidus to attract other such data contributions from retiring or deceased colleagues, so as to become the available common archival source for data for psychoanalytic therapy research study. Thus far, other contributions have indeed been made, and members of CAMP who have the largest privately held collections of taped therapy sessions have likewise promised to make PRC the beneficiary of their holdings upon their retirement from active research study. At the time, PRC was created as a separately registered non-profit organization outside the official framework of the APsaA (though all of its governing body, including myself as its vice-President, were CAMP members) because of difficulties—such as the handling of liability issues and proper insurance—that then concerned the officers of the APsaA. Now, almost a decade later, and in an altered climate, negotiations are underway to dissolve PRC as a separate corporate entity and to bring it in as a committee within the structure of the APsaA, thus better ensuring its stability and long-term continuity.

After a decade of responsibility for chairing CAMP, and on my retirement from practice and from major administrative responsibilities within organized psychoanalysis, I asked to resign my chairmanship—though I intend to continue my active attendance as long as my health permits—and to turn the leadership role over to Wilma Bucci, a staunch and very hardworking member from the beginning, who has assisted all along in many of the arrangements involved in the CAMP meetings and in the contacts with outside groups as well. An interim of shared leadership was arranged. By the December 2001 meeting, at which my original presentation (of which this is a reconstructed and much expanded version) was made, the leadership had passed entirely to Wilma, and with the cooperation of Bert Freedman, she decided to make this an all-day Symposium marking my research career and my role in the history of CAMP. For that, I am deeply grateful. I felt extremely rewarded by all my colleagues in psychoanalytic research who came from around the world to participate in this programme, and by all the other colleagues—researchers in fact or in spirit—who chose to attend.

Afterword

I end with a note for the future. What do I see as the best possible directions for psychoanalytic research at this time—or, more particularly, for psychoanalytic therapy research, and for the continuing role of CAMP (now restructured as RAAPA–CAMP, Research Associates of the American Psychoanalytic Association Collaborative Analytic Multi-site Program) within that research future? No one can realistically predict long-term directions for any profession or academic discipline, but, at least for the near future of psychoanalytic therapy research, I hold to the original vision of CAMP, articulated now almost two decades ago. It is a vision that we have never been able to fund fully and to pursue adequately, but the experience of CAMP since its creation in 1989, in its many fruitful partial collaborations among its members and in the scientific interchanges at its regular meetings in all the years since, has, for me, more than confirmed the ongoing productivity as well as the potential promise inherent in that vision.

The vision itself I have already stated: to coordinate the research endeavours of the committed psychoanalytic therapy research community, ultimately literally around the world and preferably under the even wider auspices of the IPA, all working within their preferred conceptual frameworks (and with their own methods, and their own instruments, measures, scales, etc.) around a shared database of properly transcribed analytic therapy sessions, towards three basic, interlocking ends:

1. To assess convergences and divergences, to reconcile apparent differences where evident, and to arrive ultimately at that array of process measures that, in ensemble, provide the most comprehensive and integrated overview of process-in-action;
2. to link that integrated array of process measures conceptually and methodologically to a similarly arrived-at array of outcome measures (for before, during, and after, cross-sectional assessments), so that
3. the outcomes achieved in therapies (the answers to the *what* has changed question) can be tied conceptually and empirically to the described processes (the answers to the *how* the changes have come about, or been brought about, question), towards an ever fuller understanding of the mechanisms of psychic change that

> is consequent on psychoanalytic therapy, in all their extents and limitations—and in appropriate fulfilment, then, of the aspired-to principle of P–T–O congruence.

This is what I have elsewhere (2001b) called the task of the coming "fourth generation" of psychotherapy research.

Is all this achievable? I think that it is, given the spread, the commitment, the energy, and the intelligence of the new generation, worldwide, of trained and dedicated psychotherapy researchers. Will it be achieved? I think that it can be, if sufficient resources—material, intellectual, and emotional—can be mobilized towards that end. That is my hope and my conviction for the future of this enterprise, to which I have devoted a professional life, and I look confidently to CAMP (now RAAPA–CAMP) to be one of its central carriers.

II

From Topeka onward

5

Bob Wallerstein in Topeka

Otto F. Kernberg

It is a particular pleasure as well as a great honour to be able to contribute a few words to this celebration of Bob Wallerstein's work. I owe it to him that I was able to come to live and work permanently in the United States. I owe him very personally for his help in overcoming my writing inhibition at an early stage of my professional work at the Menninger Foundation. He was a significant influence in my appointment as Training Analyst at the Topeka Psychoanalytic Institute, and he strongly stimulated and supported my work as part of the administrative leadership of the International Psychoanalytical Association. But beyond everything else, it was my work in the Menninger Foundation Psychotherapy Research Project, under the leadership of Bob Wallerstein, that permitted me to develop my own studies of severe personality disorders—my explorations of the psychopathology and psychoanalytic psychotherapy of borderline conditions.

The Psychotherapy Research Project of the Menninger Foundation was the flagship of a first generation of research on the process and outcome of psychoanalysis and psychoanalytic psychotherapy—a major project that has perhaps not had its equal in terms of scope, depth, and sheer persistence of the work on the part of a distinguished group of theoreticians, clinicians, and clinical researchers.

The planning for this project had started in 1952; in 1954 the actual project was set up, under the leadership of Robert Wallerstein and Lewis Robbins. When Robbins left Topeka in 1958, Wallerstein took on its sole leadership, until he also departed from Topeka in 1966. The basic methodology was influenced by Helen Sargent and Wayne Holtzman and, more indirectly, by John Benjamin. The early brain trust of the project included, in addition to Bob Wallerstein, Lester Luborsky, Gardner Murphy, Helen Sargent, Lewis Robbins, and Gerald Ehrenreich.

A total of 42 patients were studied in depth over many years, half of them in standard psychoanalysis and half in psychoanalytic expressive or supportive psychotherapy, as described by Wallerstein (1986). Careful evaluations of over 150 variables regarding the patient, the treatment, and the patient's life situation were carried out at the initial point of treatment, at the end of the treatment, and a two-year follow-up. Each session of these treatments was documented with extensive typed summaries, so that each case included three large volumes of material to evaluate all those variables. The patient variables included, among others, anxiety and symptoms, ego factors, motivational factors, and relationship factors. The treatment variables included techniques, subject matters, goals, therapists' skill, global change, and transference resolution. The situational variables included stress, conflict triggers, material support, interpersonal support, need congruence, mutability, and opportunity.

A basic question was, which of these patient, treatment, and situational variables contributed to significant patient change, and, in this connection, which would be the most important measures to evaluate patients' changes over time? Here, the method of "paired comparisons", which permitted us to compare individuals in the entire patient population with each other in terms of an ordering of the degree of change in each variable from minimal to maximal, led to one of Dr Wallerstein's brilliant ideas: namely, to carry out a paired-comparison study of all the patients in terms of a global, clinical judgement of overall change, comparing each patient with each of the others in a series of "batches" that would, eventually, permit us to line up the entire patient population in terms of maximal to minimal change obtained.

I must confess that it was sobering to discover that one of our scales—namely, Luborsky's Health–Sickness Rating Scale (HSRS), the original scale that has now been transformed into the standardized GAF score for overall patient's functioning—replicated quickly the laborious, time-consuming paired-comparison study of overall change that I carried out, over many months, with Dr Ester Burstein, in our small outpatient offices at the Menninger Foundation, at times with unfriendly feelings about Bob Wallerstein, who had assigned to us this lengthy and at times monotonous and frustrating work. We discovered that the HSRS not only replicated exactly our paired comparisons of global change, but also confirmed the power of that scale in practically equating the complex overall qualitative evaluation of patients' changes carried out by senior clinicians, evaluated quantitatively by our paired-comparison study.

Bob Wallerstein supervised, coordinated, and consulted on all aspects of the project, continually meeting with the various teams working on patient, treatment, and situational variables; and he developed new methodological approaches as well as hypotheses for specific analyses of the material throughout all that time. Perhaps his most original contribution to the vexing question of how to evaluate jointly, in terms of some general hypotheses, the many variables explored by the project was his decision to consult with Louis Gutmann, the director of the Israel Institute for Applied Social Research in Jerusalem, Israel, in 1965. Jointly, they developed an overall methodology consisting in combining facet analysis and multidimensional scalogram analysis into an overall frame that permitted the construction of a profile, for each case, in terms of a "mapping sentence"—that is, an overall qualitative statement that defined the "high" or "low" status of that patient on each of 156 variables. By jointly projecting those individual patient profiles onto a virtual multidimensional space, reduced to a two-dimensional space by means of a specific computer programme, it became possible to analyse which variables "divided" the space, in terms of which variables were close to each other within that space: closeness indicated relatedness; separation, by a previous hypothesis, a specific relationship.

After careful evaluation of the hypothesized relationships among all the variables, we selected 50 variables for an overall hypothetical statement and subjected the corresponding profiles to the computerized multidimensional scalogram analysis. In September 1967 Ann Appelbaum, Lolafaye Coyne, Leonard Horwitz, and I spent one month in Jerusalem, carrying out the corresponding analyses that led to the conclusions of the quantitative study of the project. For the first time we were able to confirm and disconfirm some generally held psychoanalytic hypotheses about the relationship between treatment technique, severity of illness, and outcome. That quantitative study was complemented by a qualitative study, the careful evaluation of the relationship between process and outcome of each case that Bob Wallerstein brilliantly presented in his book, *Forty-Two Lives in Treatment*, pointing to the importance of supportive factors throughout all psychoanalytically oriented treatments. The quantitative study, in turn, helped me to develop my theoretical formulations regarding borderline personality organization and the optimal psychoanalytic psychotherapy for these cases. At this time, we are testing this psychoanalytic psychotherapy and supportive psychotherapy in comparison with each other and with a non-analytic, cognitive behavioural therapy for borderline conditions, in a major, randomized, empirical study.

But what I would like to stress at this point, in addition to the important contributions to research in psychoanalysis and psychoanalytic psychotherapy that took place in Topeka under Bob Wallerstein's leadership, is the impact of his personality on all of us: his creative power, the warmth and generosity that helped all of us grow throughout those years. I have already mentioned that he spearheaded the project in 1954 and took over its sole leadership in 1958, when Lewis Robbins departed for New York. In 1959, during what turned out to be one of the most memorable dinners of my life, Bob invited me to join the Psychotherapy Research Project of the Menninger Foundation, which I did in 1961. In 1966, after Bob Wallerstein left for San Francisco, first, to take the leadership of psychiatry at the Mount Zion Hospital, and then, to become Chairman of the department of psychiatry of the University of California in San Francisco, I replaced him as director of the project, until its completion in 1972. In short, I have had the privilege of working directly under Bob Wallerstein and indirectly under his spiritual leadership from 1961 to 1972.

Perhaps the major impact of Wallerstein's personality throughout those years was his capacity to keep a very disparate, potentially conflictive, highly individualistic team of clinicians, researchers, and methodologists together. He had an enormous capacity for conciliation among mutually antagonistic and potentially combative senior researchers. He elegantly protected the project against influential, envious outsiders whose criticisms could have damaged our morale without his sensitive intervention. He always remained calm and friendly, not responding to provocations, and protected all of us who worked in the project from interferences and even persecution, beyond our own awareness. Bob was able to keep in the project some rather idiosyncratic characters, while enabling their considerable skills to come into maximum play. He had an unusual degree of tolerance of envy and competitiveness on the part of both research members and other senior clinicians at the Menninger Foundation, who envied his meteoric rise to fame throughout the national and international psychoanalytic community. He was able to maintain collegial relationships, while not succumbing to a dangerous, self-defeating naïveté in dealing with such challenges.

Robert Wallerstein's approach to psychoanalysis combined a scholarly knowledge of the literature and deep convictions about basic psychoanalytic theory with an openness to alternative hypotheses and the limitations of our field. Particularly after leaving for San Francisco, in his frequent travels back to Topeka, he warned us about "the world out there", which was highly critical about psychoanalysis and required a serious effort on our part not simply to remain contented with psychoanalytic affirmations, but to carry out empirical research to evaluate psychoanalytic theories, techniques, and findings. He foresaw major challenges to psychoanalysis many years before the psychoanalytic community became aware of their importance, and stimulated many of us to reinforce our commitment to research.

Bob was an expert on a broad spectrum of issues of daily living: providing helpful and candid advice on how to deal with various people in authority whose ongoing good will towards the project in general, and towards me in particular, was well worth cultivating. Bob Wallerstein introduced me to the Atchison, Topeka, and Santa Fe Railroad depot for damaged furniture, where wonderful things could be obtained extremely cheap; he guided me to "Bobo's", a little diner where the best hamburgers I have ever had in the United States, or elsewhere, were prepared.

Above all, he helped me to overcome my writing inhibition. After carefully listening to my concern over the chaotic and confusing text that I would produce when attempting to dictate my thoughts into a Wollensack machine (the latest advance in audio recording at that time), he recommended to me to write a "draft 0"—that is, a draft that, horrible as it might be, would be totally safe from ever being seen by anyone else and would only be used by me to sort the information out sufficiently for a Draft 1, which could then be worked on. While this did not resolve my obsessive-compulsive tendencies altogether, it definitely helped me to overcome my inhibition.

Bob Wallerstein always looked interested, relaxed, and open to new knowledge, and we all wondered how, where, and when he got to do all the impressive writing and contributions to psychoanalytic and psychiatric literature that he was carrying out. He made all of us feel inferior, and while we reacted with varying degrees of envy and admiration, in my case, I dare say, it was an undiluted sense of gratitude, loyalty, and admiration, mixed with an unrestrainable curiosity about his way of working. Close observation finally led me to discover that, in boring professional meetings, while I struggled to remain awake, Bob Wallerstein was quietly opening, reading, and making notes on the incoming mail that he had brought to the meeting (a technique I copied and have maintained to this day). When he was preparing to leave Topeka to go to San Francisco, I spent some time with him in his office on one of the last days with us. I noticed, while he was emptying his desk, an enormous number of crumpled papers in various corners, which he had evidently shoved aside over an extended period of time. This observation gave me an exhilarating sense of relief.

Looking back on Bob Wallerstein's Topeka years, what emerges strikingly for me is the gradual development of several features of his professional work and leadership style in psychiatry and psychoanalysis that have come to be fully expressed in later years. First, his openness to new ideas and his consistent effort to avoid allowing personal controversies and hostilities to restrict our willingness to consider and explore unfamiliar territory. He taught us to maintain equanimity in the face of personalized or defensive attacks on ideas and to remain loyal to the intellectual and scientific principle of examining all sides of an issue on their own merits. Second, his remarkable tolerance of human envy and limitations, not out of weakness or naïveté, but out of a deep respect for each individual, and in an effort to get the best from everybody, without, at the same time, letting oneself be exploited or manipulated. He was perfectly capable of bringing into line, without alienating them, errant team members who shirked their responsibilities. Third, and most importantly, coming from within a sheltered psychoanalytically oriented fortress like the Menninger Foundation, Bob rapidly assessed the changing nature of the professional and cultural environment that psychoanalysis was facing in the United States and internationally, and he was the first to raise the alarm over the need to respond to professional, scientific, and intellectual challenges with a broad effort at scientific research. This led to his crucial influence in shifting priorities onto the investment of resources in research on the part of the APsaA and the IPA, and the corresponding changes in the programmes of the International Psychoanalytic Congresses. Last, but not least, Bob Wallerstein has provided us with a model for a creative, strong yet flexible, generous, and generative leadership of work groups and organizations, which has helped many of us to mature, not only in our professional work, but as human beings.

6

The evolution of some short stories

Hartvig Dahl

Hartvig Dahl, In Memoriam

"Psychoanalysis has a long way to go, it is under assault from philosophers, analysts and hermeneuticists alike for its claim to be a science, but we will get there." These were the words spoken by Hartvig Dahl to one of his colleagues some 30 years ago. Hartvig died on 17 March 2007, at the age of 83. Hartvig was a psychoanalyst-researcher, a man of original ideas and strong passions, whose entire career was devoted to empirically guided psychoanalytic inquiry. He was a powerful advocate of the need for recordings of psychoanalytic treatments, and he developed the first systematic archive of verbatim session transcripts, including the famous case of Mrs C. He was a pioneer in the application of computer-assisted methods and linguistic analysis for the monitoring of the psychoanalytic session. This work was elaborated and expanded in his collaboration with his wife, Virginia Teller, a linguist and computer scientist, as, for example, in their early work that he referred to as *murder by syntax* (Dahl, Teller, Moss, & Trujillo, 1978), which identified systematic linguistic indicators of transference and countertransference.

Hartvig was a strong advocate for microanalytic and collaborative research; this vision inspired the first international conference on Psychoanalytic Process Research Strategies held in 1985 in Ulm, Germany, as a pre-conference to the Hamburg IPAC. A single session of the Mrs C. case, Hour Five, to which Hartvig referred as the "specimen hour" of psychoanalysis, was the subject of intensive study by psychoanalytic researchers from around the world; this conference was a golden hour for psychoanalytic process research. The proceedings were published in the famous "blue book" (Dahl, Kächele, & Thomä, 1988), legendary among psychoanalytic process researchers and now hard to find.

While his contributions are too many to list, we must mention two of his major original works: his emotion theory, in which emotions are viewed as appetitive wishes and beliefs about their fulfilment, which provided a basis for classification of emotion words that is in active use in empirical research today; and his development of the concept of FRAMES—Fundamental, Repetitive And Maladaptive Emotion Structures—which provides a systematic basis for the identification of underlying emotional themes in the stories that people tell; this work was carried out collaboratively with Virginia Teller and built on their joint discoveries. The search for the discovery of "fundamental" underlying structures, the inclusion of the notion of "repetition", the appreciation of pathogenesis in the use of "maladaptive", all built on the dynamic processes inherent in emotions, were powerful manifestations of Hartvig's view of the psychoanalytic process.

Many of Hartvig's accomplishments were rooted in his early training in Topeka, as is evident from his brief essay here, his last work in print, in which he relished his contact with Karl Menninger. At the Menninger Clinic he had common origins with Bob Wallerstein. However, his collaboration with Wallerstein came later. Having introduced the strategy of collaborative application of multiple measures to verbatim recordings early in his career, Hartvig was a natural comrade-in-arms for Bob during the struggles in the forming of CAMP. He sat at the table in the formative—even turbulent—meetings, as described in Wallerstein's account in this volume, and he lent his commitment and his expertise to this work. As Hartvig knew, the shared session transcripts could become the territory in which researchers could apply their own methodologies and explore divergent, often contradictory explanatory hypotheses. This goal still remains more an ideal than an actuality, but, in Hartvig's words, "we will get there".

Finally, for us, Hartvig was a valued friend and a strong colleague, whose contributions have found their way into many of our writings. We can hear his voice and sense his passion as we write.

Wilma Bucci & Norbert Freedman

I have always imagined, from noting Robert Wallerstein's career, that he prudently planned it that way, because that is the kind of person I have always thought him to be. I believe that he carefully studied what the Menninger and Winter VA Hospital in Topeka had to offer in psychiatric residencies, and he deliberately decided to go to what he considered to be the best place—a path that eventually led him to become chair of the Department of Psychiatry at the University of California Medical School in San Francisco.

Whether or not my beliefs about Bob are correct, they contrast markedly with my own path. I arrived at Topeka almost by accident. The story of my own career could hardly be more different, as were he and I as psychiatric residents in Topeka, where we did not know each other well. I told parts of the culmination of my own story in a chapter entitled, "The Voyage of el Rubaiyat to the Discovery of FRAMES" (Dahl, 1998).

After my medical internship at Gorgas Hospital in the Panama Canal Zone, I had to serve in the army for two years. With no previous training in psychiatry, I was assigned to the US Army hospital on Okinawa and appointed the island psychiatrist! We were housed in a Quonset hut which, in addition to three small offices, contained a padded cell that was used mainly for violent alcoholic soldiers. I was able to get a few psychiatric textbooks, but I think I learned mostly the way one picks up a foreign language in another country—by confrontation and trial and error. After about a year, the army sent a replacement who had some psychiatric training, and I spent the last six months in an isolated dispensary treating bruises and colds and what I did not then recognize as recurrent depressions among the enlisted men of an occupying force.

I returned to see my parents in Jamestown, North Dakota, where I also bought my first car, a Plymouth suburban station wagon, planning to drive south to San Antonio, Texas, to fulfil my last few months of army service. It was only then that two accidental memories changed my future. First, I realized that my Uncle Leif, one of my father's brothers (whom I had always imagined to be my mother's secret lover—but that's another story), lived in Fulton, Missouri, not far from Kansas. Second, I somehow remembered that one of the books I had read on Okinawa was a 1945 edition of *The Human Mind* by Karl Menninger, and that the Menninger Clinic was in Topeka, Kansas. So I decided to phone them to ask about psychiatric residencies and was told that these were available at the local Veterans Administration hospital and, if I wished, I could come to apply and be evaluated the following week on my way to San Antonio.

I have two sets of lasting memories from this trip. First, in Missouri, not far from Fulton, where Uncle Leif was a professor of French at Westminster College, and where Winston Churchill gave his famous "Iron Curtain" speech, a state trooper stopped me and took me to the local jail, claiming that I had stolen someone's car. It was the only time in my life that I have been arrested, but my uncle came to identify me, and I was released after a few hours. The following day I drove to Topeka, where, early on Monday morning, the next set started. Two psychologists, Bob Holt and Lester Luborsky, spent two 8-hour days interviewing and testing me to see whether I was a fit candidate for a psychiatric residency at the VA hospital.

I don't recall being particularly troubled by that, but what makes it indelible is that a number of years later, after I had finished my residency and moved on to practise in Seattle, Washington, they published a book (Holt & Luborsky, 1958) on the methods of evaluation and asked me for permission to include their data on me as an illustration of their procedures and tests. I was flattered indeed both that they thought I was acceptable and that I had the kinds of psychopathology they wanted to illustrate.

In the first year of our residency Dr Karl, as we all called him, gave a course based on a new book he was writing on the subject of how to conduct interviews and write up case histories. We met in his huge office, which had a long massive wooden table set diagonally, with his desk at one end facing the residents sitting around the table. (My memory is that Robert Wallerstein was not in this class, so it is not clear to me whether Dr Karl's case write-up methods later influenced his *42 Lives* case descriptions.) One day our assignment was to write a description of a patient, and as the class began, he asked for volunteers to read what they had written. I raised my hand, and he called on me. I began to read, "The patient was a warm, friendly 28-year-old white male . . ." He interrupted me, "What do you mean, *warm*?" I answered, "I think you know what I mean, Dr Karl." He didn't say a word but leaned over his desk and held his head in his hands, silent for fully a minute, but it seemed almost an eternity. Then he sat up and called on someone else, as though nothing untoward had happened.

After the class it was time for lunch, and we all walked to the cafeteria. Several of my classmates asked me where I was going to go after my brief stay in Topeka, assuming that I would be terminated from the programme for my transgression. When I returned to my ward, I was handed an envelope with a personal note from Dr Karl, written on three sheets of a memo pad with his letterhead. It read:

> *Dear Dr Dahl—*
>
> *There is no way for you to know how much I want to get certain ideas across in a too short period. As one of the more alert and responsive students, you surprised me so with your reaction that I was thrown off balance. I don't mean to justify myself or neutralize this apology with this explanation.*
>
> *I know you are working hard and trying to cooperate and improve. You've been a distinct help to me in the course. I'd be very sorry to think I did anything to discourage or hurt you permanently.* *KAM*

Needless to say, he did not discourage or hurt me permanently, but in retrospect it is quite clear that my own aggressive wishes rivalled those of Dr Karl.

Another truly significant learning experience in Topeka came during a period of brief psychotherapy that I had sought because I was having trouble with a new girlfriend and it aroused a great deal of anxiety. I went to see Bill Rottersman, who was then practising at the Menninger Clinic. One night, after perhaps 20 sessions, I had a dream that taught me the central importance of understanding the stories that patients tell and represented my first true encounter with the power of transference long before it became a fashionable topic. In my dream I was accompanying the US Army retreating from the North Korean Army to the tiny Pusan perimeter in the southeast corner of Korea. I got to the ocean and started wading out into the breakers, with artillery shells exploding all around. By the time the water was up to my chest, I was extremely frightened and truly expected to drown (as I had on el Rubaiyat—see Dahl, 1998). Then I noticed some approaching landing craft in the distance. As they got closer, I recognized that it was the Israeli Army coming to our rescue. In almost a flash I understood the meaning: I thought of Bill Rottersman as Jewish, and I understood that I trusted him and that he had indeed rescued me, if not from death, then from feeling afraid and unprotected. I smiled at him and he smiled at me and we both knew then that I had got what I needed from the psychotherapy.

How, then, did Wallerstein's career and mine differ so markedly? I think partly because our goals were radically different at the beginning, and our Topeka experiences were different. After my residency I moved to Seattle, where I felt a profound need to perfect my clinical skills. To that end I entered and finished psychoanalytic training, with monthly flights to San Francisco for supervision but no contact with Wallerstein. After a dozen years I decided that without a firm scientific foundation, the analytic profession was in serious trouble. Whenever we disagreed clinically, there were no objective methods to decide the validity of one clinical explanation versus another. What we needed then—and still need now—were such methods, but I did not know where to get them or how to provide them myself. Finally, I tried to see whether I could educate myself.

I applied to NIMH for a fellowship to go to New York University, where two other Menninger alumni, Bob Holt and George Klein, had established the Research Center for Mental Health. I was accepted, and, fully a decade after Wallerstein had joined in starting the Menninger Psychotherapy Research Project (PRP), I began to get the research training I would need to help build a foundation that I could not then even envision. Indeed, I spent eight years on research fellowships learning how to study psychotherapy and psychoanalysis scientifically.

Meanwhile Wallerstein, deeply involved in the PRP, also joined the Psychiatry Department at the University of California in San Francisco, where he became chair. On two fellowships at the Center for Advanced Study in the Behavioral Sciences in Stanford, California, he devoted himself to writing up the very important detailed and extended summaries of 42 case studies (Wallerstein, 1986) that beautifully illustrate a traditional way of reporting clinical data (along with other data analyses, which he summarized in his introduction and which reflect the state of the art of dealing with clinical data then, at a time when tape-recording psychotherapy sessions was viewed, if not with alarm, at least with trepidation).

On the other hand, probably largely due to the nearly decade-and-a-half time lag in the beginnings of our scientific careers, I was able to take seriously George Klein's urgent and repeated injunctions to start with primary data. So I committed myself to tape-recording an entire six-year psychoanalysis. Later, at Downstate Medical Center, Virginia Teller, a linguist, and I explored how to analyse the transcribed texts of this case, which led us eventually to discover a unique, rigorous scientific method to represent the stories told by people in analysis or psychotherapy (Dahl & Teller, 1994). A succinct description (Dahl, 1998) illustrates the central difference from the traditional methods of case descriptions and measures, such as the Health–Sickness Rating Scale that was used in the PRP.

A psychotherapeutic "talking cure" relies essentially on a patient's storytelling. Thus, the principle of free association as the "basic rule" of psychoanalysis is to sample stories that are characteristic or typical of a person's emotional experiences. FRAMES, as defined and described by Dahl and Teller (1994), are **F**undamental **R**epetitive **A**nd **M**aladaptive **E**motion **S**tructures that capture the plots of these stories. These plots recur again and again with different people in different situations under different circumstances. And it is the repetition of these plots in and out of the therapeutic situation that makes possible inferences about what clinicians call a patient's basic psychodynamics. Their maladaptive character lies mainly in their invariance. Their tendency to recur over and over makes for a typically inflexible, neurotic patient.

A full century after Freud's case reports and nearly a half-century after the beginning of the PRP, the advantages of starting with primary data (in this case transcripts of tape-recorded treatments) are clear to researchers but still await the true commitment of the psychoanalytic community, where typical society meeting programmes consist of arguing theoretical points of view, with case material used to bolster the contentions. On the other hand, the kind of work we urgently need was superbly captured by a general principle proclaimed by Strupp, Schacht, and Henry (1988) for those of us who have been trying to explain *how* psychotherapy works:

> *The principle of P–T–O Congruence proposes that the intelligibility of psychotherapy research is a function of the similarity, isomorphism, or congruence among how we conceptualize and measure the clinical problem (P), the process of therapeutic change (T), and the clinical outcome (O).* [p. 7; italics in original]

My claim is that FRAMES are strong candidates for a coherent method (1) to represent each patient's unique **P**athology, (2) to evaluate the psychotherapeutic **T**reatment process, and (3) to evaluate the **O**utcome. They are a reliable, relatively simple, yet coherent and cogent statement of the patient's *pathology*. To evaluate the *treatment*, one can study to what degree, how, and with what consequences the therapist focuses on a patient's particular FRAMES. And, finally, one can directly measure *outcome* on the basis of whether the FRAME structures change or disappear after treatment.

So, back to the beginning of this story. Everyone in the psychotherapy enterprise is inevitably committed to trying to understand the stories of patients' lives—the stories they tell us in treatment. I believe that the central difference between Robert Wallerstein's career and mine boils down to essential contrasts in the methods we had available to understand our patients' stories. He used a traditional way of persuasively telling the stories of 42 lives, but I had what in retrospect is the conspicuous advantage of another generation of trial and effort. Researchers now have tools that Wallerstein did not have. But, after all, that's the way of science—building on what has gone before, trying to answer old questions with new methods.

7

Two too-little-known events in Bob Wallerstein's contributions to the Penn Psychoanalytic Treatment Collection

Lester Luborsky

There is so much Robert Wallerstein and I have shared for so long. We first came to know each other about 1950, when Bob arrived at the Menninger Foundation from his medical education in New York to continue his psychiatric and psychoanalytic education at the Menninger Foundation, and Bob has been a friend, and the kind of leader who is always there for helping friends. Much has happened in the long time that we have shared, but I will limit myself here to two events that we know best.

Event 1

The first of these events was that in 1990 Bob wrote the Foreword to my book, *Understanding Transference—The Core Conflictual Relationship Theme Method* (Luborsky & Crits-Cristoph, 1990). It was a fitting book for him to comment on because in that book I present the Core Conflictual Relationship Theme (CCRT) method—an attempt to develop a method similar to the usual clinical transference pattern, but with the advantage over the clinical method of being reliable. The idea for the CCRT method actually arose with my participation in the Menninger Foundation Psychotherapy Research Project. As noted in Bob's 1986 book, *Forty-Two Lives in Treatment*, Bob had appointed me head of the team assigned the task of evaluating our sample of 42 patients at the termination of their psychotherapy. It was in that role that I helped to construct a form that required an assessment of the transference pattern (Wallerstein, Robbins, Sargent, & Luborsky, 1956). The form was filled out three times: initially, at termination, and at a follow-up. It called for a formulation of the essence of the "transference paradigms". Looking back now, I can see some of its themes in the form in an area that is also expressed in the CCRT. The form calls for paragraphs on the essence of the "transference paradigms" and, within that, on the "kinds of interpersonal expectations that the patient will have recreated in the transference situation" and, in the earlier models on which these are based, ". . . the impulses that are being defended against and simultaneously want gratification".

Wallerstein began his Foreword to *Understanding Transference* by recognizing that Freud thought of psychoanalysis as a "natural science", yet Freud never "encouraged empirical research". Bob observed that although Freud "never encouraged empirical research", the contribution of the Penn Psychoanalytic Collection of 17 cases was actually intended to encourage empirical research. But even now few present-day psychoanalysts have a background like Bob's that helps them to be accomplished in this.

Bob happily ended his Foreword to my CCRT book that "those of us interested in the ultimate fate of psychoanalysis as a science can certainly fully agree . . . that this (CCRT measure) is precisely the kind of research that is necessary to be able to answer these questions properly and fairly". In fact, the hundreds of studies that have used the CCRT, clinically or in research, imply that many researchers, whether in psychoanalysis or related fields, have also found the CCRT approach useful, as I did for the description of the cases in the Penn Psychoanalytic Collection.

Event 2

The second event was that I gave two helpful presentations to the CAMP group on my Penn Psychoanalytic Collection of recorded psychoanalytic cases before its publication. Over a period of at least six years, I have made a presentation each time the size of the collection had grown some, and I wanted to hear suggestions about possible additional recorded cases and methods of analysis. Ultimately, I collected 17 completed cases—10 from the psychoanalytic research group of the Institute of Pennsylvania Hospital and 7 additional completed cases (Luborsky et al., 2001). Of all the influences on that collection, it was Bob's invitation to give presentations to our CAMP group that kept my morale high and boosted my efforts for adding to the collection.

In the course of that collection, several principles were discovered:

Principle 1: *It is a very, very difficult job to achieve a collection of tape-recorded psychoanalytic cases.*

It's an obvious conclusion, yet even though I tried very hard, it took me about 30 years to collect and to analyse the data for these 17 completed cases. Another person who tried is Sherwood Waldron, but his collection of completed cases is fairly small. Our field has mostly followed Freud's negative view about the drawbacks of research cases.

Principle 2: *It is especially hard to collect tape-recordings of completed psychoanalytic cases.*

In these 30 years, 17 cases was the largest number of *completed* cases I could assemble.

Principle 3: *The improvement-in-treatment rate in this sample is about 75%.*

That is about the same as was found for the Menninger Foundation set of 42 cases. Therefore, this rate is probably a *usual* base rate.

Principle 4: *It is important to become an expert in the preservation of a tape's voice quality.*

Many of these tapes are now about 30 years old, as I said! To copy them, I first had to transfer each session to a cassette and then transcribe it.

Principle 5: *Our types of analyses will be expanded.*

Several introductory analyses have been done with these findings: (1) The early Health–Sickness rating predicts the outcomes of psychoanalysis, and (2) the level of benefits of outcomes in our collection is similar to that of other studies.

My plans for the future of the collection are (1) to collect an even larger sample than the 17 in the Penn Psychoanalytic Collection and (2) to apply the Penn Collection in more new studies. At the present time, there will be applications in several studies with the 17 cases that are being analysed for comparing *early with late in treatment*, including changes in defences from early to late in treatment (Roy & Perry, 2004) and changes in the course of the development of mastery (Grenyer, 2002).

So, to sum up, I am happy to share with Bob my gratitude for his friendly overseeing of my transference pattern measure in Event 1, which played such an important part in leading me to the CCRT method. And in Event 2, to invite presentations on the psychoanalytic collection of cases, so that this volume allows all of us to express our appreciation of Bob's support of the growing relative strength of empirical psychoanalytic research.

III

Outcome measures for structural change

8

The development of the Scales of Psychological Capacities: a work in progress

Kathryn N. DeWitt

For over twenty years, it has been my privilege to be part of a research group formed by Robert Wallerstein to follow up on the pioneering efforts of the Psychotherapy Research Project of the Menninger Foundation (Wallerstein, 1986). As is the case with most researchers of psychoanalytic therapies, our group had companion interests in both the process and outcome of the therapeutic enterprise. This chapter provides a summary of the results of our research collaboration. Our work is one of many testimonies to the unique contribution of Dr Wallerstein to the field of Psychoanalytic Research. As a researcher, he is unflaggingly enthusiastic and determined in his mission of discovering verifiable evidence of the processes that can be brought to bear to foster changes in human beings that will relieve their suffering and maximize their chances for positive participation in life's opportunities. We are all grateful for his leadership.

The research group formed by Robert Wallerstein at the University of California, San Francisco, followed up on the pioneering efforts of the Psychotherapy Research Project of the Menninger Foundation (Wallerstein, 1986). As is the case with most researchers of psychoanalytic therapies, our group had companion interests in both the process and outcome of the therapeutic enterprise, and in this chapter I summarize the results of our research collaboration.

Selecting a research focus

The general goal of our research group was to continue and update the work of the Menninger Psychotherapy Project by conducting research that would help to determine what attributes of patient and therapist, before and during the process of psychoanalytic therapy, would be associated with the various changes that could be detected in the patients during and after treatment. We placed special emphasis on the kinds of pervasive, enduring changes that are the objective of intensive analytic therapy and had a continuing interest in examining the relative contributions of the so-called Expressive and Supportive techniques.

Feasibility considerations played a significant role in the group's selection of a specific research focus. For the members of the group—Robert Wallerstein as leader, with a workgroup that included Nate Zilberg, Dianna Hartley, Saul Rosenberg, and me—the work was a voluntary commitment, added to already busy professional lives. Our financial resources, during an era of scarce funding, consisted of a patchwork of small grants from private individuals, psychoanalytic organizations, and public institutions that Bob located and helped us to secure.[1] After much discussion, we decided that a viable initial task for the group was the development of a well-constructed and appropriate outcome measure.

From the beginning, we, as others, had been struck by the lack of available standardized measures of clinically meaningful change in patients who had undergone long-term psychotherapy or psychoanalysis. Although the field of psychotherapy research had settled on relatively standard measures of symptoms (reviewed by Strupp, Horowitz, & Lambert, 1997), there were no similarly accepted measures of change in the more enduring aspects of personal functioning—the so-called "structure" of the patient's personality. Without such measures, it was not possible to assess the outcome of treatments designed to have an impact on the character disorders or to address the currently pressing practical demand for evidence of the "added value" of the more intensive treatment approaches over the briefer (and cheaper) time-limited treatments.

Our measurement strategy

Our initial search of relevant literature located three types of measures, all of which had some drawbacks for our purposes:

1. *Global measures,* such as the Health–Sickness Rating Scale (Luborsky, 1962), did not provide the level of detail needed to pinpoint process–outcome associations.
2. *Idiographic measures,* such as the Core Conflictual Relationship Theme (Luborsky, 1977), work well for within-patient studies but are not as well suited to *between*-patient or between-group studies.
3. *Nomothetic scales* were developed for use with one particular patient population (e.g. Kernberg, 1981) or seemed to us to employ concepts that were too abstract or too wedded to one theoretical orientation (e.g. Bellak, Hurvich, & Gediman, 1973; Karush, Easser, Cooper, & Swerdloff, 1964).

In the absence, at that time, of a satisfactory measurement approach, we set about the task of designing a set of scales that we hoped would provide a relatively comprehensive assessment of character functioning.

The conceptual background for our measurement strategy was first described in detail at the Thirty-Sixth Congress of the IPA, in Rome, in July 1989, and reported in full in 1991 (Zilberg, Wallerstein, DeWitt, Hartley, & Rosenberg, 1991). We began by noting that there is a general lack of theoretical consensus as to the meaning of psychological "structure" as a construct. (Wallerstein, 1995, pp. 459–479, provides an updated summary of issues and discussion in this area.) This lack of a theoretical consensus, in combination with difficulties due to varying levels of abstraction and to unclear relationships between constructs and observable behaviour, had impeded the development of any generally accepted measurement approach. Meanwhile, psychoanalytic research could not proceed without some relatively acceptable and meaningful measure of patient change.

In response to this dilemma, our research group adopted the practical strategy of proposing the use of a set of theoretically neutral psychological constructs: the "psychological capacities", which, when assessed together, should reflect psychological structure, however defined. Our aim was to describe a set of dimensions that adherents of all prevailing psychoanalytic perspectives could accept as providing a relatively comprehensive description of personal functioning. To maximize usefulness as a research tool, we decided that the "capacities" should be low-level constructs, readily inferable from observable behaviour, which would include reportable mental states and feelings.

We defined a "psychological capacity" as an "accessible psychological resource that contributes to the achievement of adaptive intrapsychic and interpersonal functioning". Capacities were assumed to develop to differing degrees in different individuals and to be relatively stable over time. Each capacity was defined as attained in its optimal state. Our goal was to produce a set of capacities that would be both comprehensive and nonredundant.

Scale development

Scales were constructed to include a definition of each capacity, along with three anchored points of divergence from the optimal, often in two directions, one of exaggerated and one of inhibited expression of the capacity. For example, the *Capacity for Affect Regulation* would deviate from the *Modulated Experience and Expression of Affects* in the direction either of *Out-of-Control Affect Storms* or of *Hyper-Controlled, Flat Affect*. Our initial set included a total of 38 four-point scales used to rate degrees of departure from the optimal presence of 17 capacities; of these, 11 capacities had two subscales, 5 had three, and one was unitary.

The scales were initially constructed to be rated from samples of the patient's functioning obtained via the customary initial evaluative interviews that are carried out by examining clinicians for the purpose of establishing a psychodynamic formulation of the status and illness of a prospective patient as a basis for the development of a tentative treatment plan. They were intended for use with persons whose reality testing was reasonably intact. It is important to note that the scales were not designed to detect the presence of psychopathological conditions *per se*; rather, they were to be used to assess the presence of a set of attributes that should have relevance to both psychopathology and normal functioning.

In designing the scales, we had in mind the possibility that a patient could deviate from optimal on any capacity in more than one direction at the same time. For example, on the *Self-Esteem* scale, a person could display *Grandiosity* while also having feeling of *Self-Depreciation*, either simultaneously or successively. Appendix A presents a sample scale. It shows one subdimension of the *Capacity for Trust* scale. This dimension deviated from *Openness to Others* in the direction of increasing *Suspiciousness.* Appendix A demonstrates certain characteristics of scale construction.

Each Scale was formulated in the following manner:

- The *zero*, or centre point of each scale, defines optimal presence of the capacity.
- The degrees of deviation from optimal are defined as follows:

  1. Scale Point *One* describes difficulties that occur sometimes or to some extent. The difficulties can be overcome without external support, and adaptive functioning can be restored, at least temporarily, but with some discomfort. Overall functioning is not overtly compromised.

  2. Scale Point *Two* describes difficulties that occur often or to a significant extent. The difficulties can be either: (a) frequent or pervasive but overcome temporarily with external support, or (b) less frequent or quite circumscribed but could not be overcome when they do occur. In either case, overall functioning would be compromised in some discernible way.

  3. Scale Point *Three* describes difficulties that occur all the time or are very pervasive. Functioning is consistently maladaptive in that area with significant dysphoria and/or substantially impaired relationships. Overall functioning is seriously and obviously compromised.

- Scale point definitions were written in ordinary English, without use of technical vocabulary, such as terms for psychopathological syndromes. Each of the scale point definitions is "anchored" by one or more clinical vignettes to provide an example to use in rating clinical material. These vignettes were intended to be illustrative, rather than comprehensive or exhaustive.
- In designing the scales, we were aware that they would inevitably be infiltrated, to some degree, by the values of Western culture. This would emerge most clearly in the delineation of the zero-point definitions and might limit the application of these scales to other, non-Western cultures.

Content validity study

Our first step in refining the scales for use as a practical research tool was to conduct a Content Validity study (DeWitt, Hartley, Rosenberg, Zilberg, & Wallerstein, 1991). Since our original intent was to define a set of capacities that would be acceptable to proponents of all psychoanalytic perspectives, we decided to survey representatives of all major theoretical approaches to determine the degree to which we had succeeded. We tried to select representatives of each perspective who would be sympathetic to the needs of empirical research and would, therefore, be willing to perform a significant task.

We asked a group of 110 judges from 7 countries to do two things: first, rate the scale set, as a whole, in terms of its *comprehensiveness*, listing any dimensions that needed to be added or deleted; second, rate each defined capacity in terms of its *importance, clarity,* and *vividness*. Responses from 62 judges[2] indicated that the group found that, in general, we had met our comprehensiveness goal. The ratings and comments concerning individual capacities were used to drop one capacity and substitute another and to make changes in scale definitions and in the examples. Upon completion of the Content Validity study, we settled on the set of capacities shown in Appendix B. The set consists of 36 scales, measuring deviation from the optimal presence of 17 capacities.

Interview development

As a next step, we focused our efforts on the task of developing a data collection method that could be used as a basis for reliable and valid ratings of our set of scales. Having found that the use of completely unstructured interviews often produced spotty and incomplete information, we developed an approach in which we began with a free-flowing clinical interview and shifted into a more structured interview with a manual of suggested "probe questions" that were designed to solicit specific information on each scale point. The probe questions were refined in a series of trials. Modifications in the scale point definitions and in the anchoring vignettes were also made in early informal attempts to attain reliable ratings among the members of our research group. During this period, we had a change in group composition: Dianna Hartley relocated, and Daniel Weiss agreed to take her place.

Interrater reliability studies

Two interrater reliability studies were conducted. The first study (Rosenberg, DeWitt, & Wallerstein, 1996) used 10 patients who had been treated in a previous study of brief psychotherapy and were returning for post-therapy follow-up interviews. Since the subjects had been screened for suitability for brief psychotherapy, they tended to be in the neurotic range and complained of problems with depression and self-assertion. Three members of our group (SR, DW, KD) served as judges, rating videotapes of interviews that had been conducted using the specially constructed set of probe questions. The results were promising: of the 36 scales, 22 achieved interrater reliabilities of 0.50 or better, using the Intra-class Correlation Coefficient (Strout & Fleiss, 1979) (a coefficient of 0.50 or better is suggested by Cohen, 1988, as a cut-off for large effect size). Six scales had very poor reliabilities—that is, less than 0.20. These scales were from dimensions that showed little or no variability in this relatively homogeneous sample.

The second reliability study was begun in 1995. At this point in the work, Connie Milbrath came on board to fill out our research team, which had been reduced by the departure of Nate Zilberg, Saul Rosenberg, and Daniel Weiss, who needed to attend to other priorities. The study design was informed by the previous study:

1. We used the interview format and probe questions that had been explicitly designed to gather information needed to make the scale ratings.
2. We solicited a sample with a wide range of functioning, from well-functioning nonpatients to those with mild, moderate, and severe problems.
3. We used judges who had not participated in writing the scales, so that their understanding of the material and rating process would be limited to the information in the scale manual itself.
4. We provided extensive practice sessions rating non-study subjects, to ensure that the raters understood the scales and rating process.

Interim results were reported in 1997, at the Seventh IPA Conference on Psychoanalytic Research, and final results were made available in 1999 (DeWitt, Milbrath, & Wallerstein, 1999). The findings, based on a 30-subject sample and 4 clinically experienced raters, showed that all 36 scales reached Cohen's ICC cut-off of 0.50. In fact, 28 scales had reliabilities at or above 0.70, the intraclass correlation level recommended by Lambert and Hill (1994) as a standard cut-off score for scales that do not have a low level of inference.

Concurrent validity study

Subjects in the interrater reliability study also completed a battery of self-report measures at the end of their clinical interview, including: the Inventory of Interpersonal Problems (Horowitz, Rosenberg, Baer, Ureno, & Vallasenor, 1988), the Reciprocal Attachment Questionnaire (Bartholomew & Horowitz, 1991), and the Patterns of Relating (West & Sheldon-Keller, 1994).These measures were selected to have some area of conceptual overlap with the Capacities Scales so that they could provide a test of concurrent validity for the scales. The interrelationships of the various scales are described in detail by DeWitt, Milbrath, and Wallerstein (1999). They show that subject data collected via a variety of self-report questionnaires elicits information that is conceptually consistent with that gathered via the semi-structured, clinician-rated interview of the SPC.

Test–retest reliability study

Under the direction of Connie Milbrath, our research group completed a test–retest reliability study. The stability of ratings over time is an important requirement for a measure of any enduring psychological characteristic, such as "structure". A sample of 20 subjects who were not participating in any ongoing psychotherapy was recruited from staff, patients seeking treatment for physical ailments, and patient relatives at the outpatient department of a large, independent, urban medical centre. Subjects were interviewed and rated with the SPC procedure twice, at 4-month or longer intervals (range 4–7, mean 5.2). The interval was chosen to be long enough to dampen the subject's memory of the first interview, while also being short enough to make the study practical and to minimize the opportunity for life-altering relationships and events to take place.

Different interviewers and raters were used at the two interviews in a counterbalanced design to minimize the effect of memory on the interview process and ratings.[3] Results, analysed using the Spearman–Brown measure of split-half reliability, yielded a very acceptable correlation of 0.73 between the pattern of scores of the 20 subjects at the first and second testings. In addition, the alphas for the whole scale at Times 1 and 2 were 0.72 and 0.73, respectively, indicating that the scale acted with a high level of coherence.

Allied research projects

During the course of the SPC developmental projects, we have been especially grateful for the interest, efforts, and significant research contributions of individuals and groups within the psychoanalytic research community. Early in our work, Eva Sundin and colleagues in Sweden (Sundin, Armelius, & Nilsson, 1994) explored the interrater reliability and utility of the SPC as part of their Borderline Psychotherapy Project. In Germany, Dorothea Huber and Guenther Klug conducted an ambitious series of well-designed studies of the interrater reliability, concurrent validity, and discriminant validity of the SPC (Huber, Klug, & von Rad, 1997) and report results using the measure as a pre-post treatment device in the Munich Psychotherapy study (Huber, Klug, & von Rad, 2002). Leslie O'Connell (O'Connell, 2001) examined the relationship between the SPC and self-reported adult attachment status. Finally, in chapter 9 in this volume Marianne Leuzinger-Bohleber and Tamara Fischmann describe the experience of the German Psychoanalytical Association (DPV) using the SPC as part of a large follow-up assessment of patients who completed psychoanalyses.

The results of all of these research efforts have been uniformly positive, supporting the psychometric properties and research utility of the instrument. The SPC is now in use among numerous other psychotherapy research groups around the world. Brian Greenfield and colleagues at McGill have modified the SPC examples for use with an adolescent population, and the measure has been translated into Finnish, French, German, Italian, and Swedish.

Discussion

Psychometric work on the Scales of Psychological Capacities has indicated that the measure may fulfil its promise as a tool for assessing the kinds of "structural" changes in personality organization that are thought to come about as a result of intensive long-term treatments, such as the psychoanalytic psychotherapies. The work began two decades ago with a content validity study that established the proposed psychological capacities as critical dimensions that are characteristic of normal and abnormal functioning and are highly relevant to psychotherapy process and outcome. This work was followed by the development of a semi-structured clinical interview, to be used in obtaining information about functioning on 17 dimensions of the SPC. More recent studies indicate that the SPC is a reliable instrument and that many clinicians in multiple settings can be trained to make the judgements from videotaped interviews that it requires. In addition, the SPC has been found to correlate in predicted ways with conceptually similar and dissimilar measures, to discriminate successfully between diagnostic groups, to show positive test–retest stability, to function well as a descriptor of follow-up status of patients who have completed intensive treatments, and to reflect changes in patient functioning from pre- to post-treatment. The measure has gained a level of international acceptance and is now under study and/or in use among other psychotherapy research groups around the world.

It is important to note that since this work began, other research groups have developed alternative approaches to measuring the kinds of significant changes in functioning that are the aim of intensive treatments. They include (but may not be limited to): the Differentiation-Relatedness in Self and Object Relations Scale (Blatt & Auerback, 1988), the Karolinska Psychodynamic Profile (KAPP) (Weinryb, Rössel, & Asberg, 1991), the Change in Dynamic Psychotherapy Scales (Hoglend, Bogwald, & Amlo, 2000), and the Operationalized Psychodynamic Diagnostics (OPD Task Force, 2000). In addition, Barber, Crits-Cristoph, and Luborsky (1990) have developed a classification system for the Core Conflictual Relationship Theme (CCRT) analysis that can be used as a basis for nomothetic change ratings, Shedler and Westen (1998) have developed the Shedler–Westen Assessment Procedure (SWAP-200), a Q-Sort approach to describing patient functioning, and Clarkin and associates have developed the Structured Interview of Personality Organization

(STIPO), both of which can be used to describe changes brought about by intensive treatments (Clarkin, Caligor, Stern, & Kernberg, 2002). All of these approaches are welcome contributions to the progress of research in this area.

Overall, our group's efforts to develop a well-constructed and appropriate outcome measure seem to have been successful. With the exception of a paper that provides further clarification of expressive and supportive techniques and how they intersect with mechanisms of change (Wallerstein & DeWitt, 1997), we have had to leave work on the process aspects of psychoanalytic research to other able colleagues. Though the bountiful days of the well-funded, large-scale project are past, the work continues, nonetheless.

NOTES

1. This research has been supported over nearly ten decades by grants and donations from the Columbia Foundation, the Swig Foundation, the Fund for Psychoanalytic Research of the American Psychoanalytic Association, the Research Advisory Board of the International Psychoanalytical Association, the Windholz Fund for Psychoanalytic Research of the San Francisco Psychoanalytic Institute, Mrs Patricia Costello, Dr Cloyce Duncan, Dr Norman Stone, Mr Fred Whitman, Mr Al Wilsey, and three anonymous donors.

2. The authors wish to express their most sincere appreciation to the following persons, who provided the ratings used in this study: Adrienne P. Applegarth, Howard A. Bacal, Henry M. Bachrach, Edward S. Bordin, Lou Breger, Arnold M. Cooper, Paul A. DeWald, Theodore L. Dorpat, Morris Eagle, Terttu Eskelinen de Folch, Aaron H. Esman, Norbert Freedman, Merton M. Gill, Arnold Goldberg, Jay R. Greenberg, James S. Grotstein, Stuart T. Hauser, Philip S. Holzman, Mardi J. Horowitz, Leonard Horwitz, Irving Janis, Enrico Jones, Otto F. Kernberg, Paulina F. Kernberg, Joseph D. Lichtenberg, Morton Lieberman, Lester Luborsky, James F. Masterson, Robert Michels, Nancy Miller, Stephen A. Mitchell, Arnold H. Modell, Rafael Moses, Thomas Ogden, Anna Ornstein, Paul H. Ornstein, Herbert Pardes, Ethel S. Person, Donald Rinsley, Fred P. Robbins, Allan D. Rosenblatt, Harold Sampson (with Joseph Weiss), Louis Sander, Anne-Marie Sandler, Joseph Sandler, Nathan Schlessinger, Evelyne A. Schwaber, Estelle Shane, Morton Shane, Donald P. Spence, Robert J. Stoller, Robert D. Stolorow, Leo Stone, James L. Thickstun, Paul L. Wachtel, Sherwood Waldron, Jr, Edward M. Weinshel, Joseph Weiss (with Harold Sampson), Myrna Weissman, Daniel Widlöcher, Ernest S. Wolf, and David Wolitzky. Many of the above provided us with extensive comments. An additional 11 who offered comments in lieu of ratings included: Robert N. Emde, John G. Gunderson, Robert R. Holt,

Jane Loevinger, Martin Mayman, Morris B. Parloff, Emanuel Peterfreund, Fred Pine, Calvin F. Settlage, Paul H. Tolpin, and Marian Tolpin.

3. The members of our research group would like to thank the following psychologists who served as interviewers and raters in our research studies: Mary Ewert, Tina Gutterman, Steve Hibbert, John Lundin, Leslie O'Connell, and Cathy Rose.

APPENDIX A
Capacity for Trust Scale: Subscale A

From openness to others to extreme suspiciousness

0. Willing to relate to others with no undue expectations of betrayal, frustration, or disappointment, nor feelings of being too exposed and vulnerable. Does not question others' motives without good evidence. If feelings of scepticism or suspicion do occur, the person can step back and realistically assess the situation and decide whether to trust the other person.

   For example: *A woman having lunch with a new acquaintance for the first time wants to talk with her about an important, personal subject. She begins with relatively distant or neutral aspects of the situation, watching how the other person reacts, and only when she sees a positive response, does she tell the whole story.*

1. Usually realistic in trusting appropriate people, but has nagging doubts or is excessively cautious in some situations or with some people. Even when such doubts are seen by the person to be unjustified, they persist or recur. Relationships with others and ability to function are not noticeably affected.

   For example: *A divorced woman is extremely cautious in establishing new relationships with men. She realizes that her generalized mistrust of men is unfairly applied in many cases and she is able to socialize appropriately.*

2. (a) Frequently questions the motives, honesty, or reliability of others on the basis of slight evidence or as an overgeneralization about certain groups of people. Such unrealistic suspicion can be overcome with external support, such as confrontation, additional evidence, or reassurance. Relationships are sometimes strained by guardedness, and functioning may be compromised by the repetitive need to address issues of trust.

For example: *A man is guarded with people he does not know well, and takes a long time to really trust anyone. Over time, he has developed open, trusting relationships with his wife and with longstanding friends.*

(b) In most situations, is able to judge realistically whether individuals are trustworthy, but encounters certain situations which seem always to trigger fears of being disappointed or abused in some way. These fears are intense and not easily overcome, even with a great deal of external support.

For example: *A woman is usually relatively open, but begins to mistrust men after she becomes sexually involved with them, fearing that they will do or say something that will ruin her reputation. She drives men away with her constant questioning and requests for reassurance in this area.*

3. Extreme distrust of others and misconstrual of behaviours. Feels very anxious and vulnerable in any situation that calls for disclosure or relying on another person. Convinced that others will act against self, and is not reassured by promises or evidence to the contrary. Not able to tolerate feeling exposed to others. Relationships and daily functioning are seriously impaired by suspiciousness.

   For example: *A man questions the motives of everyone he knows, and never assumes that intentions are positive. He is always searching out ways others may be taking advantage of him and cannot maintain any friendships because others become aware of his suspiciousness.*

APPENDIX B
Scales of Psychological Capacities

I. Attributes of Self
   1. Self-Coherence
      A. From Coherence to Inconsistency of Behaviour and Experience
   2. Self-Esteem
      A. From Modesty to Grandiosity
      B. From Self-Respect to Self-Depreciation
   3. Zest for Life
      A. From Appropriate Restraint to Overexcitement

B. From Appropriate Enthusiasm to Drudgery
C. From Investment in Life Activities to Apathy

4. Hope
   A. From Realistically Hopeful Outlook to Extreme Optimism
   B. From Realistically Cautious Outlook to Extreme Pessimism
5. Flexibility
   A. From Open- to Closed-Mindedness
   B. From Confidence to Confusion and Self-Doubt
6. Attribution of Responsibility
   A. From Taking Appropriate Responsibility to Overexternalizing
   B. From Appropriate Disclaiming of Responsibility to Overinternalizing
7. Effectance and Mastery
   A. From Pursuit of Meaningful Goals to Drivenness and "Overachievement"
   B. From Resourceful Mastery to Underachievement, Inhibition of Success
8. Commitment to Standards and Values
   A. From Tolerance to Moralism
   B. From Altruism to Selfishness
   C. From Principled Behaviour to Delinquency

II. Self-Regulation

9. Affect Regulation
   A. From Modulated Affects to Out of Control "Affect Storms"
   B. From Tolerance of Affects to Hypercontrol
10. Impulse Regulation
   A. From Ability to Inhibit Impulses to Compulsive Overindulgence
   B. From Ability to Indulge Impulses to Constricted Overinhibition
11. Regulation of Sexual Experience
   A. From Volitional Sexual Experience to Impulsive or Driven Expression

- B. From Active Sexual Interest and Expression to Inhibition

12. Self-Assertion
    - A. From Proper Self-Assertion to Aggression and Bullying
    - B. From Ability to Freely Pursue Goals to Inhibition and Timidity

III. Relations with Others

13. Empathy
    - A. From Appropriate Distance to Emotional Absorption
    - B. From Emotional Responsiveness to Emotional Blunting
    - C. From Taking the Perspective of Others to Egocentricity
14. Trust
    - A. From Openness to Others to Extreme Suspiciousness
    - B. From Adaptive Scepticism to Extreme Gullibility
    - C. From Trustworthy to Untrustworthy
15. Reliance on Self and Others
    - A. From Secure Reliance on Others to Rarely Able to Rely on Others
    - B. From Secure Self-Reliance to Rarely Able to Rely on Self
    - C. From Security in Having Others Rely on Self to Rarely Able to be Person Relied Upon
16. Commitment in Relationships
    - A. From Flexible Engagement to Compulsive Overinvolvement
    - B. From Secure to Limited, Tenuous Commitment
17. Reciprocity
    - A. From Comfortable Giving to Others to Exploitation of Others
    - B. From Comfortable Taking from Others to Surrender of Self

9

Application of the Scales of Psychological Capacities in a multiperspective, representative follow-up study

Marianne Leuzinger-Bohleber & Tamara Fischmann

It was a great pleasure and honour for me to be invited to contribute to a panel honouring Bob Wallerstein. I will never forget my first personal meeting with him: it was during the IPA Congress in Barcelona in the summer of 1997. At that time we just had decided to perform a large follow-up study of psychoanalyses and psychoanalytic long-term therapies studying a representative sample ($n = 401$) of all the patients who had finished their treatments between 1990 and 1993 with a member of our society. Being in charge of this research enterprise, I felt quite burdened by this new responsibility. Thus I wrote to Bob, whom I admired very much as one of the most experienced and competent psychoanalytic psychotherapy researchers. I asked him for a short meeting. We met and could not find an place to sit down: Bob—uncomplicated and friendly—suggested that we should just take a seat on the public stairs of the congress centre—and there we were: talking about research—about the possibility to use the Scales of Psychological Capacities in our study without having the chance to use videotapes—and so on. Bob had a way of listening to me with a bright, open mind: interested and with a very personal attitude: I felt understood, comforted, and surrounded by warmth, friendliness, and professional competence. Then he talked about his youth in Berlin, his emigration to the States, and—without many words—the sadness and incapability to really understand afterwards what had happened in Germany during the time of National Socialism was spreading out between us.

I feel gifted that a professional and personal exchange developed in the following years. I had several occasions to meet him and Judy again: for example, in London, in Frankfurt, in Munich, Nice, and New York. I feel grateful for all he has given to us—to me personally—but also to me as a member of a younger generation of psychoanalytic clinicians and researchers. For me he is one of the best examples for intergenerational fertility in psychoanalysis.

Now: let me turn to the scientific part of my chapter: to summarize briefly what has become of our Barcelona plans: applying the Scales of Psychological Capacities in our study. Tamara Fischmann, the second author of this paper, has been responsible for the statistical analyses which will be presented here.

The SPC: a psychoanalytic research instrument exemplifying the combination between conceptual and empirical research

Motivation for applying the SPC in our follow-up study

We preferred to apply the Scales in our study instead of other instruments of current psychotherapy research for the following reasons:

- *Relevance for psychoanalytic process and outcome studies ("structural changes")*: We probably all agree that structural change is one of the major criteria in evaluating the outcome of psychoanalytic treatments.
- *Closeness to clinical practice*: The different items are very close to psychoanalytic practice and relevant for the evaluation of the outcome of psychoanalytic treatments (see below). This fact proved to be enormously helpful in our study, since many of the instruments usually applied in psychotherapy research are based on non-psychoanalytic concepts and are thus not suitable to really measure relevant and characteristic changes of psychoanalytic treatments.
- *Consideration of the pluralism of psychoanalysis today*: phenomenological level of item description, an instrument not limited to specific psychoanalytic schools, but consideration of the theoretical richness of psychoanalysis today.

When Katherine DeWitt introduced the Scales at the Research Conference in London 1997, I was immediately struck by the research idea of trying to describe structural changes in psychoanalyses on a manifest, descriptive level—that is, on the level of psychic and psychosocial functioning—which is important for the different psychoanalytic schools today, even if each school uses its own terminology, a different language, and special conceptualizations to characterize these functions.

- *A sophisticated combination of conceptual and empirical research*: I was also fascinated by the sophisticated way the researchers combined clinical knowledge (by interviewing experts of the different psychoanalytic schools), conceptual research (conceptualizing and defining the different items), and, finally, the construction of an instrument for empirical research (the Scales).[1]

In my opinion, the Wallerstein group offers a starting point for the epistemological discussion between the two research subcommittees of the IPA: the one on empirical research, and the other clinical, conceptual, epistemological, and historical research. The Wallerstein group illustrated, in constructing the Scales, that clinical, conceptual and empirical research may be three separated steps within a research process, but can finally be integrated in different ways. This is an epistemological problem that was discussed during an international congress in Frankfurt in 2002.[2]

Application of the Scales in our study

The clinical, conceptual, and empirical strength of the Scales proved to be successful in our follow-up study (see below).

Screening instrument between the two follow-up interviews

We used a variety of combinations of psychoanalytic and non-psychoanalytic, qualitative and quantitative instruments in our study, as shown in Figure 9.1.

The Scales are the only quantitative instrument constructed by considering mainly psychoanalytic concepts. At the same time, by using a manifest, descriptive level, the Scales offer a bridge to other

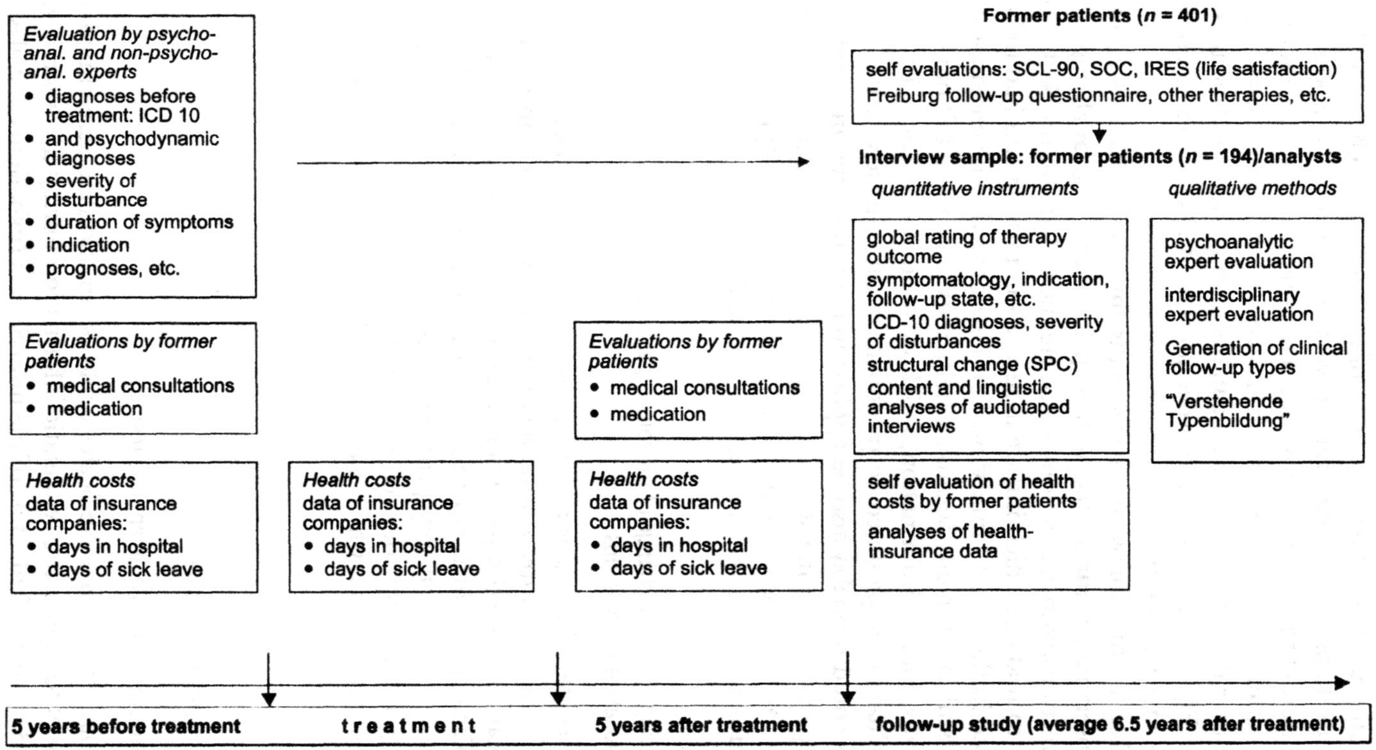

Figure 9.1. Psychoanalytic long-term treatments: a representative, multiperspective follow-up study (design and methods).

psychotherapeutic schools. Because of its theoretical richness and its closeness to psychoanalytic practice, we were able to use the Scales in two different ways in our study: as a screening instrument gathering information in the two follow-up interviews, and as an instrument evaluating the outcome of psychoanalyses and psychoanalytic treatments. Figure 9.2 outlines the procedures used to evaluate outcome in the interview sample.

After the first follow-up interview the interviewer made notes on his observations during the follow-up interview (e.g. analysing his countertransference reactions, etc.). He then filled out the Scales in order to find out which information was still missing and had to be covered in the second interview. This idea proved to be enormously successful in our study because it helped us to gain the full range of clinically relevant information, which we needed in order to be able to evaluate therapy outcome psychoanalytically. In view of this, the Scales could probably also be applied to clinical studies in a fruitful way—perhaps even in psychoanalytic supervision or training sensitizing the analysts for scotomization in their clinical perceptions, missing information in the clinical material, and so on.

Evaluating structural change of the former patients in the local research groups

We also used the Scales at the end of our evaluation process in the local research groups. All the members of the research group used the Scales to rate the patients independently, and this was followed by a discussion in order to find the so-called "consensus rating". This discussion was often very productive, because it helped us to trace missing information or even contradictions in our clinical psychoanalytic evaluations, which we had tried to summarize earlier (see below).

Experiences and results

Excellent screening instrument in our study

The expectation that the Scales could be an excellent screening instrument for gathering systematic information during the interviews proved to be justified. Most of the interviewers (experienced analysts

1. In the *first follow-up interview* we open an intermediate space for the former patients by a more or less unstructured interview to communicate to us (consciously and unconsciously) their views of their experiences with their psychoanalytic treatments. We try to obtain manifest as well as latent (unconscious) information about the interaction between the former patient and the follow-up interviewer. In the last part of the interview some follow-up topics are addressed (e.g. asking for the reasons and motives for treatment, their subjective evaluation of the therapy, motivation for participating in our study etc.). The interviews are tape recorded.
2. *After the first interview* the follow-up analyst records his impressions and information offered by the interview (on important subjects, psycho-dynamics, hypotheses, taking into consideration countertransference re-actions, etc.) on tape. He also rates some questions concerning his first global evaluation of the possible outcome of the former psychoanalytic treatment and the Scales of Psychological Capacities (Wallerstein et al.) in order to find out which subjects should still be inquired in the second interview because of still missing important information.
3. He then meets with one member of the *research group* for a supervision and narratively summarizes the interview. In the subsequent dialogue the two exchange their impressions, evaluations, psychodynamic hypotheses, open questions, etc. in order to help the interviewer to test some of these hypotheses in the second interview clinically and gather more information in order to deepen or correct the preliminary hypotheses.
4. The second interview is in the beginning unstructured again in order to be able to observe and reflect the possible effect of the first interview on the former patient. The interviewer then poses a set of questions regarding the patient's view of the former therapy, the therapist–patient relationship, the symptoms, the personal significance of the treatment for the patient, the life events before, during, and after therapy, the global evaluation etc. is asked (part of the semi-structured interview).
5. Another member of the research group (semi-structured interview) *interviews the former analyst of the patient* without having any information about the patient.
6. Afterwards the local *research group* meets.
   a. The interviewer reports his experiences, observations and hypotheses gained in the two interviews narratively. Afterwards the group listens to 5 minutes of the tape recorded interview. Then the (6–8) members of the research group rate the global evaluation questions before starting discussion. Afterwards a thorough exchange of ideas concerning the diagnosis, the indication, the results of the treatments, etc. follows. The interviewers of the former patient and his analyst are silent—only the other group members are associating and discussing (30 minutes).
   b. Now the group member who has interviewed the analyst summarizes his findings.
   c. All the group members are discussing again and finally try to find a common clinical view of the follow-up (about 15 minutes).
   d. Finally the different members of the group independently rate their "global evaluations" again and the Scales of Psychological Capacities. Afterwards the group tries to find a "consensus" concerning the Scales (according to the method developed by Leuzinger-Bohleber, 1987).
   e. After the session one member of the group summarizes the discussion and hands his summary back to the members of the group to be corrected.

Figure 9.2. Procedure for the evaluation of outcome in the interview sample.

of the DPV) reported their experience filling out the Scales after the first interview as being of great help for realizing which information was still missing and had to be gathered in the second interview.

Evaluating structural change

Interrater reliabilities. At the meeting of the Society for Psychotherapy Research in Chicago (25 June 2000) we had discussed the results on the interrater reliabilities in our study. Because we have a wide range of different therapy outcomes, diagnoses, and so on in our sample, we also had quite a large range in the different interrater reliabilities, although the average ICC (Horst coefficient) was "good enough" (if ICC > 0.5) (Table 9.1).

A contribution to the content validity of the Scales. We compared the global ratings of the analysts of the local research groups on structural change with the results of their ratings of the Scales, as shown in Figure 9.3.

Because the Scales are conceptualized on an ordinal level (Ordinal scale) statistical instruments measuring means cannot be used, but comparing groups of patients as defined by the measured categories may be useful. According to the definitions of the Scales, Ratings 0 and 1 indicate "normal, adaptive functions" and Rating 3 "pathological adaptive functions". The number of 2 and 3 ratings seemed to be a good indicator of low psychological capacities or a pathological level of adaptive functioning for the former patients in our sample.

Thus we compared two extreme groups of patients (Group A: Scale Rating 0 and 1; Group B: Scale Rating 2 and 3) according to the evaluations of the analysts. We found that Group A showed "very large structural change" and Group B coincided with those who were rated to have "little structural change".

The global rating of the analysts in respect to structural change are in agreement with the findings of the Scales, as shown in Figure 9.4. We consider these results as a contribution of our study in testing the content validity of the Scales.

Table 9.1. Interrater reliabilities for scales

		DeWitt[a] reliability	Follow-up study (*n*=25) reliability	*SD*
Hope	Optimism	0.76	0.52	0.33
	Pessimism	0.85	0.52	0.33
Zest	Overexcitement	0.42	0.66	0.28
	Drudgery	0.79	0.59	0.26
	Apathy	0.87	0.65	0.28
Responsibility	Overexternalizing	0.57	0.60	0.31
	Overinternalizing	0.69	0.52	0.28
Flexibility	Closed-mindedness	0.65	0.62	0.32
	Self-doubt	0.76	0.64	0.22
Persistence	Drivenness	0.72	0.73	0.27
	Giving up	0.90	0.62	0.32
Standards	Moralism	0.54	0.50	0.27
	Unprincipled	0.72	0.63	0.30
Commitment	Overinvolvement	0.59	0.61	0.24
	Tenousness	0.51	0.53	0.34
Reciprocity	Exploitation	0.56	0.49	0.33
	Surrender	0.78	0.56	0.35
Trust	Suspiciousness	0.70	0.68	0.29
	Gullibility	0.64	0.59	0.33
Empathy	Absorption	0.77	0.42	0.27
	Blunting	0.81	0.53	0.30
	Egocentricity	0.50	0.51	0.22
Affect	Out of control	0.77	0.48	0.31
	Hypercontrol	0.63	0.59	0.33
Impulse	Indulgence	0.84	0.52	0.22
	Inhibition	0.45	0.41	0.26
Sexual	Impulsive	0.44	0.44	0.11
	Inhibition	0.87	0.39	0.31
Assertion	Bullying	0.70	0.49	0.31
	Timidity	0.86	0.49	0.23
Reliance	Not on others	0.71	0.59	0.26
	Not on self	0.77	0.49	0.13
	Not relied upon	0.70	0.50	0.23
Self-Esteem	Grandiosity	0.47	0.72	0.33
	Self-depreciation	0.75	0.46	0.23
Coherence	Inconsistency	0.84	0.68	0.31
	ICC (Horst coefficient)[b]		0.61 *	0.61

Note: Reliability = goodness of concordance of the raters concerning item *i* (Fleiss, 1971).
[a]DeWitt, 1997; [b]Langer & Schulz von Thun, 1974.
* "good enough" when ICC > 0.5.

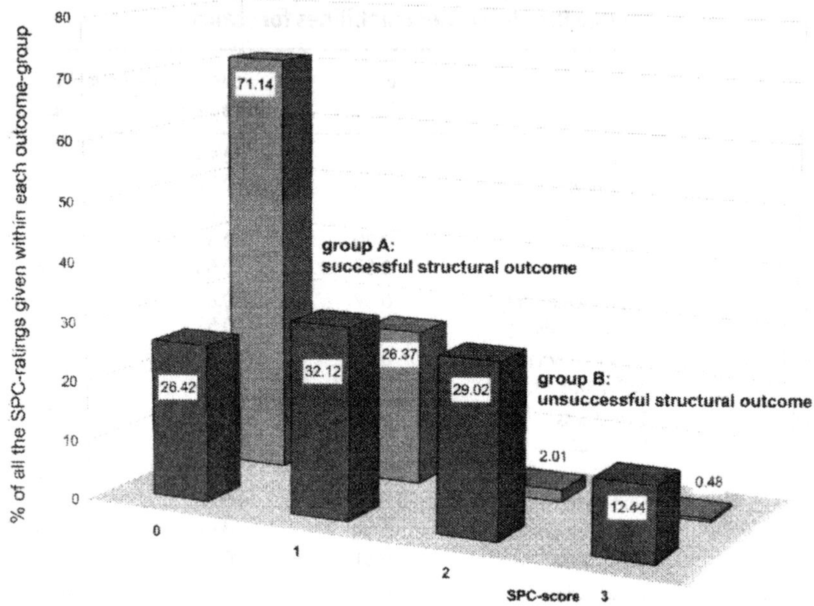

Figure 9.3. SPC scores of extreme groups.

Unexpected finding: the Scales as a diagnostic instrument

As already mentioned, although we did not expect that the Scales would prove to be of high diagnostic value in our study, they indeed proved to be so, as shown in the following three very brief examples:

Mr PU

According to the different outcome criteria, the psychoanalysis of Mr PU had been highly successful. He belonged to the large group of 51.2% of patients in our sample who were diagnosed with "personality disorder" (ICD-10: F6). In his psychoanalysis he found out that his narcissistic personality disorder (combined with phobic anxieties of becoming ill with cancer, suicidal impulses, inability to work, and promiscuity) had been unconsciously connected with his severe infantile traumatization (his father being killed on the Russian front before he was born, his mother then

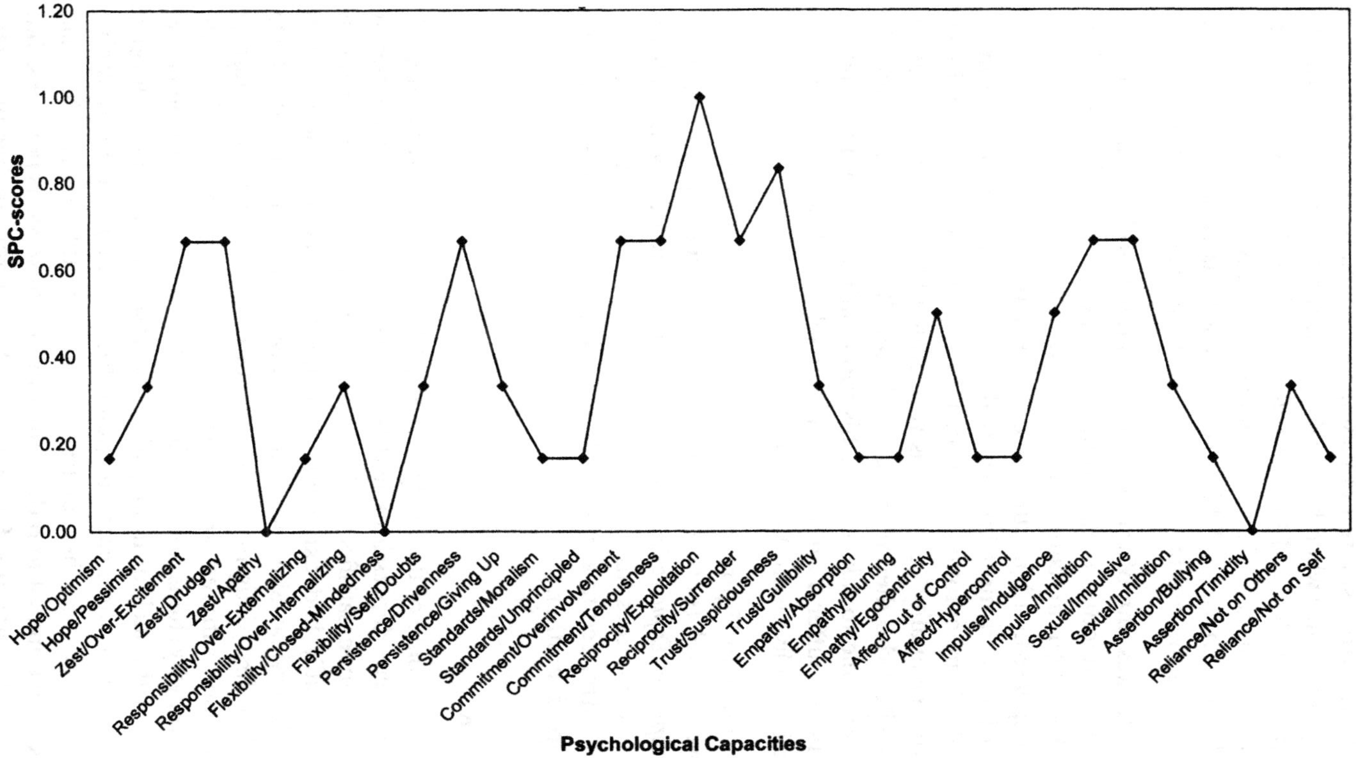

Figure 9.4. SPC: Mr PU.

suffering from severe depressions for years, the dramatic loss of his grandfather when he was 4 years old, etc.). He is very grateful that "my analyst and I have survived analysis: I had gone through a long sequence of extreme hatred and destructivity and nearly killed my analyst . . ." He also had a serious accident in connection with the reactivation of his (self-)destructive impulses.

Mr PU was one of the 63% of our study who had suffered from severe infantile traumatizations (Type II according to Terr, 1994—often in connection with the Second World War—an unexpectedly high number of such patients in our study). He considered it most important that analysis had enabled him to "re-find my emotions and an inner space—a centre within my own personality". He also is very grateful that—after the loss of his wife (who died from cancer in Mr PU's first year of analysis) he was able to take care of his two children—"avoiding that my children suffer a similar fate as I myself did: losing a parent and having to live with the other who is depressed".

As shown in Figure 9.4, Mr PU was rated to function on a normal psychic level (between 0 and 1) on the Scales; on the Subscale *Reciprocity/Exploitation of Others* he has a score of 1, which means that sometimes his adaptive functions are still disturbed but can be rearranged to a "normal functioning" by himself—without the help of another.

Mrs KU

The outcome of the analysis of Mrs KU was evaluated as "mixed". Her severe depressions had been moderated, and consequently she is quite satisfied with therapy outcome—but "nevertheless I originally had expected more positive changes", she said in the interview. She terminated analysis shortly before the birth of her first daughter. After the birth of her second daughter she again suffered from depression for two years—which is one reason why she is not completely satisfied with therapy outcome. Due to the lack of money after the insurance company stopped payment for the treatment (after 300 sessions), she was only able to continue with her analysis for another 120 sessions. She had asked her analyst to reduce the number of sessions per week, but the analyst was not flexible enough to agree. In her interview, she considers her analyst's decision a mistake. The therapist asks herself whether the end of therapy could have been a kind of re-traumatization for the patient. Mrs KU—independently from her analysts—expresses a similar feeling: the "loss of her analyst" was unconsciously probably somehow similar to the loss of her father, who divorced from her mother when she was 11 years old. "He just disappeared from my life and took all his vitality and warmth with him. I was dependent on my severely depressed mother for years and did not have a chance to escape. When I had to give up work after the birth of my second daughter, I probably felt abandoned again—but I was not able to ask my analyst for help once more. Somehow she also sent me away.... This was not good—it took me two years to get over my depression. Since I took up work again—I feel better."—We evaluated the outcome of the psychoanalysis only as medium. Filling out the Scales, we were able to see the differences in the outcome according to the ratings of the different items (see Figure 9.5).

Mrs X

Mrs X is one of the 4% of patients in our sample with a negative outcome according to her own evaluation, the view of her former analyst, and the psychoanalytic and non-psychoanalytic experts. Although we agreed on negative therapy outcome in the local research group, we were not able to find agreement regarding the diagnosis of this former patient. One part of the group thought that analysis had just not been successful because the analyst had not understood the patient well enough: analyst and analysand had not "met emotionally"—no psychoanalytic process had been established. The other part of the group was convinced that the patient had either been sexually abused or psychotic, and that the analyst had not been able to understand the dynamics of the patient—Mrs X had broken off her analysis after she, by chance, had discovered a report of the analyst for her insurance company and felt deeply insulted ("abused") by her analyst. Normally she had been living a life as a highly competent secretary—but several times she had gone through strange states of depersonalization. One day, for example, she had suddenly left her husband and her daughter in order to live with an alcoholic who abused her sexually and lived in a desperate state of neglect. We were not able

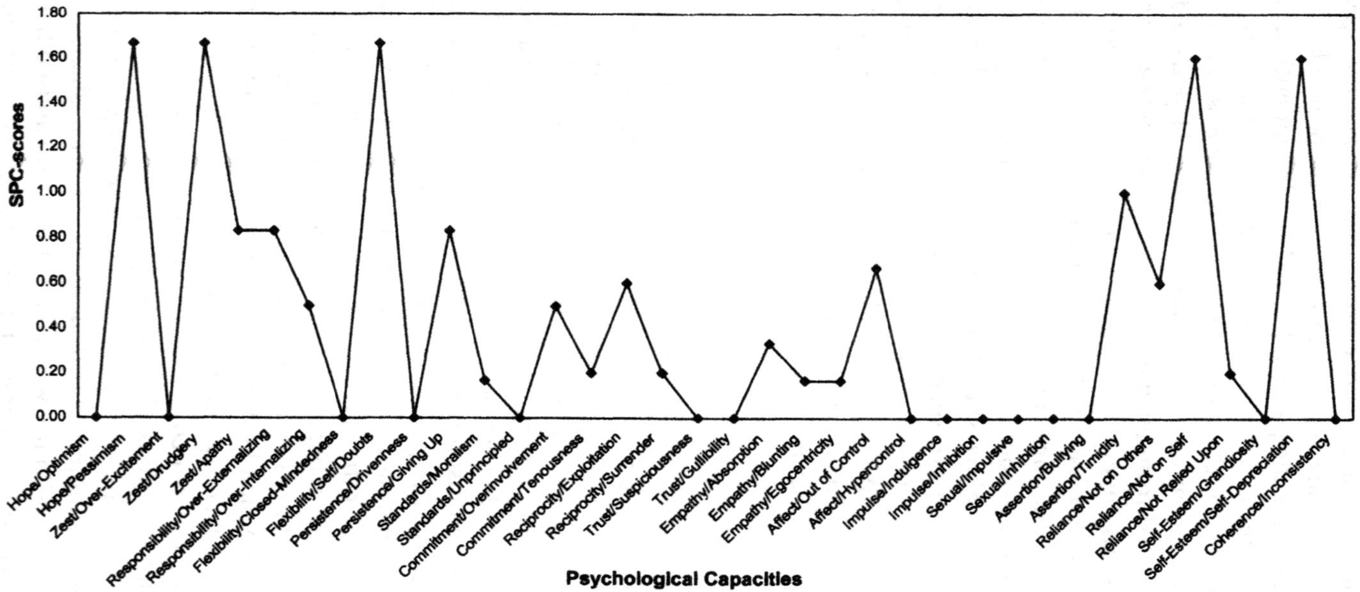

Figure 9.5. SPC: Mrs KU.

to decide whether this had been an unconscious repetition of a sexual abuse (she suffered from repeated nightmares of someone coming up the stairs and opening the door, then waking up in panic) or whether she suffered from psychotic episodes. *When trying to rate the Scales, all the members of the group discovered that they were not able to do the rating.* Thus, the members of the part of the group who had disagreed with the diagnosis of sexual abuse or psychosis now also became convinced that the patient suffered from an unintegrated psychic state. At least two different, and contradictory, parts of her psychic functioning, became visible.

This is an example of the excellent diagnostic capacity of the Scales to distinguish patients with integrated psychic functioning from those who are suffering from severe splittings or depersonalizations (severely traumatized patients, psychotic patients, some borderline patients, patients suffering from a multiple personality disorder, etc.).

Conclusions

We hope that we were able to give a short impression of how we applied the Scales in our study and what results and observations were achieved. We might add that most of the clinicians, the members of the local research groups, first felt an intensive resistance to understanding the philosophy of the Scales—they tried, for example, to characterize structural change on a descriptive, manifest level, which they felt to be quite different from our "normal" psychoanalytic evaluations of structural change within our patients. But particularly the open-minded, curious colleagues in our study discovered that applying the Scales may be an interesting supplement to our normal psychoanalytic way of perception and evaluation in a clinical situation (as our follow-up interviews showed). They began to appreciate the possibility of looking at psychoanalytic processes from an additional perspective—a possibility that seems promising for screening and evaluation processes in other psychoanalytic studies.

The Scales are applied in different ongoing psychotherapy studies in Germany, thanks to a German translation of the manual that Dorothea Huber and I have published (see, e.g., Huber, Brandl, & Klug, 2004). Thus, the Scales are already contributing to the growing research culture in psychoanalysis, thanks to its sophisticated theoretical background, its closeness to clinical practice, and its ability to bridge psychoanalytic and non-psychoanalytic methods in psychotherapy research.

NOTES

1. I felt reminded of the work of Joseph and Anne-Marie Sandler in London or Ilka von Zeppelin and Ulrich Moser—two different research groups. Both tried to combine clinical, conceptual and empirical research on a very sophisticated theoretical level (see, e.g., the work on a psychoanalytic dream theory by Ulrich Moser over a period of 25 years of his career).

2. The Congress "Pluralism of Sciences. the Psychoanalytic Method between Clinical, Conceptual and Empirical Research" is organized by the Sigmund-Freud-Institute in Frankfurt in cooperation with the Subcommittee for Clinical, Conceptual, Epistemological and Historical Research of the IPA.

10

Scales of Psychological Capacities: the Munich contribution to their psychometric qualities

Dorothea Huber & Guenther Klug

Our survey of the Scales of Psychological Capacities (SPC) starts with a brief introduction to the general topic of structural change and its assessment, using as an example a controversy in US psychoanalysis in the early 1950s. A very concise description of the SPC is followed by a more detailed overview of our studies on the principal components of their psychometric qualities: interrater reliability, test–retest stability, convergent and discriminant construct validity, and sensitivity to change.

But before we going into detail, we would like to give a little outline of our transatlantic cooperation, which began in 1995. We were launching a comparative process–outcome study and were looking for a measure of structural change when we came across a series of articles on the SPC by Robert Wallerstein and his PRP II group. We were interested in the measuring device that in our view seemed to combine a genuine psychoanalytic way to get relevant data with empirical rigor. We met Bob Wallerstein in person at the annual IPA Conference on Psychoanalytic Research in London where, at the end of the conference, he gave his incomparable summary of all presentations, giving a unique and fascinating display of his ability to link people together, to find people's "common ground"—to use the well-known term from his presidential address. This ability created the basis for our productive cooperation.

Freud formulated, most succinctly, the outcome of psychoanalysis as: "to be able to love and to work" or, in terms of structural theory, "Where Id was, there shall Ego be". Later on, this simple formula significantly evolved into that highly narcissistically cathected term: "structural change".

Moore and Fine (1990) defined structural changes as "modifications within each of the major agencies of the psychic apparatus that reduce the conflicts among those agencies". The more fine-grained analysis of the mechanisms that are necessary to bring about such changes owe very much to Bibring's thoughts, presented at the Marienbad Symposium in 1936. There, he stated that changes of the id consists of ". . . loosening fixations of the id, removal of regression and every sort of replacement, weakening or removal of repetition compulsion and thus restoration of the possibility of natural instinctual development". He added that changes in the superego mean that ". . . its archaic severity must be reduced; its great tension in relation to the ego must be lessened, and it must in part be amalgamated with the ego. Its attitude of good will, its understanding and its kindly care must be increased; its functions must be better adapted to the ego's condition of life and to reality". And, finally, changes in the ego are ". . . a mitigation of its defensive attitude and a modification of its defensive mechanisms", which leads to ". . . a resolution of anxiety, an increased toleration of affects and instincts, an increased security with regard to the superego and the external world, a removal of pathogenic defence mechanisms, and finally a restoration of the natural range of modificatory methods at the disposal of the conscious ego". A new equilibrium is established by changes within all three structures, not the ego alone, although it is the principal focus of analysis (Bibring, 1937).

These changes are said to be *deep* and *permanent*, and *resistant* against pathogenic environmental influences. Sounds good! Sounds too good, thus indicating a very well-known problem in psychoanalytic theorizing, namely of overburdening constructs with too-high expectations. Structural change has to some degree shared this fate.

Eissler's (1950) analysis of the psychic change of Jean Valjean, the hero of Victor Hugo's *Les Misérables*, is a good example. Alexander (Alexander & French, 1946) had chosen the life of Jean Valjean to demonstrate the far-reaching effects of corrective emotional experience. By contrast, Eissler tried to demonstrate that these effects are not associated with structural change, because this can only be achieved by psychoanalysis proper. Jean Valjean, a poor nurseryman living in Northern France, is condemned to five years' forced labour in the galleys for having stolen a loaf of bread. After having spent, all in all, 19 years in the galleys, he is released, his heart full of hatred. Meeting Mr Bienvenu, the bishop of Digne, the ex-convict exploits his friendliness and steals his silverware. When Jean Valjean is caught by the police, the bishop reacts with unexpected generosity, causing Jean Valjean's conversion from criminal to a respected, heroic man. We will further elaborate on Eissler's sceptical conception of change in Jean Valjean as being merely a superficial change in behaviour. Eissler doubts the *depth* of this change and remarks critically that the dichotomy of either becoming an angel or a monster indicates merely "changing the indices". He objects that Jean Valjean has, desperately, to be an angel in order not to be a criminal, but he has to be exceptional in any case: either the worst of criminals or the saintliest of men. Supposing this is the case, an unresolved ego-ideal problem still remains. Nevertheless, being an angel instead of a criminal is a dramatic change of intrapsychic forces and of the superego, which ensures much better social adaptation. Eissler further argues that Jean Valjean could never be free from his "therapist", the bishop; even on his deathbed he asks whether he merited the bishop's approval.

But how truly "free" are successfully analysed patients who adopt an analytic stance in the form of a self-analytic capacity and who very often contact their former analysts, and not only internally (Schachter & Brauer, 2001)? Jean Valjean never has a romantic relationship, it is true, but he develops a very strong positive emotional attachment to a child, Cosette, whom he loves sincerely. Victor Hugo informs us that Jean had lost his mother very early and that he lived thereafter with one of his widowed sisters and her seven children, for whom he acted like a father. Perhaps having a bishop as a therapist interferes with poor Jean solving his oedipal problems and finding a spouse. Still, he does regain his ability to love children. When Cosette falls in love with rebel student Marius, Jean heroically saves Marius's life during the battle on the Paris barricades in 1832 (the well-known unresolved ego-ideal problem!). However, seen from another perspective, he saves Cosette's love object, makes the wedding possible, and thus endures losing Cosette in the end. Is this not a deep change? A structural change?

And what about *resistance* against pathogenic environmental influences? According to Eissler, Jean Valjean reacts with a selfish manipulation of Cosette after he hears heard that she has fallen in love with Marius and is thrown into deep conflict. After the wedding of Cosette and Marius, he withdraws entirely from life, and purposely makes Marius, the fiancé, believe that he had continued his criminal career, thus overshadowing the happiness of the newlyweds. This, of course, indicates an intrapsychic crisis and a problem in handling oedipal aggression, but Jean Valjean nevertheless suffers neither criminal relapse nor depression.

And what about *permanency*? Jean Valjean met bishop Bienvenu in 1819 and died in 1833—that means the change remained stable for 14 years, without a single "post-therapeutic" contact!

We hoped to demonstrate that structural change, as a sort of shibboleth of psychoanalysis, has been highly cathected narcissistically in the past, with all the disadvantages that ensue from such an overcathexis. Perhaps its most conspicuous feature is the radicalism of its assumptions, following the "all-or-none" law of narcissism. Eissler argues that the conflict should be demolished, that it should no longer exist. It is not enough that Jean Valjean was able to use reaction formation as a more mature defence mechanism, whereas earlier he had suffered from severely disturbed impulse control and used projection as a dominant defence mechanism. Warded-off aggression will always become apparent behind reaction formation, it is true, but nevertheless reaction formation guarantees a far better social adaptation than does projection. As another example, Eissler argues that after his "cure", Jean Valjean is still unable to have a significant intimate relationship. This is correct but, on the other hand, he is able to have a loving relationship with Cosette, whom he has adopted as his daughter. He had never been able to have such a relationship before, which signifies an undeniable progressive step towards an object relational mode of relationship—a fact Eissler does not recognize at all.

Merton Gill has cast his more realistic view of structural change in the ironical remark: "we still recognize our good friends after a successful analysis"; but I think that rather than ironical distance, empirical scrutiny of psychoanalytic outcome studies has turned out to be the best antidote against an idealistic stance. This potential structural change of psychoanalysis itself has led to more cautious formulations about structural change.

For example, Pfeffer, after a careful follow-up study of satisfactorily completed psychoanalyses, spoke more modestly of a loss of poignancy of old conflicts that are still discernible but more manageable (cited in Wallerstein, 1986). In this sober and realistic vein, Wallerstein stated that, for the time being, the different theoretical perspectives in psychoanalysis can agree neither as to definitions of structure nor as to definitions of structural change and their respective operationalizations. The solution to this theoretical dilemma has been to create theoretically independent, consensually agreed-upon, and reliable indices of intrapsychic structure that will necessarily shift if there is "underlying" change in intrapsychic structures. The sum total of these indices are the "psychological capacities", which constitute the degree of adaptive or maladaptive overall personality integration and functioning. They will necessarily change if underlying psychic structure changes, irrespective of how it is conceived. The result has been a set of 17 psychological capacities.

The SPC (Wallerstein, 1988a; Wallerstein et al., 1986) are an expert-rating measure that evaluates psychic structure on a general rather than a specific theoretical basis. The Scales were developed from the research methodology of the Psychotherapy Research Project (PRP) of the Menninger Foundation (Wallerstein, 1986) and are an attempt to operationalize the concepts "psychic structure" and "structural change" as independently as possible of the differing theoretical perspectives in psychoanalysis, so that they can yield reliable assessments of specific changes after psychoanalysis irrespective of the therapist's theoretical adherence. Based on an empirical research strategy, these Psychological Capacities are constructs designed to be theoretically as low-level (experience-near) as possible and readily inferable from observable behaviour and conscious states of mind, so that the underlying intrapsychic structures and changes in them after treatment can be reliably identified.

The Psychological Capacities consist of 17 dimensions, of which 13 are divided into 2 subdimensions and 3 into 3 subdimensions; one dimension is not divided (see Table 10.1). The assessment of all 36 subdimensions is based on a 1-hour clinical intake interview recorded on tape, together with a 1–2-hour semi-structured SPC interview with probe questions. The material is rated for each subdimension, on a 7-point scale, from 0 for "normal" or fully adaptive functioning to 3 for seriously disturbed functioning, with half-points in-between. The dimensions are constructed so that one subdimen-

Table 10.1. The Scales of Psychological Capacities

Dimension		Subdimension	
1	Hope	a	Excessive optimism
		b	Excessive pessimism
2	Zest for life	a	Over-excitement
		(b)	(Drudgery)
		c	Apathy
3	Attribution of responsibility	a	Over-externalizing
		b	Over-internalizing
4	Flexibility	a	Closed-mindedness
		b	Confusion and self-doubt
5	Persistence	a	Drivenness
		b	Giving Up
6	Commitment to standards and values	a	Moralism
		b	Absence of principles
7	Commitment in relationships	a	Compulsive overinvolvement
		b	Limited, tenuous commitment
8	Reciprocity	a	Exploitation of others
		b	Surrender of self
9	Trust	a	Extreme suspiciousness
		b	Extreme gullibility
10	Empathy	a	Emotional absorption
		b	Emotional blunting
		c	Egocentricity
11	Affect regulation	a	Out-of-control "affect storms"
		b	Hypercontrol
12	Impulse regulation	a	Over-indulgence
		b	Over-inhibition
13	Regulation of sexual experience	a	Impulsive or driven expression
		b	Inhibition
14	Self-assertion	a	Bullying
		b	Timidity
15	Reliance on self and others	a	Rarely able to rely on others
		b	Rarely able to rely on self
		c	Rarely able to be person relied upon
16	Self-esteem	a	Grandiosity
		b	Self-depreciation
17	Self-coherence	a	Inconsistency

sion covers various degrees of inhibited functioning and the other various degrees of exaggerated functioning. Both directions have to be assessed, and both subdimensions can be rated simultaneously. An extensive manual is available for the rating procedure, with a detailed description of each subdimension, together with one or more clinical vignettes to anchor each scale point.

Each psychological capacity is the bond that links explorable, conscious, and preconscious psychic surface (the capacities), on the one hand, with only inferable, unconscious psychic depth (the structure), on the other. On the upper pole of the unit we check reliability: are the capacities experience-near enough that raters can agree; at the lower pole of the unit we check validity: are the capacities deep-reaching enough so that their change, reflect a change in underlying structure? Does psychic surface change when structure has changed? Or—perhaps more relevant—has structure changed when psychic surface has changed? We begin with the upper pole, the reliability of the SPC.

Interrater reliability study

Method

The sample was recruited as a sub-sample of the Munich Psychotherapy Study (MPS). In this comparative process–outcome study of psychoanalysis and psychoanalytic psychotherapy with a diagnostically homogenous sample of depressive patients (Huber & Klug, 2002; Huber, Klug, & von Rad, 2002), therapy outcome was measured with the SPC. It consisted of a homogeneous group of 38 depressed patients aged between 25 and 45 (M = 33 years, SD = 6.4 years), of whom 70% were female, 72% were single, 16% married, 12% divorced, and 29% had children. Of the total, 53% were employed full-time and 13% part-time, 5% were unemployed, and 29% had other types of employment.

The diagnosis was made by an experienced clinician (psychiatrist and psychotherapist), who used the IDCL classification scheme and a checklist for ICD-10 and DSM IV diagnosis (Hiller, Zaudig, & Mombour, 1995) after having discussed the interview with two other experts. All patients were diagnosed as suffering from a depressive disorder: 60% with moderate or severe depressive episodes, 40% moderate or severe recurrent depressive disorder; nearly half of the patients (47%) had a double depression, with dysthymia as second diagnosis.

Procedure

The authors received rater training according to the formal method (Mercer & Loesch, 1979) from Wallerstein and his coworkers. A member of the PRP-II group assessed a transcribed German SPC interview, translated into English, in order to use it as a master rating for rater training. Three German raters were then trained, in accordance with Lambert and Hill's recommendations (1994). These raters had a rather varied professional background: one was a psychology student without psychotherapy training but with a particular interest in psychoanalytic theory; another was a postgraduate psychologist undergoing behaviour therapy training; and the third was a physician undergoing advanced psychoanalytic training. They rated three videorecorded American SPC interviews and compared their ratings with the expert ratings. After having rated three German tape-recorded SPC interviews together with the respective clinical intake interviews, they assessed the above-mentioned master-rated German SPC interview independently and agreed satisfactorily, meaning that they did not differ by more than 0.5 scale points in any subdimension. After the rating of every fifth patient there was a recalibration session when the three judges and the two trainers met to correct for judges' drift.

Results and discussion

Interrater reliability among the three raters was calculated separately for each subdimension by means of the Intra Class Correlation Coefficient (ICC: Strout & Fleiss, 1979).

The mean ICC was 0.82, with a range from 0.54 to 0.89 (see Table 10.2). Using 0.70 as a standard cut-off for scales that do not have a low level of inference, in accordance with the recommendations of Lambert and Hill (1994), only 4 of the 35 subdimensions had a reliability score under 0.70. These subdimensions were *Over-Externalizing, Unprincipled Behaviour, Tenuous Commitment in Relationships*, and *Inconsistency*. All 35 subdimensions reached Cohen's cut-off point of 0.50 (Cohen, 1988).

Table 10.2. Descriptive statistics and intra-class correlation for interrater reliability study

Dimension		Subdimension		Mean	*SD*	ICC
1	Hope	a	Optimism	.56	.58	.86
		b	Pessimism	1.62	.53	.82
2	Zest of life	a	Overexcitement	1.01	.67	.85
		b	Apathy	1.18	.63	.82
3	Responsibility	a	Overexternalizing	.54	.50	.58
		b	Overinternalizing	1.54	.63	.82
4	Flexibility	a	Closed-mindedness	1.05	.70	.84
		b	Self-doubt	1.61	.91	.81
5	Persistence	a	Drivenness	1.44	.69	.86
		b	Giving up	1.16	.67	.83
6	Standards	a	Moralism	.83	.63	.83
		b	Unprincipled	.36	.38	.54
7	Commitment	a	Overinvolvement	1.61	.53	.74
		b	Tenuousness	.93	.53	.65
8	Reciprocity	a	Exploitation	.62	.64	.80
		b	Surrender	1.45	.66	.87
9	Trust	a	Suspiciousness	1.23	.67	.85
		b	Gullibility	.99	.63	.83
10	Empathy	a	Absorption	1.12	.73	.89
		b	Blunting	.85	.69	.83
		c	Egocentricity	.79	.76	.87
11	Affect	a	Out of control	1.03	.65	.86
		b	Hypercontrol	1.29	.67	.85
12	Impulse	a	Indulgence	.80	.67	.88
		b	Inhibition	.79	.61	.76
13	Sexual	a	Impulsive	.24	.41	.83
		b	Inhibition	1.14	.60	.82
14	Assertion	a	Bullying	.89	.62	.88
		b	Timidity	1.32	.54	.76
15	Reliance	a	Not on others	1.56	.95	.79
		b	Not on self	.74	.62	.88
		c	Not relied upon	.72	.53	.84
16	Self-esteem	a	Grandiosity	.33	.51	.81
		b	Self-depreciation	1.63	.44	.76
17	Coherence	a	Inconsistency	.65	.39	.65
	Average			1.02		.82

Note: $n = 38$. ICC = Intra-Class Correlation.

Test–retest reliability study (stability)

When an instrument is developed to measure change, it is necessary to demonstrate the stability of test scores over time. Scores must significantly correlate between one measurement point and scores on the same instrument after a particular time interval has elapsed, if there has been no intervention in the meantime (Kazdin, 1998).

Method

Procedure

Our study of stability is designed as a test–retest procedure. A so-called external investigator, experienced with the administration and assessment of the SPC, performs a clinical intake interview and a semi-structured SPC interview. After a time interval of 2–3 months, another comparably experienced interviewer repeats the semi-structured SPC interview. We decided in favour of a more authentic interview situation and an elimination of memory effects on the interviewer's side by changing interviewers, accepting an increase in error variance on the interviewer variable. We consider a 2–3 month time span to adequately control for memory effects on the patient's side, without running a risk that any intervention may have led to a structural change in the meantime. Between Measurement Point 1 and Point 2 the patient was on the waiting list for psychotherapy without any treatment.

Two raters rated each interview independently. If they disagreed by more than one scale point, a senior rater (one of the authors) rated the scale again—a method recommended by Jones, Cumming, and Horowitz (1988). This is our *standard procedure*, used for all following psychometric studies with the SPC.

The sample consists of 20 depressed patients aged between 25 and 45 years, again recruited as a sub-sample of the Munich Psychotherapy Study.

Results and discussion

Table 10.3 shows the coefficients for stability calculated with the Pearson coefficient. No coefficient is under 0.50, 2 are under 0.60,

Table 10.3. Stability coefficients for the SPC

Dimension		Subdimension		rr1
1	Hope	a	Optimism	.77
		b	Pessimism	.77
2	Zest of life	a	Over-excitement	.85
		b	Apathy	.89
3	Responsibility	a	Over-externalizing	.67
		b	Over-internalizing	.82
4	Flexibility	a	Closed-mindedness	.56
		b	Self-doubt	.91
5	Persistence	a	Drivenness	.81
		b	Giving up	.71
6	Standards	a	Moralism	.77
		b	Unprincipled	.74
7	Commitment	a	Overinvolvement	.85
		b	Tenuousness	.87
8	Reciprocity	a	Exploitation	.96
		b	Surrender	.87
9	Trust	a	Suspiciousness	.76
		b	Gullibility	.65
10	Empathy	a	Absorption	.76
		b	Blunting	.82
		c	Egocentricity	.90
11	Affect	a	Out of control	.56
		b	Hypercontrol	.81
12	Impulse	a	Indulgence	.92
		b	Inhibition	.84
13	Sexual	a	Impulsive	.76
		b	Inhibition	.70
14	Assertion	a	Bullying	.91
		b	Timidity	.83
15	Reliance	a	Not on others	.74
		b	Not on self	.77
		c	Not relied upon	.71
16	Self-esteem	a	Grandiosity	.65
		b	Self-depreciation	.88
17	Coherence	a	Inconsistency	.80
	SPC Total Score			.88

Note: n = 20. 1 rr = Pearson´s Correlation Coefficient.

and only 6 out of 36 are under 0.70. At 0.88, the stability of the SPC total score (mean of the 35 subdimensions) is very satisfying.

Table 10.4 shows the comparison of means (t-test) between the two measurement points—test and retest. While the two instances of significant improvement balanced the two instances of significant deterioration, on the whole, the total score reflects a slight deterioration.

If we consider the different influencing factors, including two different interviewers for the test and the retest, and if we consider the small sample, we can regard the coefficients to be extraordinarily stable. These results are in line with the results of the stability study with healthy people, presented in this volume by Kathryn DeWitt (chapter 8).

At retesting, all patients knew that they had been accepted for therapy. Clinical and empirical data affirm that certainty about future therapy in itself leads to clear improvements (i.e. Herschbach, Henrich, & Oberst, 1994). It should be mentioned briefly that we also administered the Beck Depression Inventory at two measurement points before the therapy commenced. The depression score of the second test turned out to be highly significantly lower: $t(72) = 3.3$, $p < 0.001$. This confirms again that the certainty of a prospective therapy may improve the symptoms but does not lead to an improvement in the psychological structure revealed by the SPC. Thus we have another piece of evidence for the consistency of the ascertained parameter "structure" and the stability of the SPC.

Validity studies

Validity I: discriminant and convergent validity

In 1997 we performed a first discriminant and convergent construct validity study with 41 SPC interviews of depressed patients. This study has already been published (Huber, Klug, & von Rad, 2002) and is mentioned here only briefly . We compared the SPC with symptom questionnaires in order to evaluate discriminant validity, and with an instrument that measures interpersonal functioning to evaluate convergent validity.

The SPC was independent of current symptoms, and relevant correlations between interpersonal problems and psychic structure were demonstrable. Additionally, convergent validity was proven by comparing a hypothetical prototypical profile for a depressive patient postulated by two experienced clinicians with the empirically found profile of 41 depressed patients for the 36 subdimensions. The clinicians' prediction was correct for all but one subdimension (Huber, Klug, & von Rad, 2002).

Validity II: replication study of discriminant and convergent validity

Having demonstrated, in 2000, reliability of the SPC, we conducted another construct validity study as a replication of the discriminant and convergent validity studies—a study to be described in greater detail. We again evaluated discriminant validity by comparing the SPC with construct-distant instruments measuring symptoms (and expected a zero or only a weak correlation) and compared the SPC with construct-near instruments that measure interpersonal functioning, defence mechanisms, life satisfaction, and personality structure in order to evaluate convergent validity (and expected a medium but not a very high degree of correlation, because the instruments comprise only part aspects of structure).

Method

Sample

The sample consisted of 47 depressed patients, again recruited as a sub-sample of the MPS.

Procedure

In comparison with the above mentioned construct validity studies (Huber, Klug, & von Rad, 2002), these studies used a different sample of depressed patients, a different interviewer, different raters being trained according to the formal method for rater training (described by Mercer & Loesch, 1979), and the same as well as additional construct-near and construct-distant instruments.

Instruments

The construct-distant instruments used to assess discriminant validity were the Symptom Check-List (SCL-90-R), a widely used self-rating symptom inventory (Derogatis, Lipman, & Covi, 1973); the Beck Depression Inventory (BDI) for assessing the severity of depression (Beck, Ward, Mendelson, Mock, & Erbaugh, 1961); the Symptom Severity Score (BSS), an observer rating scale that evaluates the impact of psychic illness (Schepank, 1995); and the Global Assessment of Functioning Scale (GAF), which is also observer-rated and is an

Table 10.4. Comparisons of means between test and retest for the SPC

	Dimension		SPC Subdimension	Test M	Test SD	Retest M	Retest SD	Test statistic (t-value)	Significance (p)
1	Hope	a	Optimism	0.84	0.69	0.59	0.52	2.24	.041
		b	Pessimism	1.63	0.58	1.64	0.61	0.16	.879
2	Zest of life	a	Overexcitement	1.08	0.81	1.03	0.69	0.45	.662
		b	Apathy	1.27	0.72	1.17	0.59	1.15	.270
3	Responsibility	a	Overexternalizing	0.53	0.71	0.55	0.43	0.12	.907
		b	Overinternalizing	1.25	0.86	1.20	0.75	0.38	.709
4	Flexibility	a	Closed-mindedness	1.05	0.69	1.16	0.60	0.72	.486
		b	Self-doubt	1.64	0.90	1.55	0.74	1.00	.333
5	Persistence	a	Drivenness	1.28	0.70	1.06	0.67	2.05	.058
		b	Giving Up	1.47	0.81	1.56	0.61	0.66	.520
6	Standards	a	Moralism	0.42	0.60	0.58	0.55	1.58	.136
		b	Unprincipled	0.23	0.41	0.56	0.54	3.63	.002
7	Commitment	a	Overinvolvement	1.53	0.82	1.52	0.60	0.14	.889
		b	Tenuousness	0.95	0.98	1.05	0.78	0.76	.456
8	Reciprocity	a	Exploitation	0.39	0.65	0.47	0.69	1.58	.136
		b	Surrender	1.09	0.79	1.11	0.80	0.16	.879

9	Trust	a	Suspiciousness	1.02	0.81	1.08	0.69	0.47	.648
		b	Gullibility	0.66	0.71	0.88	0.52	1.62	.125
10	Empathy	a	Absorption	0.80	1.04	1.14	0.90	2.02	.062
		b	Blunting	0.91	0.72	0.91	0.72	0.00	1.000
		c	Egocentricity	0.83	0.81	0.84	0.75	0.17	.864
11	Affect	a	Out of control	1.11	0.80	1.08	0.66	0.18	.860
		b	Hypercontrol	1.34	0.88	1.41	0.66	0.48	.638
12	Impulse	a	Indulgence	0.70	0.67	0.78	0.69	1.16	.264
		b	Inhibition	0.64	0.58	0.80	0.56	1.91	.076
13	Sexual	a	Impulsive	0.17	0.35	0.17	0.35	0.00	1.000
		b	Inhibition	1.30	0.74	1.08	0.68	1.58	.135
14	Assertion	a	Bullying	0.78	0.80	0.80	0.68	0.19	.855
		b	Timidity	1.02	0.69	1.28	0.76	2.46	.027
15	Reliance	a	Not on others	1.25	0.90	1.30	0.53	0.30	.769
		b	Not on self	0.88	0.87	0.95	0.78	0.56	.585
		c	Not relied upon	0.80	0.77	0.81	0.64	0.11	.911
16	Self-esteem	a	Grandiosity	0.42	0.52	0.36	0.46	0.61	.554
		b	Self-depreciation	1.78	0.66	1.86	0.70	0.92	.370
17	Coherence	a	Inconsistency	1.05	0.59	0.70	0.41	3.78	.002
	SPC Total Score			0.97	0.25	1.00	0.21	0.87	.397

Note: $n = 20$
* adjusted alpha = 0.0014.

internationally used scale for assessing the influence of symptoms on global functioning (APA, 1994).

As a construct-near measure we used the Inventory of Interpersonal Problems (IIP), short version (Horowitz et al., 1988). The IIP is an internationally established instrument for the assessment of interpersonal problems and concerns. We measured quality of life with the Questions on Life Satisfaction (FLZ) questionnaire; we used the two total scores for General Life Satisfaction and for Satisfaction with Health (Henrich & Herschbach, 2000; Huber, Henrich, & Herschbach, 1988). We also compared the SPC with the Questionnaire for Conflict-Coping Strategies (FKBS), which measures 5 defence mechanisms (Hentschel, Kießling, & Wiemers, 1998). This questionnaire is similar to the Defense Mechanism Inventory (DMI) (Gleser, & Ihilevich, 1969). In addition to these self-rating questionnaires, the external investigator rated the patient's psychic structure with the Operationalized Psychodynamic Diagnostics (OPD), axis 4: Structure (OPD Task Force, 2001) on a 4-point scale (good, moderate, poorly integrated, disintegrated), and we examined the correlation of this global assessment with the SPC total score.

Statistics

Pearson Correlation Coefficient was used to calculate correlations. Because of multiple measures, we decided to interpret only findings that reached at least a 0.1% level of significance.

Results and Discussion

Table 10.5 shows clearly that there is no significant correlation between the SPC subdimensions or the SPC total score and the construct-distant instruments, thus confirming our first assumption that the SPC measure psychic functioning and not just the influence of symptoms.

There are 19 significant correlations between the IIP scales and the SPC subdimensions. They are (as shown in Table 10.6): Subdimension *Pessimism* with *Subassertive* (0.52); *Apathy* with *Cold* (0.47) and IIP total score (0.58); *Surrender* with *Autocratic* (–0.53); *Blunting* with *Cold* (0.45); *Hypercontrol* with *Cold* (0.51) and IIP total score

Table 10.5. Survey of significant correlations between the SPC and the construct-distant/construct-near instruments

Construct-distant instruments	SCL-90 (10 scales)	BDI (1 scale)	BSS (4 scales)	GAF (2 scales)
Amount of sign. correlations	0	0	0	0
Range of all correlations	.01–.38	.02–.41	.01–.37	.01–.32
Construct-near instruments	**IIP (9 scales)**	**FLZ (2 scales)**	**FKBS (5 scales)**	**OPDa (1 scale)**
Amount (range) of sign. correlations	19 (.46–.59)	3 (.46–.55)	2 (.46–.52)	1 (.49)
Range of all correlations	.00–.59	.01–.55	.00–.52	.00–.49

Note: $n = 47$.
[a]The OPD-score was correlated with the SPC total score only.
$p < 0.001$.

(0.48); *Bullying* with *Autocratic* (0.49), *Subassertive* (–0.48) and *Nurturant* (–0.48); *Timidity* with *Autocratic* (–0.46), *Introverted* (0.51), *Subassertive* (0.59), *Exploitable* (0.56), *Nurturant* (0.51) and IIP total score (0.51); *Not on Self* with *Autocratic* (0.46) and *Competitive* (–0.52).

As one can see in Table 10.4, out of the 17 SPC dimensions, 9 correlate with IIP scales. Most of the correlations (9 out of a total of 19) can be found to the SPC dimension *Assertion*, 6 of these to the subdimension *Timidity* and 3 to the subdimension *Bullying*; thus almost half are related to the SPC dimension *Assertion*, especially to the subdimension *Timidity*. So we can state that into this scale enter mostly aspects of interpersonal problems. Our results match the results of the convergent validity study of DeWitt et al. (1999). In this study, the IIP was also used, in a different and much more heterogeneous sample. The authors specify 44 correlations at a level of significance of 5%: if the same rigorous level is used as in our study, the correlations are reduced to 22 (in our study there were 19 correlations). DeWitt and colleagues also found most of the correlations to the subdimension *Timidity*.

Table 10.5 shows three significant correlations between the two Questions on Life Satisfaction (FLZ) scales and the SPC subdimensions. These are: Subdimension *Pessimism* with *Satisfaction with Health* (–0.46); and *General Life Satisfaction* (–0.55); Subdimension *Surrender* with *Satisfaction with Health* (–0.48).

Table 10.6. Significant correlations of the SPC with IIP-scales

Dimensions		SPC Subdimensions		IIP-scales							
				PA	BC	DE	FG	HI	JK	LM	TO
1	Hope	b	Pessimism					.52			
2	Zest of life	b	Apathy			.47					
3	Responsibility	a	Overexternalizing								.58
8	Reciprocity	b	Surrender	–.53							
10	Empathy	b	Blunting			.45					
11	Affect	b	Hypercontrol			.51					.48
13	Sexual	b	Inhibition			.46					
14	Assertion	a	Bullying	.49				–.48		–.48	
	–	b	Timidity	–.46			.51	.59	.56	.51	.51
15	Reliance	b	Not on self	–.46	–.52						

Note: $n = 47$. PA = Domineering, BC = Vindictive, DE = Cold, FG = Socially avoidant, HI = Non-assertive, JK = Exploitable, LM = Overly Nurturant, (NO = Intrusive), TO = IIP total score.
$p < 0.001$.

There are two significant correlations between the Questionnaire for Conflict-Coping Strategies (FKBS) scales and the SPC subdimensions: Subdimension *Pessimism* (0.46) and Subdimension *Apathy* (0.52), both with *Turning against Self*. These significant correlations, together with the absence of any other significant correlation with the remaining four scales of the FKBS (*Reaction Formation, Turning Against the Object, Intellectualization/Rationalization,* and *Projection*), confirm our hypothesis that depressives mainly show the defence mechanism *Turning against Self* and that only this scale will correlate with the SPC subdimensions relevant for depression.

There is a significant correlation between the *OPD* sum score and the SPC total score (0.49). This validates the SPC as a general measure of psychic structure.

All correlations with the SPC subdimensions were consistent conceptually, made sense clinically, and never contradicted clinical theory. So the convergent validity study provides some evidence that the SPC measures a construct similar, but not identical, to interpersonal problems, quality of life, and defence mechanisms.

However, there is only a small number of correlations between the SPC subdimensions and the scales of the construct-near instruments. This can be explained partly by the very rigorously chosen level of significance (Perneger, 1998) and partly by the different source of observation (e.g. Pilkonis, Imber, Lewis, & Rubinsky, 1984). The latter effect is even more important because the psychically very disturbed patients of our sample tend to have a very flawed self-reflection that will enlarge the difference between their and the raters' perspective.

All in all, we consider our second assumption as only partly confirmed. We therefore decided to choose another method to investigate construct validity of the SPC.

Validity III: discrimination of different diagnostic groups

Construct validity may be demonstrated through a well-established and approved method called "known-groups approach" (Lambert & Hill, 1994; Lienert & Raatz, 1998). Thus the objective of the this study is to investigate whether depressive patients differ from borderline patients and from normal controls in their empirically found SPC profiles. According to psychoanalytic theory, clear-cut differences in psychic structure are to be expected. So the following differences were derived on the basis of psychoanalytic theory: in borderline patients disturbances in impulse- and affect control and in self-coherence predominate, whereas in depressive patients disturbances in self-esteem, hope, and attribution of responsibility predominate, which the SPC should be able to reflect.

We expect therefore that there will be significant differences between the empirically found profiles of borderline patients, depressive patients, and controls.

Method

Sample

The sample comprises three groups of women, as comparable as possible in regard to age. All groups consisted of women only, because women predominated in the depressive as well as in the borderline group. A total of 36 depressed women were again taken from the MPS sample, and 33 borderline patients were recruited, all of them meeting the ICD-10 criteria for emotionally instable personality, borderline type (*F* 60.31), or a DSM-IV diagnosis of Borderline Personality Disorder (301.83), respectively. All patients were diagnosed by means of an ICD-10 and DSM IV checklist (Hiller, Zaudig, & Mombour, 1995). In addition, 36 controls were recruited from among employees in the civil service and in banking, as well as medical students. All controls were selected on the basis of a screening interview, the SCL-90-R and the IIP, to exclude those persons who had a relevant mental disorder or had been in psychotherapy. In both tests, controls did not differ from the norm values indicated in the test manuals.

Age, marital status, and professional situation of the three diagnostic groups are described in Table 10.7. Depressives and controls were equally likely to have a constant partner, whereas borderline patients were not. The significant difference in educational level is caused by the high rate of students in the control group and by the high rate (nearly a half) of borderline patients with extended elementary-school education.

Table 10.7. Sociodemographic variables of the three groups

	Borderline (n = 33)		Depressive (n = 36)		Controls (n = 36)		Test statistic (χ^2)	Signif. (p)
	n	%	n	%	n	%		
Romantic relationship	12	36	26	72	22	65	9.973	.007
Marital status							2.548	.636
single	26	79	31	86	32	89		
married	4	12	3	8	1	3		
divorced	3	9	2	6	3	8		
One or more children	6	18	4	11	1	3	4.234	.120
Education							39.591	<.001
Short-course secondary	13	48	0	0	0	0		
Intermediate-course secondary	3	11	8	26	4	11		
College-preparatory and higher	11	41	23	74	31	89		
	M	SD	M	SD	M	SD	$F(1, 102)$	p
Age	28.7	6.6	28.6	3.7	26.8	5.1	1.547	.218

Note: Women only.

Procedure

All patients were evaluated using an unstructured clinical intake interview and a semi-structured SPC interview. In order to control for interviewer variable, the same three interviewers and raters rated all three groups. We recruited new raters for this study, all being trained according to the formal method (Mercer & Loesch, 1979). In this study all interviewers/raters were women.

Statistics

Comparisons of means between the three groups for the 35 SPC subdimensions and the SPC total score were calculated with univariate one-way ANOVAS. Because of multiple testing, we adjusted alpha level with the Bonferroni correction. As univariate analyses of variance cannot take into account possible mutual correlations among the different SPC subdimensions, a stepwise discriminant analysis was used as a multivariate method to discriminate the three clinical groups.

Results and discussion

As is shown on Figure 10.1, borderline patients clearly showed the highest scores. In 18 subdimensions the borderline patients exceeded 1.5, in contrast to only three of the depressives and none of the controls. The five subdimensions that loaded highest for borderline patients are (in descending order): *Self-Depreciation, Indulgence, Affect out of Control, Inconsistency,* and *Hypercontrol of Affect.* The five subdimensions loading highest for depressives are: *Self-Depreciation, Overinvolvement in Commitments, Pessimism, Self-Doubt,* and *Over-Internalizing.*

As is shown in Table 10.8, the ANOVAs indicate highly significant differences for 32 SPC subdimensions and the SPC total score ($p < 0.001$). The controls score the lowest for every SPC subdimension and the SPC total score. They are distinguished significantly from the borderline patients, as the post-tests show for every SPC subdimension plus the SPC total score. In 12 subdimensions and the total score there are significant differences among all three groups. In 13 subdimensions the controls differ significantly from the two clinical groups; in 6 subdimensions the controls and depressives together differ from the borderline patients. In 2 subdimensions there is only a difference between controls and borderline patients, and in 2 subdimensions there were no significant differences.

In order to elucidate the different levels of psychic structure, the SPC total score (mean of the 35 subdimensions) of the three investigated groups is compared in Figure 10.2.

The stepwise discriminant analysis rendered an extraction of 7 subdimensions. The groups were classified according to two discriminant functions with a 94.3% accuracy and by cross validation with a 92.4% accuracy. As is shown in Table 10.9, 100% of the healthy controls, 89% of depressives, and 94% of the borderline patients were identified correctly. Both canonical discriminant functions explain a substantial part of the variance; the first function 85.7%, the second function 14.3%. For both functions, Wilk's Lambda is highly significant; both functions are therefore necessary for the distinction of the three groups (Function 1: Wilk's Lambda = 0.074; $\chi^2(14) = 257.7$, $p < 0.000$; Function 2: Wilk's Lambda = 0.506; $\chi^2(6)$, $p < 0.000$).

As follows from Figure 10.3, presenting the canonical discriminant function, Discriminant Function 1 especially distinguishes the borderline patients from the controls. The depressives are in-between, but are—according to the post-hoc test—also highly signifi-

Figure 10.1. Mean profile of SPC sub-dimensions for the three investigated groups

Table 10.8. Comparisons of means of the SPC for the three groups

Dimension		SPC Subdimension		Borderline ($n = 33$) M	Borderline ($n = 33$) *SD*	Depressive ($n = 36$) M	Depressive ($n = 36$) *SD*	Controls ($n = 36$) M	Controls ($n = 36$) *SD*	Test statistic $F(2,102)$	Signif. (p)	Multiple comparisons[a] (s^a)
1	Hope	a	Optimism	0.81	0.66	0.31	0.40	0.28	0.39	12.53	< .001	C,D < B
		b	Pessimism	1.77	0.70	1.54	0.63	0.26	0.39	67.84	< .001	C < D,B
2	Zest for life	a	Over-excitement	1.55	0.87	0.99	0.70	0.51	0.53	18.20	< .001	C < D < B
		b	Apathy	1.65	0.61	0.98	0.65	0.10	0.23	74.72	< .001	C < D < B
3	Responsibility	a	Externalizing	0.80	0.81	0.32	0.43	0.14	0.28	13.56	< .001	C < B
		b	Internalizing	1.58	0.96	1.47	0.79	0.58	0.60	16.94	< .001	C < D, B
4	Flexibility	a	Closed-minded	1.41	0.60	0.88	0.67	0.38	0.55	24.97	< .001	C < D < B
		b	Self-doubt	1.73	0.59	1.51	0.87	0.44	0.51	36.80	< .001	C < D,B
5	Persistence	a	Driveness	1.70	0.67	1.12	0.72	0.68	0.61	20.01	< .001	C < D < B
		b	Giving up	1.44	0.88	1.08	0.87	0.10	0.27	31.46	< .001	C < D,B
6	6tandards	a	Moralism	0.96	0.70	0.43	0.65	0.35	0.42	10.21	.001	C,D < B
		b	Unprincipled	1.28	0.66	0.17	0.42	0.14	0.29	63.41	< .001	C,D < B
7	Commitment	a	Involvement	1.82	0.70	1.56	0.78	0.53	0.62	33.30	< .001	C < D,B
		b	Tenuousness	1.69	0.76	0.65	0.75	0.22	0.45	44.09	< .001	C < D < B
8	Reciprocity	a	Exploitation	0.56	0.59	0.23	0.46	0.17	0.36	6.74	.002	C < B
		b	Surrender	1.67	0.77	1.25	0.80	0.51	0.61	22.92	< .001	C < D,B

9	Trust	a	Suspiciousness	1.65	0.81	1.13	0.71	0.31	0.45	35.57	< .001	C < D,B
		b	Gullibility	1.31	0.65	0.71	0.66	0.50	0.50	16.56	< .001	C,D < B
10	Empathy	a	Absorption	1.51	0.93	1.09	0.90	0.47	0.60	14.14	< .001	C < D,B
		b	Blunting	0.91	0.71	0.56	0.60	0.13	0.26	17.13	< .001	C < D,B
		c	Egocentricity	0.89	0.83	0.36	0.57	0.31	0.38	9.05	< .001	C,D < B
11	Affect	a	Out of control	2.17	0.60	1.15	0.75	0.29	0.47	80.36	< .001	C < D < B
		b	Hypercontrol	1.89	0.81	1.22	0.81	0.46	0.54	33.07	< .001	C < D < B
12	Impulse	a	Indulgence	2.18	0.70	0.74	0.61	0.20	0.44	102.39	< .001	C < D < B
		b	Inhibition	1.09	0.78	0.90	0.63	0.27	0.39	17.11	< .001	C < D,B
13	Sexual	a	Impulsive	0.22	0.50	0.06	0.21	0.01	0.04	4.36	.015	
		b	Inhibition	1.80	0.95	1.19	0.78	0.49	0.67	22.72	< .001	C < D < B
14	Assertion	a	Bullying	1.19	0.66	0.63	0.68	0.33	0.57	15.98	< .001	C,D < B
		b	Timidity	1.42	0.84	1.25	0.67	0.49	0.54	18.53	< .001	C < D,B
15	Reliance	a	Not on others	1.78	0.82	1.23	0.76	0.63	0.57	22.30	< .001	C < D < B
		b	Not on self	1.23	0.88	0.96	0.83	0.24	0.38	17.56	< .001	C < D,B
		c	Not relied upon	0.95	0.78	0.65	0.68	0.22	0.37	11.86	< .001	C < D,B
16	Self-esteem	a	Grandiosity	0.23	0.39	0.20	0.35	0.06	0.22	2.61	.079	
		b	Self-depreciation	2.25	0.56	1.74	0.60	0.40	0.48	105.28	< .001	C < D < B
17	Coherence		Inconsistency	1.92	0.65	0.83	0.55	0.06	0.15	123.74	< .001	C < D < B
	SPC Total Score			1.40	0.25	0.89	0.22	0.32	0.19	207.54	< .001	C<D<B

Note: One-way ANOVAs. Adjusted alpha-level = 0,0014. B = Borderline; C = Controls; D = Depressive.
[a]Multiple comparisons are significant on a 5% level; blank means no significance (post-hoc test: Games-Howell).

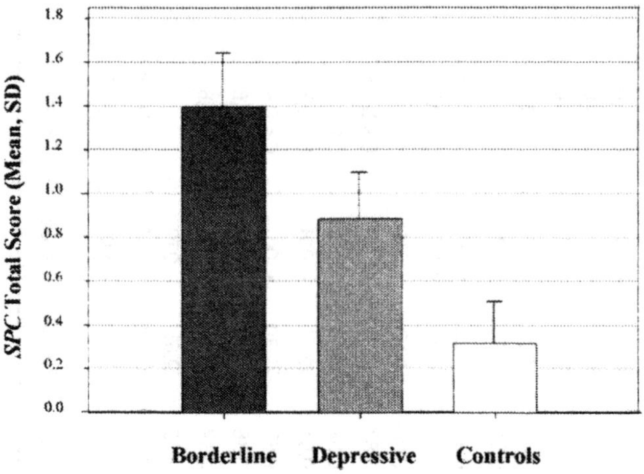

Figure 10.2. SPC total score of the three investigated groups

cantly distinguished from both groups by Function 1 (for all post-hoc tests: $p < 0.001$). This function thus comprises increasingly disturbed psychic structure, ranging—according to theory—from controls to borderline patients. As Figure 10.3 shows very clearly, Discriminant Function 2 does not differ between borderline patients and controls (post-hoc test: $p = 0.915$), but it does distinguish between depressives and controls and between depressives and borderline patients (for both post-hoc tests: $p < 0.001$). The essential distinctions among the groups—between the patients and the controls as well as between the two diagnostic groups—is accomplished by Function 1.

As Table 10.10 shows, Function 1, discriminating highly significantly among all three groups, is composed of the subdimension *Inconsistency* of the dimension *Self-Coherence*, *Indulgence* of the dimension *Impulse Regulation*, and *Self-Depreciation* of the dimension *Self-Esteem*.

Table 10.9. Classification results of stepwise discriminant analysis

	Predicted groups		
Groups (N = 105)	Borderline	Depressive	Controls
Borderline (n = 33)	94% (31)	6% (2)	0%
Depressive (n = 36)	3% (1)	89% (32)	8% (3)
Controls (n = 36)	0%	0%	100% (36)

Note: 7 SPC subdimensions selected.

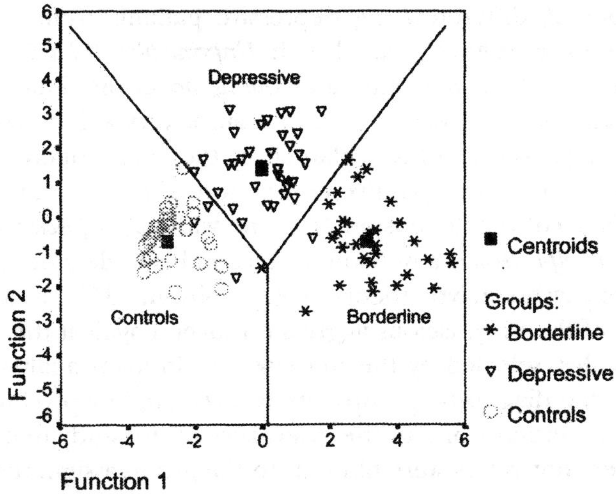

Figure 10.3. Canonical discriminant functions: Position of the individual scores and of the centroids of the three investigated groups.

Subdimensions 1 and 2 are typical for borderline patients, following Kernberg's structural analysis of the borderline personality: *Inconsistency* of the dimension *Self-Coherence* corresponds to Kernberg's identity diffusion, *Indulgence* of the dimension *Impulse Regulation* corresponds to lack of impulse control. *Self-Depreciation* is self-evidently predominant for depressive patients and corresponds to Kernberg's self-denigration, partly as reaction formation to grandiosity, in borderline patients (Kernberg, 1975).

Table 10.10. Structure matrix

SPC Subdimensions		Discriminant function 1	Discriminant function 2
17	Inconsistency	.64	−.11
12a	Indulgence	.57	−.32
16b	Self-depreciation	.57	.41
1b	Pessimism	.44	.47
6b	Unprincipled	.41	−.52
6a	Moralism	.17	−.16
16a	Grandiosity	.09	.09

Note: Pooled within-groups correlations between SPC subdimensions and canonical discriminant functions. Variables ordered by size of correlation with Function 1.

Function 2, differentiating depressive patients from the other groups, is negatively correlated with *Unprincipled Behaviour* of the dimension *Standards and Values* and *Indulgence* of the dimension *Impulse Regulation*. The absence of these traits is very well known in the theory of depression and is explained by the harsh superego of the depressed patient. The positive correlation of the second function with *Pessimism* of the dimension *Hope* and with *Self-Depreciation* of the dimension *Self-Esteem* is a well-known fact and is understood, according to ego-psychoanalytic theory (e.g. Jacobson, 1971), as a clinical indicator of the unconscious aggression turned against the self.

The scales, selected by the stepwise discriminant analysis to differentiate the diagnostic groups, are as predicted by psychoanalytic theory. It is certainly one of the drawbacks of the study that neither interviewers nor raters were blind as to the group assignment of patients and controls. Nevertheless, the consistency with psychoanalytic theory supports the validity of the SPC, since neither interviewers nor raters knew the specific research questions, so that an unconscious tendency towards confirmation or refutation of our hypotheses was ruled out.

As already mentioned, the construction of the SPC makes it possible to deviate from optimal functioning in more than one subdimension at the same time; in that case, both subdimensions have to be scored. For example, on the psychological capacity *Self-Esteem*, a patient may feel inadequate *Grandiosity* as well as intense *Self-Depreciation*, so that both subdimensions have to be scored high. If both feeling states are conscious and if they do not lead into conflict but are expressed conflict-free in experience and behaviour, they indicate splitting as a defence mechanism.

Following psychoanalytic theory, splitting is an archaic defence mechanism, used by the more disturbed patients and not by normal people. We hypothesized that borderline patients would use splitting most often, depressive patients less so, and controls the least, if ever.

We operationalized a Splitting Index as follows: each subdimension of a psychological capacity had to be clearly pathological (score of 1.5 or higher), and the difference between the two corresponding and contradictory subdimensions has to be small—that is, not exceeding one scale point. In our example of psychological capacity: *Self-Esteem*, if subdimension *Grandiosity* scored 2.5, *and* if subdimension *Self-Depreciation* scored 2, the criteria for splitting are fulfilled. Here it should be added self-critically, that we are not sure whether the SPC will be able to discriminate between splitting as a typical defence mechanism and impulse ruptures, based on affective hyper-control, as an indicator of a failure of defence.

A total sum score of splitting was calculated for each group. As is shown in Table 10.11, the groups differed highly significantly (ANOVA: $p < 0.001$—Games–Howell post-hoc test for multiple comparisons). We were able to confirm our hypothesis that borderline patients showed most splitting, depressive patients only some splitting, and controls no splitting at all.

Construct validation by proving predicted test score differences of different groups, chosen according to theory-based assumptions, has been recommended in the literature (e.g. Lambert & Hill, 1994; Lienert & Raatz, 1998). In the present investigation this form of validation clearly demonstrated the construct validity of the SPC.

Patients and controls filled out two self-rating questionnaires: the SCL-90-R and the IIP. This gave us the opportunity to test the "normality" of the controls and to have another source of observation to determine the groups. The controls were within the normal range and differed significantly on all SCL scales from the two clinical groups. There was no significant difference between the depressive and the borderline group for 8 of the 10 SCL-90 scales; only in *Phobic Anxiety* and in the General Symptom Index (GSI) did borderline patients score significantly higher than depressives.

For the IIP scales, the controls again differed significantly on all 8 IIP scales and the IIP total score from both clinical groups, and they were within the normal range as well, but for the IIP scales there were no significant differences at all between the clinical groups.

Table 10.11. Total score of Splitting Index for the three groups

Borderline (B) (n = 33)		Depressive (D) (n = 36)		Controls (C) (n = 36)		Test statistic	Sign.	Multiple
M	*SD*	M	*SD*	M	*SD*	$F(2,102)$	(p)	comparisons
4.36	2.76	0.97	1.36	0.00	0.00	59.04	<.001	C<D<B

Note: one-way ANOVAs. Post-hoc-test: Games-Howell $p < 0.001$

So, on a phenomenological basis neither the symptoms, assessed by the SCL-90-R, nor the interpersonal problems, assessed by the IIP, will suffice to distinguish between these two distinct clinical groups—namely, borderline and depressive patients. But, as was shown with this known group's validation, the SPC differentiated clearly between them.

Sensitivity-to-change study

The SPC are conceptualized especially for measuring change in psychotherapy, therefore we considered the proof of sensitivity to change to be the most important psychometric property. Sensitivity to change in outcome measurement is, according to Lambert and Hill, 1994, "the degree to which a measure is likely to reflect changes that actually occur following participation in therapy". It is the logical counterpart to the stability of an outcome measure indicating that the instrument will reflect change only when a specific intervention has been applied.

1. Our *main hypothesis*: After an approved therapeutic intervention—namely, psychoanalytic long-term therapy—structural change will take place. This structural change should be measurable with the SPC if it is sensitive to change.
2. Our *second hypothesis*: The expert judgement of two independent experienced psychoanalysts rating the patients' structural change will correlate significantly with the pre–post difference in the SPC total score.

Method

Procedure

Based on the assumption that psychoanalytic psychotherapy is the intervention to bring about structural change, we used the SPC in a pre–post design to evaluate sensitivity to change in a long-term therapy.

The therapy was a psychoanalytic long-term therapy carried out by very experienced psychoanalytic therapists, all of them with at least five years' experience as analytic psychotherapists in private practice. The frequency of treatment for 21 therapies was once a week, for 8 therapies twice a week, and for 13 therapies three times a week. The mean length of treatment was 26 months, the median was 29 months.

In addition, the SPC total score was compared with expert ratings of two experienced psychoanalysts. They assessed the degree of structural change retrospectively on a 7-point Likert scale during the follow-up interview, but prior to their administering and evaluating of the SPC. Different interviewers were used at post-treatment and at pre-treatment in order to exclude memory effects. Furthermore, the interviewers at post-treatment could not be blind as to "pre" or "post", because patients generally talked about their therapies. Both experts, who have worked for many years as psychoanalysts, are experienced clinicians and interested in psychoanalytic outcome research. Their judgement was based on a clinical interview of the patients' significant object relations, work situation, relationship with primary objects (if alive), acquaintances and friends, and spare-time and social activities. We are aware of the problem that expert rating can be regarded only as a "pseudo gold standard".

The sample consists of all 42 patients of the Munich Psychotherapy Study, who had finished therapy.

Statistics

We evaluated change not only with usual comparisons of means (t-tests) but also with standardized effect size, and—as a third proof of change—we calculated clinical significance (described by Jacobson & Truax, 1991).

Results and discussion

Figure 10.4 shows the average SPC profiles at the measurement points "pre" and "post". To give an impression of what the SPC of healthy people looks like, the SPC profile of the healthy control group (n = 60) is marked as well.

The SPC-subdimensions that had shown high values before the beginning of the treatment showed very significant improvement in psychic structure after the termination of therapy.

Table 10.12 shows means and standard deviations for all 35 SPC subdimensions and for the SPC total value at the measuring times "pre" and "post", as well as the *t*-values with the respective *p*-values and the standardized effect sizes (SES). A significant change in 20 subdimensions occurred between pre and post. In this connection, the subdimensions meeting Cohen's criterion for high effect sizes (ES > 0.8), are of special importance. These are the following 9 subdimensions (in order of their effect size): *Overinvolvement* in the dimension *Commitment*, *Pessimism* in the dimension *Hope*, *Self-Depreciation* in the dimension *Self-Esteem*, *Surrender* in the dimension *Reciprocity*, *Drivenness* in the dimension *Persistence*, *Over-Internalizing* in the dimension *Responsibility*, *Self-Doubt* in the dimension *Flexibility*, *Timidity* in the dimension *Assertion*, and *Absorption* in the dimension *Empathy*. The only significant (though no longer significant after the Bonferroni correction) worsening was to be seen in the subdimension *Grandiosity* of the dimension *Self-Esteem*; this dimension had had a very low initial value. With a standard effect size of 1.84, the SPC total value shows a very distinct change and the highest sensitivity to change altogether.

In psychotherapy research proof not only of statistical, but also of clinical significance is increasingly important. Therefore, clinical significance has been proposed as a method to safeguard that differences in psychotherapy outcome research signify clinically meaningful improvements in real life. The method does not simply rely on pre–post differences of the measure applied, but compares the values of a specific dysfunctional population with the values of a functional population (Jacobson & Truax, 1991). Even this definition of reliable change was upheld with the SPC: 81% of patients fulfilled the criteria of a clinical relevant improvement, as determined with the Reliable Change Index. This means that these changes are profound enough to have significance for the patients' lives.

For a better evaluation of the change brought about by therapy, Figure 10.5 compares means and standard deviations of the SPC totals of the test–retest study and of the sensitivity-to-change study. As already stated, there was no significant shift during the waiting period of about two months, but there was a highly significant improvement during a therapy of about two years.

An effect size about 1.84 for the SPC total score is very high and by far exceeds the average effect size of 0.85, as reported—but only for short-term therapy—in different meta-analyses (Grawe, Donati,

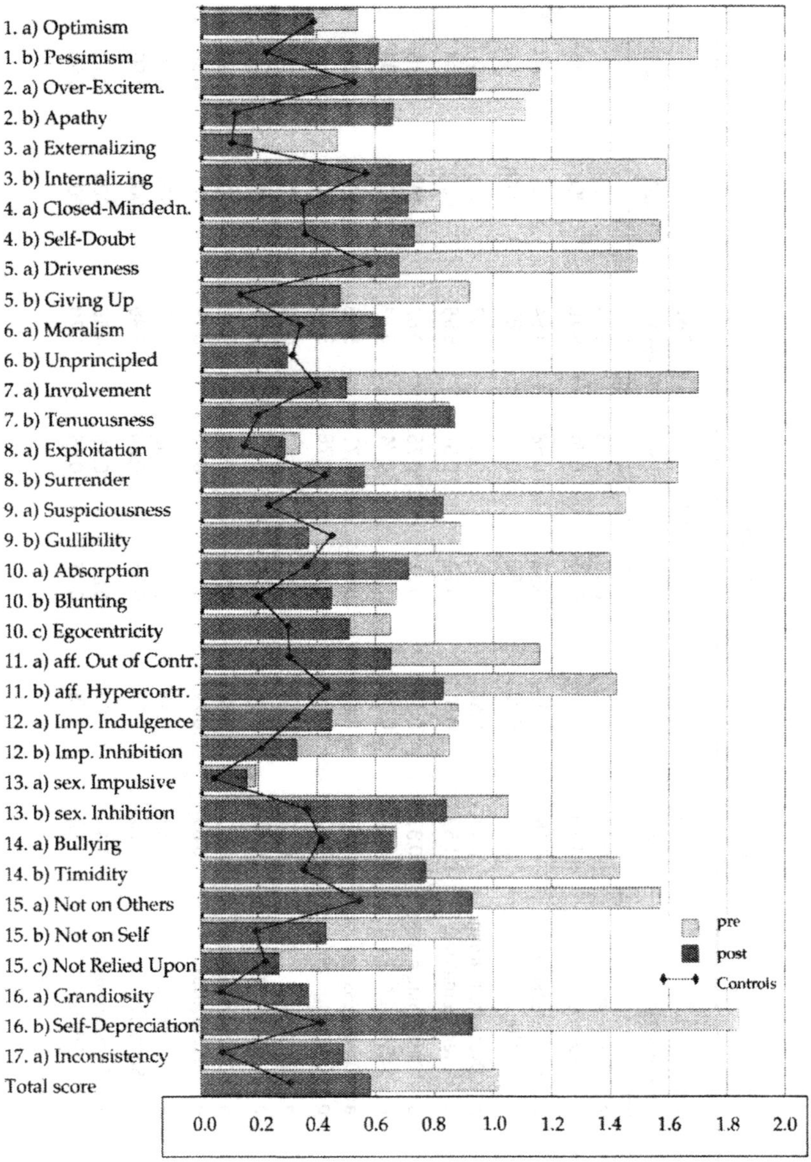

Figure 10.4. SPC profile of depressive patients (***n*** = 42), before (pre = light) and after (post = dark) psychoanalytic long-term therapy (line for the profile of the healthy controls, ***n*** = 60).

Table 10.12. Sensitivity to change

	Dimension		SPC Subdimension	Pre- M	Pre- SD	Post- M	Post- SD	Test (t-value)	Significance (p)	SES
1	Hope	a	Optimism	0.54	0.59	0.39	0.55	1.73	.091	0.25
		b	Pessimism	1.70	0.62	0.61	0.74	8.78	.000	1.76
2	Zest of life	a	Over-excitement	1.16	0.73	0.94	0.68	1.54	.131	0.30
		b	Apathy	1.11	0.72	0.66	0.73	3.81	.000	0.63
3	Responsibility	a	Over-externalizing	0.47	0.56	0.18	0.43	2.92	.006	0.51
		b	Over-internalizing	1.59	0.81	0.72	0.61	5.95	.000	1.08
4	Flexibility	a	Closed-mindedness	0.82	0.72	0.71	0.75	0.87	.391	0.16
		b	Self-doubt	1.57	0.80	0.73	0.74	6.34	.000	1.04
5	Persistence	a	Drivenness	1.49	0.67	0.68	0.71	5.48	.000	1.20
		b	Giving up	0.92	0.84	0.48	0.78	3.44	.001	0.52
6	Standards	a	Moralism	0.59	0.63	0.63	0.62	−0.37	.712	−0.08
		b	Unprincipled	0.29	0.60	0.30	0.52	−0.15	.884	−0.03
7	Commitment	a	Overinvolvement	1.70	0.64	0.50	0.72	9.49	.000	1.89
		b	Tenuousness	0.85	0.77	0.87	0.96	−0.11	.913	−0.02
8	Reciprocity	a	Exploitation	0.34	0.47	0.29	0.50	0.53	.600	0.11
		b	Surrender	1.63	0.71	0.56	0.66	7.96	.000	1.50
9	Trust	a	Suspiciousness	1.45	0.86	0.83	0.75	4.56	.000	0.72
		b	Gullibility	0.89	0.76	0.37	0.65	3.70	.001	0.68

10	Empathy	a	Absorption	1.40	0.81	0.71	0.74	5.04	.000	0.85
		b	Blunting	0.67	0.65	0.45	0.68	1.72	.093	0.34
		c	Egocentricity	0.65	0.70	0.51	0.67	1.05	.299	0.20
11	Affect	a	Out of control	1.16	0.77	0.65	0.71	4.26	.000	0.66
		b	Hypercontrol	1.42	0.82	0.83	0.75	4.55	.000	0.71
12	Impulse	a	Indulgence	0.88	0.77	0.45	0.62	3.46	.001	0.55
		b	Inhibition	0.85	0.76	0.33	0.55	4.83	.000	0.69
13	Sexual	a	Impulsive	0.19	0.43	0.16	0.39	0.37	.714	0.07
		b	Inhibition	1.05	0.84	0.84	0.92	1.15	.258	0.25
14	Assertion	a	Bullying	0.67	0.66	0.66	0.72	0.08	.933	0.02
		b	Timidity	1.43	0.73	0.77	0.73	5.26	.000	0.91
15	Reliance	a	Not on others	1.57	0.86	0.93	0.80	4.22	.000	0.74
		b	Not on self	0.95	0.73	0.43	0.55	4.20	.000	0.71
		c	Not relied upon	0.72	0.69	0.27	0.50	3.64	.001	0.65
16	Self-Esteem	a	Grandiosity	0.21	0.33	0.37	0.54	−2.05	.047	−0.48
		b	Self-depreciation	1.84	0.57	0.93	0.72	7.27	.000	1.59
17	Coherence	a	Inconsistency	0.82	0.59	0.49	0.66	2.61	.013	0.56
	SPC Total Score				0.24	0.58	0.24	10.33	.000	1.84

Note: SPC of depressive patients before (Pre) and after (Post) psychoanalytic long-term psychotherapy; $n = 42$. SES = "Standardized Effect-Size" (Diff (pre-post)/SD(pre)); adjusted alpha = 0.0014.

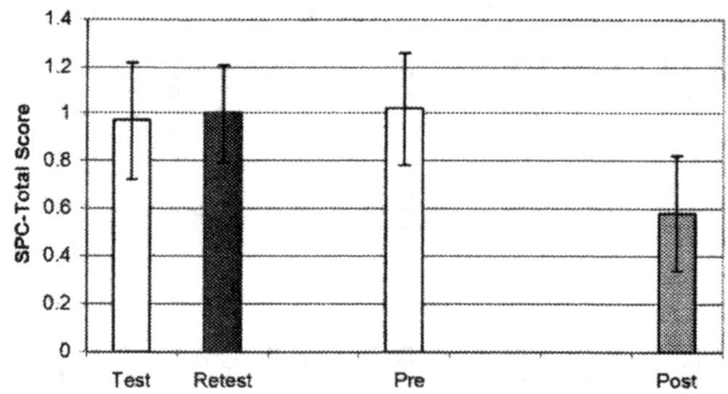

Figure 10.5. SPC-total score at test and retest ($n = 20$) compared to pre- and post- ($n = 42$)

& Bernauer, 1994; Lambert & Bergin, 1994; Smith, Glass, & Miller, 1980). Self-rating tests like the Inventory of Interpersonal Problems (IIP), the Questionnaire for Conflict-Coping Strategies (FKBS), the Questions on Life Satisfaction (FLZ), and the Symptom Check-List (SCL-90-R) help to interpret this high effect size.

In all these standardized tests, the improvements we found were generally greater than in other studies using these instruments. This indicates that long-term psychoanalytic therapy is an especially effective method for treating depressive patients. Furthermore, it should be noted that the effect size of the SPC total score (ES = 1.84), compared with other standardized instruments, is clearly the highest. The difference between SPC and the next-highest effect size in the IIP total score (ES = 1.63) is 0.21, and the difference between the effect sizes of the SPC total score and the total score from the SCL-90-R (ES = 1.49) is 0.35. This can be regarded as confirming the specificity hypothesis: the psychoanalytic therapy causes a specific change—namely, structural change—and the SPC reflects this change very sensitively, thus explaining the outstanding high effect size.

The correlation coefficient of the pre–post difference in the SPC total score and the experts' judgement of structural change at the measurement point post is 0.34 and is significant at the 5% level. This numerically rather low correlation may be attributed to the generally low reliability of difference values. This result points again to the problem initially discussed: the judgement of two experts cannot be considered a "gold standard" in examining a new measure.

All in all, we think we convincingly demonstrated that the SPC are sensitive to change.

In addition to these psychometric studies, we conducted an intercorrelation matrix and a factor analysis with our 133 depressive patients. The intercorrelation matrix and the factor analysis of the 35 SPC scales demonstrate that there are only very few relevant intercorrelations and that there is neither a general factor nor a few relevant factors. To explain 80% of the variance, 16 factors are needed. These results confirm that it makes sense to describe patients with the 35 SPC subdimensions to encompass the concept psychic structure.

Summary of results

1. The interrater reliabilities calculated with the intraclass correlation coefficient (ICC) come to a mean ICC of 0.82, with values between 0.54 to 0.89, and are thus in a very satisfactory area.
2. The stability coefficients (determined with the product–moment correlation coefficient of Pearson) range between 0.65 and 0.96 for the 35 subdimensions; for the total value it is 0.88, thus demonstrating excellent stability.
3. Construct validations I and II were accomplished through the comparison of the SPC with construct-distant (in the case of discriminant) and construct-near (in the case of convergent) validation tests. This replication study showed that the SPC are not correlated with instruments measuring symptoms and are to some extend correlated with instruments measuring interpersonal problems, life satisfaction, defence mechanisms, and global rating of structure.
4. Construct Validation III was done by comparing three different groups (depressives, borderline patients, and healthy controls). With stepwise discriminant analysis the three groups can be classified correctly on the basis of the SPC values to 94%, and the discriminant functions can be interpreted meaningfully.
5. For the proof of sensitivity to change we compared the SPC values before and after long-term psychoanalytic therapy. All SPC subdimensions relevant for depression show a clear improvement (i.e., a high standardized effect size). The improvement of 81%

of the patients met the criterion for the reliable change index, thus demonstrating clinical significance.

6. Norm values for 133 depressive patients in need of treatment and 60 healthy controls are available. Age, sex and education have only a minimal influence on the SPC.
7. A factor analysis comes to a 10-factor solution with the clarification of 65% of the variance. Because of the small size and homogeneity of the sample, we suggest studying more patient groups before reducing the number of scales.

To summarize, these findings suggest that the SPC add a genuine intrapsychic dimension to the array of outcome measures already applied. This dimension should no longer be neglected in order to account for the more subtle and enduring effects of psychotherapy.

NOTE

We want to give our thanks to the Research Advisory Board (RAB) of the IPA, which supported our studies three times and enabled us to perform them. But even more—although money makes the world go round—we want to express our deep gratitude to Bob Wallerstein, who generously provided us with the SPC material and a rater training in San Francisco and encouraged us to do all this work with the SPC.

IV

The CAMP initiative and looking ahead

11

The Open Access Project: origins and new directions

George Klumpner
with Thomas Klumpner & Ethan Graham

Robert Wallerstein's contributions to my professional development began in 1971 when, as President of the American Psychoanalytic Association (APsaA), he called a meeting of all committee chairmen. The Indexing Committee—of which I was Chair—which had been set up to help guide researchers through the vast psychoanalytic literature, had never fitted in well among the many diverse activities of the Association, and when Bob learned of this, he suggested I join the Committee on Scientific Activities in order to provide a liaison between the two committees.

In the mid-1970s Bob was the ideal Chairman of the Committee on Scientific Activities (CSA), and his experiences in research, in administration, and in the APsaA augmented his personal integrity, his consideration for others, and his ability to focus on basic issues. In the late 1980s he asked me to chair a Joint Committee to establish a Fund for Psychoanalytic Research, after which we served six years together as Directors of the Fund. This was my first experience with the complexities of evaluating research applications. Under Bob's direction, the Directors of the Fund worked hard to establish enduring procedures as we simultaneously reviewed specific research applications.

When I became Chair of Scientific Activities, Bob agreed to continue as an active member and made many contributions that were both helpful and valuable. During this time Hartvig Dahl, who had previously been a member, contacted the CSA about the potential loss of a treasure trove of audio-recorded analyses (some of which had already been transcribed) unless a repository could be established to preserve them physically and also safeguard their confidential nature.

Bob Wallerstein played a key role in creating the Psychoanalytic Research Consortium, even locating controlled storage facilities in a Kansas salt mine that was also used for archiving by the Menninger Foundation. We served together as Directors of PRC for three years. Our semi-annual meetings were unusually spirited because of differences of opinion about how to describe the varied materials entrusted to the Consortium. The Board finally agreed to centralizing the PRC Board by choosing members who were in frequent contact. Woody Waldron's research group in New York replaced the original directors.

Later, Bob Wallerstein and I worked closely in an effort to establish local committees willing to raise money for psychoanalytic research. Each group was co-chaired by a local analyst and a friend of psychoanalysis who was well connected in that community. Thanks to Bob's wide range of professional contacts, we were able to establish 25 of these committees in regions all across the country. We even had procedures in place for representatives of these groups to meet and exchange ideas in conjunction with the meetings of the APsaA. After the network was established, the Executive Committee of the Association decided that someone else should be responsible for the venture, and we were thanked for our efforts.

Bob and I also shared the excitement that extended over a number of years of the illusory million-dollar grant for clinical research in psychoanalysis that ultimately led to the formation of CAMP. Bob's enthusiasm, optimism, and patience were so infectious that this remarkable organization may indeed still fulfil its promise in spite of being disappointed in not receiving the original funding.

New directions in research: the Open Access Project

While I was not a member of any participating research group, Bob knew of my interest in trying to automate procedures for studying psychoanalytic transcripts and suggested I attend the CAMP meetings as an auditor. Since that time, I have worked to develop and validate a method to facilitate open sharing of session data and further Bob's vision of an empirical psychoanalytic science. This method, the Open Access Project, is a collection of procedures and tools designed to facilitate psychoanalytic research.

With my collaborator, Thomas Klumpner, I have devised methods to extract quantitative data from transcripts of audio-recorded psychoanalytic treatments. We use computer programs to transform transcripts into standardized data—sets of single words and phrases—that can easily be analysed. Unlike transcripts, our quantitative data and measures can be safely shared and widely distributed because no continual discourse that might be revealing on a clinical level is presented. The programs provide a form of public data that can be further evaluated by others. The database can be easily manipulated and studied by anyone using a personal computer. Our tools have the potential to help researchers identify verbal patterns that represent clinical processes, and locate where they occur.

The group of programs in the Open Access Project may be used to generate and test psychoanalytic hypotheses. They also provide a quantitative basis for evaluating hypotheses already in the literature. We believe that clinicians, with their considerable experience in discovering and describing patterns in patient data, will be interested in using tools that quantify those patterns so they can be adequately tested. Our hope is that extracted data developed through our procedures may be used to anchor and clarify clinical opinions and impressions.

Our computer programs process both number-based and word-based data. For example, with respect to word-based data, any distinct word, group of words, repeated sequence, or group of repeated sequences can be grouped, sorted, or screened by any word-based variable, combination of variables, or summary statistics based on the variables. These data can then be manipulated to compare information about patients and analysts across and within sessions or whole treatments over varying durations of time. In all, Open Access can evaluate five types of comparisons:

1. similarities and differences among psychoanalytic treatments;
2. changes in individual psychoanalytic treatments that occur over time;
3. periods within psychoanalytic treatments when features of the treatment deviate from their usual baseline;
4. comparisons of analyst's activities and patient's activities;
5. correlations among variables found in psychoanalytic treatments.

Comparisons are based on three types of data:

1. the total number of words spoken by the analyst and patient;
2. the frequency of individual words or unique groups of words used by the analyst and patient;
3. word sequences repeated during a specified period.

The nature of the Open Access Project

The project is open-ended in every sense. The computer programs are standardized, automatic, and very efficient. They are written so they can readily be modified or expanded. The database, extracted from the transcripts, is expandable essentially without limits, easily accommodating new collections of transcribed data. The standardized tables can be modified by adding new variables or augmented with additional extracted data. All newly added data or procedures can automatically be merged with existing data and procedures. These additions and changes will broaden the clinical evidence available for evaluating psychoanalytic treatments. Statistical summaries facilitate screening and selecting clinical samples of special interest.

Extracted data ensures confidentiality

Transcribed audio-recorded materials are not generally available to researchers because of their sensitive nature. Once a transcript leaves the hands of the treating clinician, there is no guarantee that confidentiality will not be compromised. The extracted data in the Open Access Project are free from all risks of breaching confidentiality because not only the identities of both patient and analyst, but also the clinical material itself, are completely obscured. Therefore, all extracted data can be widely shared and freely discussed.

The three tools of Open Access

The project is based on three computer programs: Data Extractor; Data Explorer; and Data Analyser.

Data Extractor: building the database

Our first program, Data Extractor, extracts words and phrases from psychoanalytic texts and creates a table with five standard items based on quantified linguistic variables. The example in Table 11.1 demonstrates how data were extracted from a collection of 80 transcripts selected from Mrs C's 1,114-session analysis. This data set includes eight groups of 10 consecutive sessions from each year of the analysis. The five listed items provide extracted data *per hour* for all the variables. This could also be provided per units of uninterrupted speech, 5-minute intervals, or any other type of segmentation.

Data Explorer: selecting extracted data for data analysis

Data Explorer, our second program, allows analysts to focus on the frequencies of specific words or phrases in the extracted data. Data Explorer simplifies complex data manipulations, prevents accidental erasures of data, procedures, and results, and can create any number of spreadsheets to organize and reorganize data. The frequency of words or word sequences used by the patient or analyst is quickly extracted. The "Counted Item" data includes a variety of analyst and patient information, including the total number of questions asked, total number of words ("tokens") used, total number of distinct "types" of words, total number of distinct (different) repeated word sequences, and the number of speaker changes in each session.

Table 11.1. Tables created by Data Extractor for Mrs C

Tables of extracted data (extracted from psychoanalytic transcripts and can be safely shared)	Spreadsheets extracted from the tables
1 Patient's Distinct ("types") Word Table includes all distinct words used by the patient in each session and the number of times each word was used. (Number of distinct words in 80 sessions = 48,674; Total words used = 300,518.) 2 Analyst's Distinct ("types") Word Table includes all different words used by the analyst in each session plus the number of times each word was used. (Number of distinct words in 80 sessions = 8,378; Total words used = 16,696.)	Personal pronouns spreadsheets (provided automatically by Data Explorer)
3 Patient's Repeated Word-Sequences Table includes all repeated word sequences (defined as any sequence of three or more words) used by the patient in each session plus the number of times each sequence was used. (Number of distinct repeated sequences in 80 sessions =14,731; Total sequences used = 32,939.) 4 Analyst's Repeated Word-Sequences Table includes all repeated word sequences used by the analyst in each session plus the number of times each sequence was used. (Number of distinct repeated sequences in 80 sessions = 234; Total sequences used = 478.)	Custom spreadsheets created using Data Explorer (data from any combination of the five tables)
5 Counted Items Table tallies 11 constant and countable variables found in every psychoanalytic session (11 items times 80 hours) 1 Number of questions (identified by transcribers) asked by the **patient** in each session. 2 Number of questions (identified by transcribers) asked by the **analyst** in each session. 3 Total number of words ("tokens") used by the **patient** in each session. 4 Total number of words ("tokens") used by the **analyst** in each session. 5 Number of distinct ("types") words used by the **patient** in each session. 6 Number of distinct ("types") words used by the **analyst** in each session. 7 Total repeated word sequences used by the **patient** in each session. 8 Total repeated word sequences used by the **analyst** in each session. 9 Number of distinct word sequences used by the **patient** in each session. 10 Number of distinct word sequences used by the **analyst** in each session. 11 Number of speaker changes in each hour.	Counted Items spreadsheet (provided automatically by Data Extractor)

These data can be combined and compared with simple mathematical operations. The resulting manipulations are automatically saved to an Excel spreadsheet without additional computation. Using this program, analysts will be able to prepare and then analyse spreadsheets that contain all references either by patient or by analyst for any term, group of terms, or repeated sequences in the psychoanalytic transcripts.

Data Analyser: summarizing and finding trends within the database

Our third program, Data Analyser, can automatically group data into different categories and generate statistical summaries for each group. The statistical summaries include mean, standard deviation, range, coefficient of variation, variance, *t*-score, slope, and R^2. Data Analyser also identifies specific sessions where a variable deviates by more than a specified number of standard deviations from the mean for that variable. These data are presented in both a visual and a tabular format.

Using the database

The following demonstrates some of the various ways that Open Access can be useful in comparing session data across and within treatments.

Comparing treatments of different patients

By analysing the content of session hours (total number of words by analyst versus patient,[1] turn changes, number of distinct words, etc.), researchers may quantitatively compare different treatments and identify patterns as they emerge from the data. Table 11.2 contains averaged data for each set of Counted Items from the following four sets of transcripts.

- The *"15 x 14" Group* includes 15 transcribed psychoanalytic sessions from each of 14 patients.
- The *Ulm Group* includes 10 patients treated by the same analyst, 8 with more than 10 transcribed sessions.
- *Mrs C*'s data is based on 80 transcripts in groups of 10 consecutive sessions from each year of her 1,114-hour analysis.
- *Case A2* contains transcripts for all 324 hours of that treatment.

Table 11.2. Comparing linguistic variables among 26 psychoanalytic treatments

	15 x 14 Group	Ulm Group	Mrs C	Patient A2
Number of hours	210	153	80	324
Number of cases	14	10		
Hours per case	15	6–36 (range)	1	1
Dyad's activities				
Ratio of patient to analyst words				
Mean (approx.)	6	7	18	3
Range	2–24	3–23	NA	NA
Speaker changes				
Mean	75	47	18	180
Range	14–114	20–77	4–50	48–425
Analyst's activities				
Questions				
Mean	14	10	5	37
Range	4 - 23	2 - 20	0 - 19	14 - 85
Analyst's total words ("tokens")				
Mean	688	315	209	1,644
Range	144–1,301	206–403	14–1,083	322–3,719
Analyst's distinct words ("types")				
Mean	216	131	105	407
Range	81–342	98–168	14–311	159–684
Analyst's total sequences				
Mean	40	17	6	115
Range	9–79	6–27	0–58	2–382
Analyst's distinct sequences				
Mean	19	8	3	54
Range	2–37	3–13	0–29	1–178
Patient's activities				
Patient's questions				
Mean	15	6	3	17
Range	5–46	1–18	0–11	2–51
Patient's total words				
Mean	4,067	2,304	3,756	5,430
Range	2,890–6,435	1,301–5,049	2,113–5,988	943–7,695
Patient's distinct words				
Mean	721	461	608	921
Range	492–902	344–595	429–877	319–1,206
Patient's total sequences				
Mean	417	258	412	550
Range	228–794	109–865	181–840	35–4,004
Patient's distinct sequences				
Mean	194	115	184	241
Range	105–352	49–379	82–359	17–414

The data compiled in Table 11.2 give us great power to identify the unique characteristics of specific treatments and to generate hypotheses. For example, one might wish to assess the technical qualities of given analyses. In attempting to pin down such a broad analytic concept as "neutrality", one could use various linguistic measures to examine the relative amounts of patient and analyst involvement. We could begin to pursue this topic by examining the gross amount that certain analysts speak relative to their patients. In averaging across the first two groups of treatments in Table 11.2, we note that these analysts tend, on the whole, to speak 6 to 7 times less frequently (measured in numbers of words) than do their patients. In stark contrast to the general average, Mrs C's analyst spoke 18 times less frequently than did Mrs C. And contrasting in the opposite direction, in Case A2, the analyst spoke only 3 times less frequently than did the patient.

With this breakdown of information in Table 11.2, we may deepen our technical assessment across treatments by looking not only at analyst involvement as indicated by speech quantity, but also as based on the type and structure of the interactions. As demonstrated in the tables, we may, for example, look at average numbers of questions by analysts relative to their patients, as well as the average number of speaker changes within the dyad. As we see again, the cases of A2 and Mrs C stand out as atypical in terms of these variables when compared with those of other treatments. All aspects of the A2 analyst's activity were more than double those of any other treatment group; in contrast, all categories of activity of Mrs C's analyst were below those of any other sample. Though perhaps a somewhat rough way to approach such complex analytic concepts, it does provide a useful beginning for the difficult process of quantifying and contrasting the varying analytic qualities of different treatments.

Examination of clinical claims

We may illustrate the application of the Open Access approach by examining a claim presented by Shapiro (2002). He posits that the analyst generally "becomes more of a participant as an analysis is prolonged". Based on this claim, we would expect to see increases in analysts' activity over time; Open Access gives us the means to empirically examine this assumption. Using the variables of analysts' spoken words, questions, and speaker changes, we may assess the veracity of such a claim.

While Shapiro envisions a general, relative increase in analyst participation, the data, by contrast, reveal three distinct patterns of change. The first pattern falls in line with Shapiro's hypothesis: in five of the treatments from the data sets mentioned above (15×14 group, Ulm Group, Mrs C, A2), analysts did, in fact, become relatively more active over time, as measured by all the following variables: Total Words ("tokens"), Distinct Words ("types"), Total Sequences, Distinct Sequences, and Speaker Changes. The majority of the data, however, portray a different sequence of events. In 10 of the treatments, there was no change at all for either analysts or patients along all variables. And for seven of the treatments there was no change in analyst variables, but there were *decreases* in *all* of the patient variables. These kinds of result powerfully suggest the ways in which clinicians and researchers may put assumptions to empirical test, allowing them to revise and expand ideas when needed.

Exploring treatments of single patients: the example of Mrs C

Pronoun frequencies

In addition to looking at data across treatments, we can also focus on single cases in depth. Open Access can provide valuable information concerning individual patients. For example, we may examine the number and type of personal pronouns used by a given patient over the course of an entire treatment. By doing so, we might explore the patient's level of object relatedness and attention to the "other" in the room based on their use of the pronoun "you" versus impersonal pronouns such as "it". In the case of Mrs C, we note her strong tendency to use the word "it" (28,417 instances) over "you" (7,780 instances). Though by no means a complete description of object relations in itself, it does provide a useful means with which to examine the particulars of language in a treatment without revealing confidential information. One could also conduct these types of analyses in comparison to the patient's analyst and also to other patients.

Differences in the frequency with which patient and analyst used the same words

In addition to analysing the patient's and analyst's use of particular pronouns, Open Access also allows us to tabulate and compare the patient's and analyst's use of individual words or word groups. While patients have overall higher word frequency than analysts, the ratio of analyst:patient usage of specific words varies widely. In looking at the data from Mrs C, we can easily identify a cluster of words that she uses with much greater frequency than does the analyst. For example, she uses the words "child", "enjoy", "confident", "responsibility", "parents", "response", "husband", and "hurt" at least 25 times more frequently than does the analyst. In contrast, she uses another cluster of words, including "punish", "sex", "penis", "orgasm", and "rape", no more than four times as often as the analyst. Though not providing a final conclusion about this particular analysis, the results open the door to future exploration. Perhaps the relatively high incidence of a cluster of sexual language used by the analyst suggests the degree to which the analyst steered the treatment in a certain direction; perhaps it suggests the degree to which the patient may be defended against certain types of material. A wide range of interesting hypotheses may be formed and explored in greater depth.

For example, Open Access can also compare the most frequently used words (such as those above) with words referenced in *A Guide to the Language of Psychoanalysis* (Klumpner, 1992) to determine how many of the *Guide*'s references included each word. Strikingly, words in the former cluster that were most frequently used by the patient were generally not referred to in this guide, whereas those in the latter group were. From these data, one might speculate on the degree to which the language, and the course of the treatment, is strictly driven by or centres around theory or around the individual patient's issues. It will also be interesting to use Open Access, in the future, to compare the usage of these same words across different treatments.

Word sequences clarify a word's meaning

The Open Access Project may also be used to evaluate psychoanalytic hypotheses already in the literature. For example, in the case of Mrs C, one might be curious about the degree to which the theme of penis envy was suggested by the analyst or by the patient's material. With the programs, one can draw out key words in a meaningful context by searching for certain word sequences.

One could explore the topic of penis envy, in this case, by searching for different phrases. The phrases "your penis" and "his penis", clearly have different meanings. Mrs C repeated the word "penis" in six different word sequences: "your penis", "he has a penis", "his penis", "get a penis", "have a penis", and "a penis and". The program identifies the specific session in which a word sequence was used, providing additional context. As demonstrated previously, this information could also be compared to the usage of those same words and word sequences by the analyst.

Open Access can also generate a list of the most frequently occurring word sequences, and information about their changing frequencies over time, which may be used to form or test hypotheses. While Mrs C used the sequence "I don't know" and variations of the word "think" ("and I think", "I was thinking", etc.) very frequently in all 80 sessions of our sample (averaging 28 times per session for the former sequence and 60 times per session for the latter), the phrase "you know" appeared only infrequently in a small proportion of the first block of ten sessions. It appeared only once in the 50 sessions reflecting the next five years of her treatment. It then appeared very frequently (270 times) in the seventh 10-hour block and extremely frequently (910 times) in the last 10-hour block.

Given the striking pattern of the sequence "you know", we were curious about the context of the surrounding words and found that it was frequently embedded with words commonly connoting tentativeness, such as "uh/uhm", "sort of", "just", "but", and the expression of a sigh (290 times)—we might posit that "you know" also reflects a similar emotional state. One would have to examine other data from Mrs C's analysis to evaluate whether her emotional state and level of tentativeness at the beginning and end of her treatment paralleled the pattern of changing frequency in her use of "you know".

Ratios that change over time may reveal psychological trends

An indicator for changes in passivity and ambiguity

On the topic of Mrs C's possible changes in tentativeness, we wondered if we could identify whether and when Mrs C changed from speaking ambiguously or passively to expressing more responsibility for what she felt, thought, or did. We thought her use of the pronouns "I" and "it" might reflect such changes. Therefore, we compared the ratios of the frequencies of her use of "I" divided by the frequencies of her use of "it" in eight blocks of 10 consecutive hours. Mrs C's data do not support the hypothesis that these ratios changed over the course of her treatment, on the one hand perhaps suggesting a revision or clarification of our above hypothesis about Mrs C's tentativeness or, on the other, suggesting that this linguistic indicator may not have the expected connotation.

An indicator for changes in caution or evasiveness

Ronald Carpenter, a professor of English, became curious about changes during the Carter–Ford presidential debates after Ford incorrectly said that the Russians had no influence over Eastern Europe (personal communication). In subsequent debates, as the candidates became either evasive or more cautious, they used fewer words overall, and they also selected their words more carefully, which resulted in using a larger number of different words. These two differences in word usage reinforce each other when combined as a ratio. Carpenter interprets this "type–token ratio" generally as indicating a change in the level of cautiousness or evasiveness.

Table 11.2 makes it possible to compare the ratios of the number of distinct "types" of words divided by the number of total words used in each session for both patient and analyst.[2] If Carpenter's hypothesis is correct, it appears that Mrs C's analyst was substantially more cautious than she was—hardly surprising, given the nature of the psychoanalytic situation. His type–token ratios varied considerably in all eight blocks of text but were always 3 to 4 times larger than hers.

The type–token ratio also provides another important lens through which to describe and contrast treatments. Based on the data in Table 11.2, we can compare this ratio for patient and analyst between treatments. We note that Mrs C averages 608 distinct words compared to a mean of 3,756 tokens per session, yielding a ratio of 0.16; Case A2 averages more types (921) and more tokens (5,430) per session, but her type–token ratio of 0.17 is essentially equivalent to that of Mrs C. However, we also note the substantially higher type–token ratio of Mrs C's analyst over that of A2's (0.5 vs 0.25, respectively). This finding raises some key technical psychoanalytic questions. It would be most interesting to explore the relationship between the degree of an analyst's neutrality (as explored in the section on "comparing treatments") and the corresponding level of evasiveness. Can the degree of an analyst's adherence to the technique of neutrality be gauged by caution and evasiveness? Does this evasiveness serve a therapeutic end? Might there be different sorts of neutrality that can be distinguished along the above lines?

Conclusion

We have devised uniform methods for the quantitative analysis of psychoanalytic texts without breaching confidentiality. Our methods were able to identify variations among four different sets of transcripts, and these could be examined in relation to clinical variables as well as other linguistic variables. We have also identified trends within one set of transcripts, Mrs C, including:

1. patterns in the most frequently repeated distinct sequences—as in "I don't know", "and I think", etc.;
2. unusual word patterns within a set of transcripts—such as Mrs C's use of the phrase ". . . you know . . .";
3. differences in the frequency with which patient and analyst used the same words—such as "child", "enjoy", "sex", "penis";
4. an indicator that may identify changes in passivity and ambiguity—for example, changes in the use of first person versus second-person pronouns;
5. an indicator that may identify changes in caution or evasiveness—Carpenter's application of the type–token ratio.

The findings above were previously unrecognized. Our programs provide new approaches to psychoanalytic research; these new techniques potentially have the special value of permitting analysts to develop research projects using their own clinical materials.

We hope our quantitative approach will enrich current research endeavours. Perhaps this number-based perspective will serve as a standard for comparing past, present, and future treatments. To this end, our programs are highly flexible, allowing for the addition of essentially unlimited types of number-based comparisons. This work is, however, only a beginning. We have demonstrated what can be done, but we must leave it to others to decide what will be done, and hope that this approach will contribute to advancing the field of process research that Bob Wallerstein was so instrumental in cultivating.

NOTES

1. We are grateful to the late Hartvig Dahl, Erhard Mergenthaler, and Woody Waldron for helping us gain access to transcribed material. We are especially grateful to Dahl, who first provided such access, without which this project would never have been possible.

2. It is not clear whether type–token ratios can be validly compared for different-sized data sets. The purpose of this study is to demonstrate how questions can be raised and addressed in an exploratory way. We leave it to others to address the questions further.

12

First steps towards a clinical research library

Andrés Roussos, Wilma Bucci, & Bernard Maskit

The field of psychoanalytic treatment research has been expanding greatly in many directions during the past decade, fuelled by economic and institutional changes in the field of mental health care and methodological advances in psychotherapy research, and stimulated as well by developments in psychoanalytic theory and technique.

There is now a recognition "that analytic therapy can go on under . . . observed circumstances—that is, that a properly therapeutic process can nonetheless evolve" (Wallerstein, 2001b, summarizing Wallerstein & Sampson, 1971). Researchers are embarking on new data collections as well as using archival material; interactions between clinicians and researchers are increasing, and new modes of such interaction are being developed; new measures, including process and outcome measures, are being developed and existing ones refined; and simpler, more economically efficient electronic techniques are being utilized for recording, managing, and transmitting clinical material. Considerable incentive and support for psychoanalytic treatment research has been provided by the recent initiatives of the International Psychoanalytical Association and the American Psychoanalytic Association (APsaA). The Research Training Programme of the IPA has, since its inception in 1995, inspired its Fellows to initiate and foster research programmes in their institutes and societies in the United States and around the world. The funding provided by the Research Advisory Board of the IPA and the funds available through the Fund for Psychoanalytic Research (FPR) of the APsaA have provided support for this work (Wallerstein & Fonagy, 1999).

Along with this positive and promising expansion in psychoanalytic treatment research, problems have proliferated as well. Recorded clinical and quasi-clinical material exists in many different sites, with different owners, different formats, and different technologies. Scientific goals and administration of the sites vary widely, with no generally accepted standards for organizing and preserving the data or monitoring their use. In addition to the recorded session material, in some cases including video as well as audio recordings, the various studies have accumulated transcripts, clinical notes, test materials, and data from applications of research measures; these materials are spread over the different centres, with few if any links among them.

The lack of a shared database is a major obstacle to the development of psychoanalytic research. Only a small proportion of the data that are collected is actually analysed, and a still smaller proportion of the results that are achieved actually appears in published form, so that the large-scale research efforts are yielding limited results in providing a knowledge base for the field (Bucci, 2005; chapter 13, this volume). In an attempt to provide an overview of the field of psychoanalytic treatment research, descriptions of studies carried out by a wide range of active research groups were collected in the IPA *Open Door Review* (Fonagy et al., 1999, 2002). The sections on "Process" and "Process–Outcome" include brief reports of studies by 15 different groups covering different data sets and measures. There is, however, no discussion of interaction among the various approaches—no indicators of the extent to which different groups use the same source material or how one study might relate to another so as to build a coherent field. Despite a wealth of potentially interesting results, the specific contents and findings of the different archives remain unknown, the field remains fragmented, and the research carried on thus far has had little impact on clinical work (Bernardi, 2003; Wallerstein, 2001b).

Many of our current scientific goals and questions could be addressed using the treatment data that have already been collected, or whose collection is now actively under way, in studies such as those mentioned in the *Open Door Review*. In the most basic terms, in order to evaluate a treatment and potentially develop more effective treatment techniques, we need to know, for a wide range of patient groups, (1) *what the nature is of the change that occurs* and (2) *how change comes about*. To answer the first question, we need data on treatment effectiveness, including pre-treatment assessment; systematic and objective change criteria and assessment procedures; and measures of treatment effects over time, with outcome at termination separated from effects in the post-analytic phase. To answer the second question, we need data on the treatment process, including tape recordings and transcripts of session material, objective measures applied to this material, and clinical reports representing different perspectives, including impressions of the therapist as well as clinical observers.

Both archival and ongoing treatments are needed to provide these data. Archival collections of completed treatments provide material that cannot easily be replaced, if at all, given the characteristic length of psychoanalytic treatment and the costs and difficulties of assembling such a collection. The current studies incorporate external measures of effectiveness, permit longitudinal follow-up, and are responsive to the broadened perspectives concerning clinical–research interaction.

We are now in a situation where there are valuable and extensive psychoanalytic treatment data, including both archival and ongoing treatments, representing great expenditures of money, effort, and passion, that could provide a basis for collaborative research, but that remain largely unprocessed and unanalysed, while, at the same time, there are researchers who have the skills and motivation to do this work but are unable to gain access to the data they require.

In order to have a viable field of scientific psychoanalytic research, the researchers in the field need to know what recordings, transcripts, and other aggregated data, including demographic data, and results of previous studies, already exist, and how access to this information may be obtained. To accomplish this, it is necessary to have a system with the capacity to include and interconnect clinical and quasi-clinical data sources. It is also necessary to develop mechanisms and standards for protecting the privacy of all participants, including patients, therapists, and research subjects, as well as for protecting the intellectual property of collaborating researchers. In this chapter we address these "housekeeping" issues, which are, on the one hand, crucial for the development of the field of clinical research, and, on the other hand, like housekeeping in general, intrinsically unexciting in themselves—something researchers all wish someone would "do something" about. We now must recognize that the people who need to "do something" about this problem, and who have the skills to do it, can only be the researchers themselves.

The following is an example of the need for preservation of archival data, and some of the problems that can arise from the evolution of ethical standards.

Max Eitingon, a colleague of Freud and a founding member of both the Berlin Psychoanalytic Institute and the Israel Psychoanalytic Society, was, among other professional interests, seriously involved in the formulation of training guidelines for the IPA. Over the course of his professional career, Dr Eitingon collected a substantial amount of diverse psychoanalytic material, including clinical notes and summaries from the analyses that he conducted in Berlin and in Israel, as well as numerous letters from several of the psychoanalytic pioneers, manuscripts of books that Freud and others sent to him for review or as presents, pictures, and other material. After his death, this archive was donated by his widow to the Israel Psychoanalytic Society. Over a period of several years, a group of people from this Society studied and organized this material.

This work on the archived clinical material forced them to face a serious dilemma: the clinical information, which had been collected mainly for Eitingon's own clinical or research purposes, dated from a period prior to the development of standard criteria for written consent and other ethical issues. Since the material does not include any written demographic data, the Israel Psychoanalytic Society has been unable to identify and contact the patients so as to obtain their permission to use the material.

On the one hand, the material is a unique source of knowledge concerning the thinking of one of the founding figures of psychoanalysis; on the other hand, the Society has the obligation to protect the anonymity of the patients and other people involved. There were two opposite positions taken in relation to this dilemma: one group suggested destroying part of the archive in order to maintain confidentiality, while another group viewed the archive as a valuable source of information and suggested opening the entire archive to the public. The compromise position that was reached was that the archive is to be stored in the Israel National Archive and is not to be opened for 120 years. While this solution clearly protects the anonymity of the patients, the thoughts of this psychoanalytic pioneer are lost to the current generation of researchers, and the significance of this material to researchers more than a century from now is uncertain.

Evolution of the psychoanalytic clinical collections

A workshop including European and American process researchers held in Ulm, Germany, in 1985 provided a model for the collaborative approach sought here (the proceedings of this workshop were published in an important volume, *Psychoanalytic Process Research Strategies*, edited by Dahl, Kächele, & Thomä, 1988.) In this workshop, a wide range of process measures, representing different perspectives, was applied to the same data—the fifth session of a classical psychoanalysis. The source data of the investigations, the written transcript of the session itself, was published in the volume. The measures included FRAMES (Dahl, 1988), Referential Activity (Bucci, 1995, 1997), PERT, a method for coding the patient's experience with the therapist (Hoffman & Gill, 1988), the CCRT (Luborsky & Crits-Cristoph, 1988), and measures of processes such as the patient's tests of the analyst, developed by the Weiss and Sampson group (Silberchatz, Curtis, Fretter, & Kelly, 1988). This was the first opportunity for these researchers to look at their measures in relation to others and to explore the construct validity of their measures and the significance of their findings. While the focus on a single session kept this study to an exploratory level, the results, published in the 1988 volume, strongly confirmed the potential value of such collaborative research.

This approach inspired the formation of the Collaborative Analytic Multi-site Program (CAMP), organized by Wallerstein in 1990 under the auspices of the APsaA.[1] Process research groups in the United States and internationally, working within the CAMP network, have applied measures of different aspects of the treatment process, including transference themes, defences, language style, and several aspects of clinical process, to a larger set of transcribed verbatim sessions from three psychoanalytic treatments. Some results of the collaborative studies have been presented at workshops of the CAMP group at the annual meetings of the APsaA, and also at meetings of the Society for Psychotherapy Research. Largely because of organizational issues, few results have as yet been published from the substantial work done by members of the CAMP group.

The CAMP effort in acquiring, transcribing, and scoring a shared set of sessions served the purpose of generating a large amount of new information and clearly demonstrating the potential of the collaborative approach. The natural next step is to develop a unified database that has the capacity to deal with the organizational problems that emerged in the CAMP initiative. In that sense, the project proposed here may be seen as an outgrowth of the CAMP initiative.

The Jacob archive, possibly the newest model of clinical archive in use, is a database belonging to the department of clinical psychology of the University of Zurich (Luder, Neukom, & Thomann, 2000). The archive was developed to organize the storage and use of the large amount of clinical material generated by the department. Video recording takes place in the video studio of the department, using five cameras operated from a separate technical room. Over the past three decades more than 10,000 hours of video material have been recorded, of which some 5,000 have been archived in the database. In addition, several thousand hours of audio-only recordings are stored in the database. It became necessary to designate physical space for storage and to involve a technician, who designed specific software for the use of this database.

The material is still being stored in analogue format. Over the course of many years of research, a substantial amount of such data has been collected. In addition to the audio and video material mentioned above, the archive also includes patient card files, transcripts of therapy sessions, extracted narratives, publications, dissertations, theses, and student research papers. Only a part of the recorded material is transcribed.

This database is used by the members of the research team of the department and by its students. They are currently studying the possibility of developing a system of accreditation for researchers from outside the department, so that accredited researchers can have access to this material.

There is a plan to move the archive to a new building, as it is currently situated in a building with temperature control, but not humidity control. Also, the collection keeps expanding and will soon outgrow its current building (B. Boothe, personal communication).

Management of archival data

Archival treatments have thus far provided the main database for process research, as in the Ulm and CAMP projects. In the 1980s, the Ulm Text Bank of the University of Ulm's department of psychotherapy and psychosomatic medicine in Germany prepared the first large-scale collection of tape recordings of clinical material (Kächele & Mergenthaler, 1984; Mergenthaler, 1985), with 28 eight psychoanalytic treatment cases.

Another collection, the Psychoanalytic Research Consortium (PRC) was developed in the United States to serve a related purpose. The mission of the PRC and the problems encountered in its implementation have been outlined by Wallerstein (chapter 4, this volume). As his description makes clear, the PRC has thus far been able to fulfil the vision of the founders and the needs of the psychoanalytic research community to only a limited degree. For institutional and other reasons, there have not been adequate resources to hold, maintain, and catalogue the material and make it a useful resource for the field.

Luborsky et al. (2001) have provided the major advances in this work by assembling a systematic organized archive of fully recorded psychoanalyses meeting specific research criteria, known as the Penn Collection. The goal of Luborsky and his colleagues was to develop a collection that was suitable for clinical research use and that was sufficiently large for meaningful statistical analyses on the set to be carried out. The essential criteria for inclusion in the collection were that the case be fully tape-recorded with all sessions available, and that the recording was done with the intention, from the beginning of treatment, to include the treatment as a research case after it was completed, no matter how the analysis had fared. Since the archival studies lacked systematic external outcome assessment, Luborsky and his colleagues (2001) developed a reliable method for assessing the effectiveness of the treatments using the session material itself. The findings of this assessment are included in the Penn Collection database, which is at present our largest organized psychoanalytic treatment resource and which provides a core component of the project proposed here. The Penn Collection includes, however, only cases meeting Luborsky's stringent requirements of completed psychoanalytic research treatments. There is the further problem that the owners have extremely limited resources for overseeing the distribution of these materials.

In general, little information is available concerning the content of the different archival collections, and there is essentially no information as to the extent to which the various collections overlap.

The "second generation" of process research

As discussed by Bucci (chapter 13, this volume), the application of multiple objective process measures to a shared database of session material constitutes the first generation of psychoanalytic process research. A new wave of process research is now emerging that is responsive to critiques of empirical research by practising clinicians and that incorporates clinical perspectives in an ongoing and integrated way. Bucci (chapter 13) has referred to this broadened approach as the "second generation" of psychotherapy process research. According to the Committee on Psychoanalytic Specificity of the IPA, addressing the question of "What is specific about the nature and consequences of analytic practice?" (Freedman, Lasky, & Hurvich, 2003), an appropriate database should include subjective and intuitive judgements of the analyst and evaluation by consultants using methods of peer review and supervision, as well as recorded texts.

In general, the archival studies do not include such components. A remarkable exception, which is not well known, was a study carried out from 1956 to 1960 under the direction of Franz Alexander at the Mt. Sinai Hospital in Los Angeles (Eisenstein, Levy, & Marmor, 1994). The project involved intensive studies of two treatments—a psychoanalysis, and a psychoanalytic psychotherapy—conducted by Alexander, using multiple observational techniques, including direct observation by participating clinicians through one-way mirrors, audio recordings, and recordings of physiological changes in therapist and patient. The data of the study include systematic and detailed impressions by the treating analyst and observing clinicians, as well as verbatim recordings and transcripts. As yet no objective research methods have been applied to these materials, although the data are collected and potentially available to qualified researchers for study (Eisenstein, personal communication).

There are currently two major ongoing studies known to the authors that incorporate these broadened perspectives: one at the Institute for Psychoanalytic Training and Research (IPTAR) in New York, and the other at the Asociación Psicoanalítica Argentina (APA) in Buenos Aires. Both involve new data collection rather than archival material, and both involve clinicians working collaboratively and interactively with researchers in the data collection and analysis. These are described in detail by Bucci (chapter 13, this volume).

Many other important archival collections and ongoing studies are being developed, including the studies of Jones and colleagues in Berkeley; Weiss and Sampson and their colleagues in San Francisco; Stern, Baucom, and their colleagues at the Lucy Daniels project in North Carolina; and many specific collections included in the Ulm Text Bank. There are also a number of innovative and focused smaller studies, such as a unique collection of transcripts and process notes for the same sessions developed by Bailey and his colleagues in Baltimore. Some aspects of these studies have been presented at the CAMP and RAAPA workshop meetings during the past decade. As yet, however, each of these studies operates as a separate entity, and collaborative work on these data sets by researchers outside the group collecting the data has not taken place.

In addition to the direct treatment studies, a wide range of other interview material has also been collected, including clinical interviews, such as intake or supervisory material; quasi-clinical interviews, such as projective or therapy analogue material; and many other types of interviews, carried out for research purposes. It is clear from published reports that very extensive stores of such interview material exist, in both clinical and research contexts. We should note that such interviews, also collected under conditions of confidentiality, are potentially of considerable value to the psychoanalytic research field if mechanisms were available for cataloguing and sharing them.

The main goal of this chapter is to outline the basic steps needed for the creation and operation of a modern system for organizing, safeguarding, and providing access to clinical and quasi-clinical information, and to discuss some of the problems involved in setting up such a system. To achieve this goal, a survey was performed to obtain information about the contents of existing collections and the standards and procedures now prevailing in these collections.

Participants in the pilot survey

Information was gathered concerning seven collections varying in age from less than one year to over 40 years and representing a range of academic, institutional, other professional, and private origins. This pilot survey was a first pass at examining the types of collections of clinical materials that exist today and does not attempt to provide a systematic or representative sample of existing data sources.

In order to obtain the pilot information for this study, 15 collectors were contacted. In addition to some collections already known, the last six volumes of *The Journal of the Society for Psychotherapy Research* were reviewed for additional sources. This review yielded 38 research projects using collections of video and audio recordings; 19 of the 38 involved psychodynamically oriented treatments or sessions. Since some of these projects used materials from the same sources, the actual number of collections identified was 15.

In addition to recorded treatments and verbatim transcripts, many of the collections represented here also include both clinical and quasi-clinical interviews; however no attempt was made to canvass collections of such materials. With one exception—an extensive database of clinical interview material—our survey focused on collections holding treatment cases; the other holdings of these collections were then also described.

A questionnaire was prepared in electronic format and sent to the 15 owners of these collections. Of the 15 owners, 7 answered the questionnaire (two additional collectors agreed to participate but did not complete their responses).

Results of the survey

The survey focused on characteristics of the contents of the collections, issues of generating, organizing, and maintaining the collections, technical aspects of their use and storage, and ethical issues associated with the use and sharing of materials.

Contents of the collections

Table 12.1 provides a summary of the information reported by the respondents to the questionnaire. The table provides data concerning the types and quantities of material that has been collected and that are potentially available for researchers, but does not enable cross referencing of the data, or characterization of the holdings of

Table 12.1. Major contents of current collections of clinical materials

	Summary of responses		
Questionnaire item		**Response category**	**Collections[a]**
Type of clinical material collected	a	Psychotherapy and/or psychoanalytic sessions:	6
	b	Clinical interviews	6
	c	Quasi-clinical interviews such as monologues, responses to TAT cards, reports of early memories and RAP (Relationship Anecdote Paradigm) interviews.	2
Types of treatment	a	Psychoanalytic	3
	b	Psychoanalytic psychotherapy	3
	c	Short-term psychotherapy	1
	d	Experiential psychotherapy	
	e	Interpersonal therapy	
Number of recorded treatment cases	a	More than 100 cases (125)	1
	b	Fewer than 100 cases (17, 12, 6, 6, 3)	5
	c	No cases	1
Number of recorded sessions	a	More than 100 sessions	5
	b	Between 50 and 100	1
Features of recorded treatment	a	Some fully recorded treatments	5
	b	Some ongoing treatments	3
Location of treatment	a	Private office	5
	b	Clinic	3
	c	Psychoanalytic institute	2
	d	Hospital	1
Format of recordings	a	Cassettes	4
	b	VHS format	2
	c	Open reel	1
	d	CDRom with audio	1
Dates of collected material	a	Before 1960	1
	b	1960–69	1
	c	1970–79	2
	c	1980–89	5
	d	1990–99	5
	d	2000–present	5

individual collections. The categories of the responses as presented in the table are not mutually exclusive; for most responses, many collections will be represented in more than one category.

The seven collections responding to our survey hold a wide range of clinical materials, including psychotherapy and psychoanalytic sessions, clinical interviews such as intakes or recall sessions, and a

Questionnaire item		Summary of responses: Response category	Collections[a]
Number of session transcripts[b]	a	Over 100	4
	b	Between 50 and 100	1
	c	Fewer than 50	1
	d	No recorded or transcribed sessions	1
Type of clinical and quasi-clinical interviews	a	Intakes	2
	b	Supervisions	1
	c	Diagnostics	2
	d	Projectives	2
	e	Monologues	1
	f	Early memories	2
	g	Recall sessions	1
	h	Parenting and attachment style interviews	1
Location of interviews	a	Private office	2
	b	University	2
	c	Clinic	2
	d	Psychoanalytic Institute	4
Number of recorded interviews	a	Over 100	1
	b	50–100	2
	c	Fewer than 50	3
Format of recorded interviews	a	VHS	3
	b	Cassette	5
Dates of interviews	a	1971–1980	1
	b	1981–1990	3
	c	1991–2000	4
	d	2000 to present	4
Number of interviews transcribed[b]	a	Over 100	1
	b	50–100	2
	c	Fewer than 50	3

[a] Number of collections. Categories are not mutually exclusive; for most items, many collections are represented in more than one category.
[b] Two of the collections have some of their older transcribed material in hard copy only rather than in computerized form; also in some cases the recordings have been lost and only transcripts remain.

variety of quasi-clinical interviews, from psycholinguistic and clinical research studies. The treatments include both short- and long-term psychodynamic cases, including some fully recorded complete, some partially recorded complete, and some ongoing treatments. The number of cases held by the collections ranges from 3 to 125; one collection does not hold session material. Four collections hold more than 100 recorded sessions, two between 50 and 100. Four collections hold more than 100 transcripts of sessions, one holds between 50 and 100, and one holds fewer than 50 transcripts of sessions. The collections include treatments dating from 1960 to the present; they were carried out in a range of locations and recorded in a variety of formats, some now obsolete (as discussed below). The collections also hold a range of clinical and quasi-clinical interviews, carried out in a variety of locations, dating primarily within the last 20 years, generally using relatively modern recording techniques.

Other materials held by the collection not represented in the table include therapist notes and research measures that have been applied to the sessions or interviews and included in the database. One collection has between 5 and 10 in-session therapist's notes; two collections have over 20 out-of-session therapist's notes; some of these are handwritten and some are on cassette. Three collections include results of psychological measures—CCRT, Defense Mechanisms Scale, EARS, FRAMES, Gottschalk-Glaser, Q-Sort, RA, SPC, and the Social Cognition and Object Relations Scale (SCORS), among others. Only two of the collections have stored the results of these measures in their archives. In addition, all the collectors reported that they had demographic data for the patients or participants.

Organization and maintenance

Cataloguing systems. Four of the collections have relatively systematic and comprehensive—although generally incomplete—cataloguing systems; the other three have more informal systems of data organization.

Storage and maintenance. Two of the collections are stored in a temperature- and humidity-controlled environment; two are stored in university laboratories; one is stored in a university office; one is stored in a private office. Only two collectors reported any deterioration of clinical material to date; this consists of some lost labels and some broken cassettes. One of the collectors reported that some of the original data have been reformatted into digital format.

Procedures for safeguarding and accessing materials

Protection of privacy. Five of the seven collections report that an Institutional Review Board (IRB) is in place that monitors the use of all data. All seven collections require informed written consent.

Publication. All seven collections permit publication of aggregate data. All collections have published or presented research based on their data. Four of them (two with prior approval) permit the publication of vignettes; and three (two with prior approval) permit the publication of direct quotes.

Use of the material by outside researchers. Each collection has its own policy regarding use of the data by outside researchers; these policies are generally informal. The basic rule appears to be that material is lent only to the collectors' students and to colleagues known personally to them. In general, there are no formal rules or protocols for use of the materials by others, and no ongoing or follow-up procedures to monitor the use of such material.

Electronic transmission of data. Two of the relatively safe file transfer methods—ftp and encryption—were not sufficiently well known to be used by the interviewed collectors. Only three out of six collectors consider email as a safe way to transmit clinically sensitive material; all the collectors agreed to the use of floppy discs and five of the six agreed to the use of CD ROMs as safe ways to transmit such material.

Interest in participating in a collaborative clinical research library. All collectors recognized the need for researchers to have access to sensitive clinical material, while maintaining its security and confidentiality, and all had dealt with these issues for their own archives. With respect to participation in a common database for the field, four of the collectors were clearly interested and saw the possibility of such a venture; two were somewhat interested but doubtful; and one was more concerned with the potential problems and was not interested in participating.

Discussion

From the point of view of researchers looking for clinical material to test their hypotheses, what we can gather from our survey is the following. There is a substantial amount of recorded clinical material held in quite a few disparate collections, and a considerable amount of this material has been transcribed. There is, however, no uniformity of format, even within a given collection. Some of the material is in modern electronic format, other material is in older, perhaps unusable format. A few of the collections have a database organization listing the contents and their formats; most have lists of varying degrees of completeness. There are no uniform rules concerning access of outsiders to the data, or concerning publication of results. Some standard psychological measures have been applied to some of the transcripts, but cataloguing of these applications is not consistently available. There is essentially no systematic way for researchers to know to what extent they are duplicating (on the same sample), or replicating (on different samples) work already done, and no systematic way to identify the gaps where new research can contribute most effectively.

The need for a clinical research library

The results demonstrate the need for an organized and catalogued "clinical library", including: primary material (video and audio tapes); secondary material (transcripts); and derived data from the application of research materials, with different and appropriate procedures for the safeguarding and distribution of materials at each level. This clinical library may be in either virtual or real form—that is, as a catalogue of what exists and where, with procedures for access; or an actual physical library containing all the original source material. There are liabilities and benefits associated with each approach, and it is likely that a functional clinical research library would incorporate both.

Because of the serious problems involved in a physical library, some of the current owners have said that they would at best cooperate to the extent of permitting the library catalogue to list their data. On the other hand, there are some holders of clinical material who are seeking well-functioning clinical research data banks to protect their materials and take over the responsibility of cataloguing, maintaining, and keeping current the format of such material. Many such owners also recognize the issue of protection and maintenance of the material in perpetuity. The heirs of the collectors may not wish to carry on the work of maintaining the collection, and, without a stable institutionally supported library that could accept it, there would be serious danger that the collection might literally be thrown out. A similar problem could exist with an institutionally owned collection, as institutions sometimes change their views of their missions.

Both the Ulm Text Bank and the Psychoanalytic Research Consortium (PRC) were intended as such physical text archives for clinical material. As Wallerstein has discussed (chapter 4, this volume), the development of the PRC was stimulated by Merton Gill's concern about the disposition of the research records, including recorded treatments, that he had accumulated throughout his career, but the PRC has not been able to fulfil Gill's vision for institutional and other reasons.

Given what we have learned from the previous experiences of other collectors as well as through our survey, it seems that our best solution would be to set up a stable institutionally supported clinical research library that has both a physical location where it maintains some amount of original clinical data and an extensive catalogue or data bank, listing not only the material it owns, but also all such material held by others that is at least under some circumstances accessible to outsiders. The physical part of the library would contain the material and auxiliary data owned by the library in a secure location. The virtual component of the library would contain listings of clinical material, including listings of available data derived from this material, the location(s) of the material, and conditions of accessibility, including ownerships and rules for use.

Issues involved in building and maintaining a clinical research library

The survey provides considerable data regarding the problems of administration and the obstacles to sharing basic data, applying to both archival and current collections. Here we discuss three broad categories of issues: (1) organizational and administrative responsibilities; (2) methodological and technological suitability; and (3) legal and ethical constraints and protections.

Organizational and administrative issues

In general, as discussed, a clinical library will require both physical and virtual aspects; some amount of material will need to be physically stored in the library, and the library will need to have a comprehensive catalogue of its own material as well as material held elsewhere that owners are willing, at least to some extent, to share.

The first and major organizational difficulty in building and maintaining a clinical research library, either physical or virtual, is the need for financial support; once that has been addressed, mechanisms for solution of the other problems do exist. The actual costs are, of course, substantially greater if a physical collection is to be developed and maintained, although considerable resources would also be needed to maintain a well-organized virtual library with a comprehensive and up-to-date database. In any case, the development and maintenance of the library would require the services of a librarian(s) or data bank manager(s) with special training beyond the usual database management or library skills, due to the specialized confidential nature of the material and the variation in the degree of sensitivity of items in the data bank (Stewart & Cervone, 2003).

We propose that a clinical library might be built gradually, starting with one or more of the known collections used by one or more research groups in a virtual way. Then, for this sample virtual collection, the requisite database could be constructed and studied, and problems of preservation and reformatting could be addressed. Our hope and expectation would be that the scientific yield of such a step would convince other collectors, clinical groups, and scientists to join and pool resources to support the project. At this point, also, institutional support would be sought, both within the psychoanalytic community and in the broader mental health field.

At this point we would also need to address the question of institutional affiliation for such a clinical research library: for example, as an independent entity; as part of some existing organization, such as the IPA; or as affiliated with a university that has significant clinical research representation. There are benefits and problems to be explored with each approach, and the final resolution is likely to depend on the availability of support.

Methodological and technological issues

The first step in setting up such a library would be to choose a database and a platform for the electronic catalogue. Some general information about these topics is currently available (see, for example, Library of Congress, 1996, or the National Science Foundation DLI II Project—NSF, 2003), and a range of standard library cataloguing systems for varied materials are currently in existence. The specialized needs concerning confidentiality of sensitive clinical material and different levels of confidentiality for different types of materials would call for modifications of these systems. The choice of appropriate platform among the standard systems such as Unix, Windows, MacIntosh, SunOS, and others, or the need for specially tailored systems, would be determined by requirements for safeguarding privacy, as well as scientific considerations. Similar factors will affect the related technological question of the choice of backup system.

In establishing a physical library, major technological problems associated with formatting must be considered. Each current collection has its data in its own format; any catalogue of its holdings would be in its own format as well. Some of the original recordings are on reel-to-reel tape, others are on cassettes, and yet others are digitalized. Some of the transcripts are in Microsoft Word, some are in WordPerfect, some are in other word processor formats, including formats that are or may soon be obsolete, and still others exist in hard copy only. Similarly, the associated data comes in various spreadsheet, statistical, or text formats.

In addressing the problems of multiple diverse formats, one possibility might be to leave such material in its original format and include information as to format in the catalogue. A danger associated with this approach is the issue of obsolescence. There is still valuable clinical material held in reel-to-reel format; however, machines that play such tape are no longer being manufactured, the machines that do exist are falling into disrepair, and technicians to repair such machines are no longer being trained, so that in the not-too-distant future it may simply no longer be possible to play reel-to-reel tapes. There are similar problems with computer software: for example, WordStar, once one of the leading word processors, no longer exists, and documents in WordStar format are not accessible to computers with modern operating systems. There are similar problems for spreadsheets and databases: old systems disappear.

The second option would, then, be to choose a single format for each type of data and reformat all the data into this one style. This solution would, of course, call for significant resources in time and money, particularly in the instance of backing up material currently in reel-to-reel or hard-copy format. On the one hand, this appears necessary to preserve valuable, unique, irreplaceable material; on the other hand, there is the likelihood that in some cases the material may never be used.

For the associated data consisting of results of applied measures, the reformatting is ultimately necessary for research use; otherwise a researcher who would want to use some of the associated data might be faced with the formidable or even insurmountable difficulty of dealing with data in several different formats, some of which are based on different platforms (operating systems). Fortunately, however, the reformatting of such secondary data is, both less costly and less urgent, in terms of risk of deterioration, than is the case for the primary material.

In any case, the library will need to own several different computers working on different platforms, and many different word-processing, spreadsheet, and statistical programs. If the associated data are kept in their original format, the library will need these systems in order to make the data available to researchers. This is particularly a problem for meta-analyses, where one is dealing with results coming from different sources (Wampold, 2001), potentially involving many different formats for the original data and the associated data. If the data are to be reformatted, the library will need multiple systems to do the reformatting.

Aging of collections. The issue of aging of collections and potential obsolescence has been touched on above. Fortunately, there is apparently still time to perform this reformatting; the collection that is over 40 years old has reported that there is as yet no noticeable demagnetization of the tapes.

It should also be noted that digitalization, the newest technology in this field, remains untested as to its durability in the long term. At this point the principal modern modes of storage of digitalized material are computer hard discs and CD ROMs. Computer hard discs are known to have some failure; these appear to be statistical, rather than time-dependent. CD ROMs are still being tested as to the impact of various degenerative processes on them; it is not currently clear how long one can expect them to last.

A comparison between modern digital sources and tape-recordings was conducted by Renals et al. (2003); according to this international report, prepared by a group of European and American researchers, tape recordings have limited life spans, are difficult to maintain, and lose quality when copied onto new analogue media. Also, analogue recordings can provide only linear access; they must be listened to in consecutive order. As tapes are known to deteriorate with use, the library would need to maintain separate master copies, with new working copies made from these when necessary. In contrast, material in digitally stored format can be easily accessed at different predetermined points, so that one does not, for example, need to listen to many transcripts on the tape before reaching the desired one. Also, digitally stored material can be easily copied, at little cost. However, the ease of copying of digital material raises issues of confidentiality and privacy, which will be addressed below.

Legal and ethical problems

Legal and ethical requirements present central challenges that must be addressed from the very beginning in developing a databank, whether virtual or physical. It is necessary to establish standards and procedures for evaluating the credentials of researchers and to tailor these for material at different levels of sensitivity, from unedited tapes of transcripts and interviews to verbatim transcripts that have been altered so as to disguise the patient and/or analyst, or aggregate numerical data obtained from analysing the tapes and/or transcripts. Uniform standards for informed consent need to be developed and applied. The issues of confidentiality are, of course, considerably more acute for recent or ongoing treatments.

Transmission of sensitive data. The technical issue of transmission of data is a potential Pandora's box of legal and ethical problems. On the one hand, email is widely used and now accessible to almost everyone, is the most efficient way to transmit electronic data, and is particularly useful in cases of international collaboration; on the other hand, it may be insecure and vulnerable to misuse. One possible solution to this problem is code encryption, but this entails both organizational and technical problems at both ends of the transmission; many researchers would see this technical requirement as a significant if not insurmountable barrier. Furthermore, it should be clear that any data that are subject to computer-assisted content analysis will, of necessity, be available to on-line transmission, even if initially distributed via disk.

A related issue is that of transcription headers. Most transcriptions of psychoanalytic or psychotherapeutic sessions have ownership and/or confidentiality statements at the beginning of the transcript. Especially for transcripts that have been electronically transmitted, these headers may be lost, in many cases inadvertently, thus endangering the control and regulation of the use of the material, with possible legal as well as ethical consequences.

The legal issues concerning confidentiality and privacy vary from collection to collection, as the different collections use different consent forms and/or different rules, and they also vary by national jurisdiction, as different countries have different laws in this respect. Since there are researchers and collections in different countries and many of the researchers either are currently involved in international collaboration or would like to be, this international aspect could be of considerable importance.

Ownership, access, and the rights of privacy. In view of the legal obligations inherent in any use of confidential and/or private material, one of the first steps in setting up such a library would be both to set up an initial legal consultation and to provide for continuing legal advice. Some of the crucial questions that would arise are the following. What are the rights, privacy or otherwise, of the patient? In what form must informed consent have been given? What are the rights, privacy or otherwise, of the patient's heirs? What are the rights of the analyst or therapist? What are the rights of the analyst's or therapist's heirs? What is the legal status concerning ownership, which may vary from country to country? While it is obvious that one can own the paper on which a transcript is written, under what circumstances can one own the words themselves? Also, does the transcriber or the person or organization who paid for the transcription have ownership, or any special rights and/or responsibilities? What are the responsibilities of the holder of clinical material? To what extent do the scientists who extract data from such material have the right to publish their findings? To what extent do they have the right to publish vignettes or quotations from the original material? We have only begun to scratch the surface of the legal and ethical issues involved in collaborative use of sensitive clinical material, including protection of intellectual rights of researchers as well as privacy of participants. The problems need to be solved if we are to have a suitable knowledge base for psychoanalysis and can potentially be solved with an adequate organizing structure, adequate funding, and good will by cooperating researchers.

Conclusions

The accumulation and sharing of research data and findings constitutes the lifeblood of any scientific field. Researchers must build on the work of others. In the absence of interactive scientific discourse, researchers will, on the one hand, unknowingly duplicate the experiments and computations of others, and, on the other hand—perhaps even more damaging—will lose the opportunity to build upon, confirm, question, and expand the results and findings of the field.

There is significant recognition of these issues within the psychoanalytic research community, and significant involvement in developing a collection of treatments and other clinical material for research. Even the responses to our small survey demonstrate the variety of different sites used to record treatments and other clinical material and the range of types of mental health organizations involved in this scientific effort.

The small group of collectors interviewed in this pilot study together hold more than 100 short-term cases and approximately 40 long-term cases representing several varieties of therapeutic modality, as well as a wide range of other clinical and quasi-clinical material. The authors are also aware of many other research archives, holding substantial quantities of treatment material, including complete psychoanalytic psychotherapies, which are not represented in this survey. These researchers are generally unwilling or unable, because of the conditions of their collections, to share much of their material with researchers outside their own group.

Ultimately, the scientific method depends on access to data and the establishment of a context for cross validation and verification of results. This is no less true in the field of psychoanalytic and psychotherapy research than in any other scientific field. The formidable problems that we have identified have operated as deterrents to the development of the field. We are, however, now, at a time of a new and expanding generation of clinical research, providing the basic data, the recognition of professional responsibility, and the impetus for new directions in scientific methods to meet the goals of the field. It is time to carry forward the vision of Wallerstein, in establishing the CAMP framework, in a new kind of structure that builds on recognition of the problems of the past and the application of new techniques of data management that have been developed to address these problems.

NOTES

This study was supported in part by the Research Advisory Board of the International Psychoanalytical Association.

1. The programme is now receiving additional institutional support through its inclusion in the new Research Associates of the American Psychoanalytic Association (RAAPA).

13

Building the research–practice interface: achievements and unresolved questions

Wilma Bucci

The integration of research and clinical work that has been the guiding vision of Robert Wallerstein's career has also been the theme of the work presented in this volume. Here I would like to examine the question of how far we have come in achieving this integration, what are the prospects, and how we need to proceed.

Two questions form the framework for this chapter. The first question is: "How and why do psychotherapists' theoretical and technical models change?" This question was the basis for a study carried out at the Uruguayan Psychoanalytic Institute and presented by Bernardi and his colleagues at the Society for Psychotherapy Research in Montevideo in 2001 (Bernardi, 1997, 2002, 2003). The second question is: "What is specific about the nature and consequence of analytic practice?" This was debated in the House of Delegates of the IPA during the work of the Committee on Psychoanalytic Specificity in 1996 (Freedman, Lasky, & Hurvich, 2003).

Turning first to Bernardi's question concerning changes in theory and technique, the results, based on qualitative analysis of intensive interviews with 20 senior analysts, pointed to changes derived from increasing emphasis on pluralism of theory, as discussed by Wallerstein (1989a) and others; increasing emphasis on each analyst's implicit theory, as discussed by Sandler (1983); as well as changes in technique that are not necessarily consistent with theoretical changes. Reports of changes based on research findings or systematic evidence of any type were rare. In general, Bernardi reports, analysts mention favourable evidence only in supporting their positions; there is little discussion of alternative hypotheses. There are no consistent methodological and procedural criteria available for collective processing of the changes that are occurring. As Bernardi concludes, a major scientific debate is necessary, to examine critically the quality of the evidence and the argumentation.

Bernardi's study raises crucial questions concerning the status of evidence in the development of psychoanalytic theory and technique and the related issue of the failure of empirical research to have impact on clinical work. The major shifts that have been observed in theoretical approach, such as the movement from classical drive theories to various types of relational models, and the related technical shifts, such as the change from emphasis on interpretation and the influence of therapist on patient, to focus on interpersonal interaction and bidirectional influence, have taken place essentially without the benefit of any kind of systematic research or any evidence as to differential treatment effects.

Considering the impressive amount of psychotherapy research that has been carried out over the past half-century, it is perhaps somewhat surprising that research has had so little apparent impact on clinical work. Wallerstein (2001b),[1] has identified four generations of such research.

First generation

The first generation (1917–1968) comprised simple retrospective counts of improved outcomes with outcome judgements made by the therapist, primarily based on unspecified criteria for diagnosis or improvement and without supporting evidence (United States: Coriat, 1917; Berlin Institute: Fenichel, 1930; London Psychoanalytic Clinic: Jones, 1936; Chicago Psychoanalytic Institute: Alexander, 1937; American Psychoanalytic Association: Hamburg et al., 1967; Clinic of the Southern California Psychoanalytic Institute: Feldman, 1968).

Second generation

The studies of the second generation recognized and corrected many of the flaws of the first. These were largely prospective studies, with outcome judgements made by independent researchers, based on specific criteria. Wallerstein described six American projects and three European projects in this generation.

American projects

The six US projects included three group studies of clinic cases carried out at the Boston Psychoanalytic Institute (Knapp, Levin, McCarter, Wermer, & Zetzel, 1960; Sashin, Eldred, & van Amerongen, 1975); the Columbia Psychoanalytic Center (Bachrach, Weber, & Solomon, 1985); and the New York Psychoanalytic Institute Treatment Center (Erle, 1979; Erle & Goldberg, 1979, 1984), and three individually focused studies at the New York Psychoanalytic Institute Treatment Center (Pfeffer, 1959, 1961, 1963).

The Pfeffer phenomenon. Pfeffer's studies were based on intensive individual case studies of nine patients who had completed analyses and had agreed to a series of follow-up interviews with an analyst other than the treating analyst. The interviews were open-ended, once a week, analytic in character, and ranged from two to seven in number, with the participants agreeing on a natural close. Two other research groups, one in San Francisco (Norman, Blacker, Oremland, & Barrett, 1976) and one in Chicago (Schlessinger & Robbins, 1974, 1975) replicated Pfeffer's study and reached essentially the same conclusion, termed "the Pfeffer phenomenon"—that is, in analyses considered highly successful, neurotic conflicts are not eliminated, but are regulated and handled in new ways. While making important contributions, these studies have been criticized for failing to recognize the distinct processes of a post-analytic phase and failing to distinguish effects, positive or negative, that may occur during this phase, from those observed at treatment termination, as well as for problems of validity of the outcome assessment.

European projects

Wallerstein also identified three important European studies, dating from the middle and late 1990s to the present, which fall largely in the category of second-generation research: (1) the Anna Freud Centre chart review (Fonagy & Target, 1994, 1996); (2) the German Psychoanalytical Association (DPV) study of the long-term effects of psychoanalysis and psychoanalytic psychotherapy (Leuzinger-Bohleber, 1997); and (3) the European multicentre collaborative study of long-term intensive psychoanalytic treatment (Szecsödy et al., 1997).

Third generation

What Wallerstein called "third-generation studies" combined the design and methodological approaches of the group projects with those of the individually focused studies. Like the best second-generation projects, they were prospective studies with pre-treatment assessment and systematic and objective change criteria and assessment procedures, but they also went beyond the second-generation studies in separating outcome at termination from effects in the post-analytic phase. The Psychotherapy Research Project of the Menninger Foundation (PRP), with patients entering treatment in the mid-1950s and followed up for approximately 30 years (Wallerstein, 1986) and the more recent Boston Psychoanalytic Institute studies (Kantrowitz, Katz, Paolitto, Sashin, & Solomon, 1987a, 1987b; Kantrowitz, Paolitto, Sashin, Solomon, & Katz, 1986), carried out in the 1970s and published in the middle and late 1980s, were prime examples of this third generation.

With all the advances in design, the major findings of these studies were essentially negative or null. In the Boston study, therapeutic benefit exceeded analytic benefit, and successful outcome could not be predicted on the basis of any of the predictor variables included in the study. Furthermore, looking at the post-analytic period, as Kantrowitz points out, psychological changes were no more stable over time for the group of patients assessed as achieving a successful analytic outcome, along with therapeutic benefit, than for those who achieved equivalent therapeutic benefit alone. Like any null finding, this result does not "prove" that there is no difference between therapeutic and analytic benefit but, rather, indicates that the research has not been able to show such a difference with the procedures and measures in use; nevertheless, this is a disappointing and disturbing result. Kantrowitz has continued to follow the question of analytic gain and factors affecting this in her important line of research concerning a variable not studied in the Boston project, the impact of the patient–analyst match (Kantrowitz, 1986).

The Menninger PRP findings were also essentially null with respect to specificity of psychoanalytic technique and outcome. The PRP study examined the links between the nature of change (structural vs. behavioural) and the intervention mode (expressive or supportive) by which the changes were brought about. As in the Boston study, the two types of change were difficult to distinguish, supportive modes were far more effective than had been expected, and greater stability was not found for changes achieved through the expressive modality. Again, as for any null findings, one may raise questions about the measures, as well as about the generalization of the findings from the Menninger Clinic patients to presumably less severe psychoanalytic outpatient populations. These studies have made valuable contributions in causing us to question some of our assumptions concerning the psychoanalytic process and have at least implicitly provided the basis for the pluralism that is dominant in the field, but they have not provided many answers concerning treatment effectiveness or guidance for clinical work.

Recent studies

Several recent outcome studies not reviewed by Wallerstein have produced more promising results, using different measures and statistical techniques.

The Stockholm Outcome of Psychoanalysis and Psychotherapy Project (STOPPP). In a major study by Sandell and his colleagues in Stockholm (Sandell et al., 2000), more than 400 patients were followed before, during, and for three years after psychoanalysis or long-term psychodynamic psychotherapy with interviews, questionnaires, and other measures. The major conclusion based on Sandell's study was that psychoanalysis and psychotherapy showed essentially equivalent results during treatment but diverged in the follow-up period; the improvement continued for psychoanalysis and levelled off for psychotherapy. Sandell also found effects of treatment frequency and duration and complex associations between therapist and analyst attitudes and training and treatment outcome that differentiated the two treatment modalities.

The IPTAR Effectiveness and Recall Projects. Studies covering treatment effects at termination and at follow-up after one year were carried out by Freedman and his colleagues (Freedman, Hoffenberg, Vorus, & Frosch, 1999) at the Clinical Center of the Institute for Psychoanalytic Training and Research (IPTAR), a low-cost psychodynamic therapy service staffed by candidates and members of the Institute. The Effectiveness study used a questionnaire (the EQ) developed for the Consumers' Report study (Seligman, 1995) and provided to IPTAR by Seligman's group. A total of 241 Clinical Center patients, both in treatment and terminated, were contacted, and 99 responded. An Effectiveness Score was computed based on measures of specific improvement in problems leading to therapy, satisfaction with therapy, and general or global improvement. The study found effects of frequency and duration similar to those shown by Sandell and his colleagues (Sandell et al., 2000)—for example, stronger effects were shown for session frequency for psychoanalytic therapy, compared to a broad range of treatment modalities.

The Recall component of the IPTAR project involves post-termination assessment that includes an extended psychoanalytically sensitive interview giving a qualitative account of the patients' lives after termination, as well as scales evaluating "internalization attachment" and symptom levels, and another EQ. The researchers expect to study 30 patients in the Recall study, with follow-up one year and three years after termination.

Other recent studies

In a study by Bateman and Fonagy (2001), 44 borderline patients treated with psychoanalytically oriented partial hospitalization were followed every 3 months for 18 months post-termination. Indicators of treatment effects included changes in numbers of suicide attempts, acts of self-harm, inpatient hospitalization, and a range of self-reported measures. Patients showed gains at the ends of treatment and continued to improve further after termination. A study of psychodynamic therapy for panic disorder (Milrod et al., 2000) found improvements at treatment termination and at follow-up after 6 months. Additional studies, incorporating features of the third generation and addressing issues of specificity—what specifically works for whom—have been further explored in work by Fonagy and his colleagues (Roth et al., 1996).

Fourth generation: focus on process

Wallerstein also identified a fourth generation of psychotherapy research studies that seek to answer more precisely the question of process: *how does change come about?* These contrast with the three groups of studies just reviewed, which focus on the question of treatment outcome: *what changes take place?* These questions are necessarily interlocked in many ways, as Wallerstein has pointed out: for example, the Menninger Project was designed as an inquiry into both outcome and process. As he also noted, however, new techniques have been developed since the time of that project that permit more detailed investigation of the therapeutic process and therapeutic interaction.

The major shift in the fourth generation of research was an emphasis on audio and video recording of session material, which made possible the finer-grained study of therapeutic interaction and inspired the development of a wide range of measures for such research. Wallerstein and Sampson (1971) reviewed the arguments for and against the audio recording of therapy sessions. As Wallerstein (2001b) summarized these arguments:

> The major pro arguments were the greater completeness, verbatim accuracy, permanence, and public character of the database, as well as the facilitation of the separation of the therapeutic from the research responsibility, with the possibility of thus bypassing the inevitable biases of the analyst as a contaminant of the data filter. The major con arguments were the indeterminate impact of this (research) intrusion on the "naturalness" of the therapeutic process (including the compromise of full confidentiality and the insertion into the treatment of goals other than therapeutic) and the sheer enormity, complexity, and cost of the database thus made available. [Wallerstein, 2001b, p. 261]

As Wallerstein further notes,

> It is only within the last two or perhaps three decades that an adequate consensus has emerged that analytic therapy can go

> on under these observed circumstances—that is, that a properly therapeutic process can nonetheless evolve.

At the same time, computer technology has advanced to the point where the database can be feasibly managed.

A landmark book, *Psychoanalytic Process Research Strategies*, edited by Dahl, Kächele and Thomä (1988), reported on a major workshop of German and American process researchers held in Ulm, Germany, just prior to the 1985 IPA Congress in Hamburg. The Ulm workshop initiated the approach of researchers applying a wide range of different methods reflecting different perspectives to the same treatment material. This is the basic approach that was also taken by the Collaborative Analytic Multi-site Program (CAMP) organized by Wallerstein under the auspices of the APsaA (see chapter 4, this volume). Recent work in this area is also covered in the second edition of the *Open Door Review* (Fonagy et al., 2002) and has been reviewed by Bucci (2005).

In order to look beneath the generally null results of the major "third-generation" studies, we need to examine what goes on in the room between analyst and patient and how this interaction relates to treatment effects. Process research has the potential to provide new understanding of factors leading to change in psychoanalysis, to characterize the nature of analytic change, and to provide indicators of such analytic change having occurred. However clinicians have as yet generally rejected the introduction of recording and the application of empirical research techniques and have not seen the results of research as relevant or useful for their work. Some of the reasons for this dissociation of clinical work and research from the clinical perspective have been discussed by Bucci (2005); other explanations may be found in the nature of the early phases of process research.

THE GENERATIONS OF PSYCHOANALYTIC PROCESS RESEARCH

Because of its complex and costly nature, coupled with the lack of institutional interest and financial support, Wallerstein (2001b) saw the progress of process research as relatively limited and did not identify generational transformations in this work. Here I would like to go beyond Wallerstein's evaluation. I think there have been developments, both conceptual and methodological, during the past few years that enable us to identify generational advances in psychotherapy process research and to build new bridges to clinical work (see also Bucci, 2005). I outline several phases of psychotherapy process research here that have the status of generational shifts and that also show change and advance in their own developmental lines.

First and second generations

The work mentioned by Wallerstein, as represented in the Ulm Workshop and CAMP, actually represents a synthesis of two stages of development over several decades. The *first generation* focused primarily on the development of a range of objective measures and the establishment of their reliability and validity. These included measures of transference themes (Dahl & Teller, 1994; Gill & Hoffman, 1982; Luborsky & Crits-Cristoph, 1990), defences (Perry, 1990), and language style (Bucci, 2002a, 2002b; Mergenthaler, 1996), as well as more comprehensive process scales, developed by individual researchers and applied to transcripts of therapy sessions and other clinical materials (Ablon & Jones, 1998; Hilsenroth, Ackerman, Blagys, Baity, & Mooney, 2003; Waldron, Scharf, Hurst, Firestein, & Burton, 2004).

The *second generation* focused on the application of some of these measures to shared data sets, as in the Ulm and CAMP projects described above. The collaborative approach enabled researchers to build the construct validity of their measures in relation to other measures and to outcome but also introduced its own methodological and theoretical problems; these have been discussed by Bucci (2005).

The need for integration of clinical and research perspectives: a third generation of process research

A *third generation* of process research is now emerging—one that reflects an increased recognition of the need to integrate research and clinical perspectives and to produce findings that have the potential to inform clinical practice. The focus of this research should be seen in relation to the second guiding question of this chapter: "What is specific about the nature and consequences of analytic practice?"

A discussion in the 1996 meeting of House of Delegates of the IPA during the work of the Committee on Psychoanalytic Specificity focused on the nature of psychoanalytic practice and the proper database for defining analytic process (Freedman, Lasky, & Hurvich, 2003). In spite of wide theoretical differences, the group agreed fairly readily on the following processes: transference, transference regression, interpretation, the recognition of the symbolic, and the judicious use of countertransference as specific to psychoanalysis. After lengthy debate, a position statement was developed that included four points:

1. Any effort at validation must be rooted in the history of psychoanalytic clinical thought.
2. The evaluation of process should originate in the subjective and intuitive judgement of the engaged and experiencing analyst.
3. Evaluation should be corroborated by consultants using the time-honoured methods of peer review and supervision.
4. Only then would these essentially clinical procedures receive external validity through the study of recorded texts.

The IPTAR study of recorded psychoanalysis

The IPTAR research programme is directly responsive to these four points. Here we look in some depth at a single case study being carried out in the Research Program of the Institute for Psychoanalytic Training and Research (IPTAR) as providing perhaps the most fully developed illustration to date of research developed in this context. The structure of the project and some recent findings are covered in more depth by Freedman, Lasky, and Hurvich (2003) and by Bucci and Maskit (submitted).

The study focuses on 60 sessions from the third year of an analysis of a married woman in her thirties, seen on the couch four times a week by an experienced female analyst. At the time of writing, the treatment and the research project are ongoing. Tape-recording was introduced in the second year of analysis. The analyst explained the research objectives to the patient and obtained her written consent. Aside from her role in recording the sessions, providing her impressions as described below, and delivering the tape recordings through an intermediary, the analyst has no interaction with the research team.

The case is being studied using what Freedman terms the method of "sequential specification", which includes multiple sources of data and phases of data analysis:

Phase 1: The analyst's clinical scan. Immediately after each session, with the tape recorder still on, the analyst dictates her impressions (for 3–5 minutes) of the session just ended. As Freedman, Lasky, and Hurvich (2003) describe this: ". . . the scan covers the kinds of thoughts and feelings that may permeate an analyst's consciousness just after the patient has left the room", for example: "The patient was extremely anxious at first, she saw her dilemma, and I sensed what she wanted from me, I felt I knew her . . ." or "The session didn't seem to go anywhere; the material was chaotic, I felt attacked and irrelevant" (Freedman, Lasky, & Hurvich, 2003, p. 209).

Clinically experienced analysts then listen to the analyst's recorded scans and categorize them in terms of two clusters of process qualities, which have been given the abstract terms "A" and "Z" qualities. "A" qualities generally represent processes of integration, consolidation, developmental progression, and relatively stable exploration and may reflect a range of functions such as explicit transference, affect communication, reflective function, and interpretations received. "Z" qualities indicate non-integration, regression, and destabilization and may be associated with an experience of impasse. While A qualities are generally seen as dominant in working sessions and Z in less immediately productive sessions, the abstract terms are used to emphasize the position of the Freedman group that both are clinically significant—indeed necessary—aspects of the treatment process. Thus productive treatment requires a rhythmic alternation of A and Z qualities, between and within sessions, as discussed in detail by Freedman (Freedman, Lasky, & Hurvich, 2003).

Two analysts, working independently, achieved high reliability in scoring these dimensions as reported in the analyst's scans. As expected, the scales were highly negatively correlated. A composite score was computed as the difference between the A and Z scores as assigned by the judges. A total of 16 criterion sessions, representing clearest dominant A or Z process qualities as indicated by the A–Z difference scores based on the analyst's impressions, were selected for more intensive study.

Phase 2: Clinical confirmation—direct evaluation of session material by clinical consultants. Three new raters, two analysts and one psychologist who was not an analyst, then listened to or read these 16 sessions themselves, and evaluated them directly on the A and Z dimensions. Excellent reliability among the three scorers was achieved on both dimensions (a correlation of > 0.90 between each pair).

The ratings of A vs. Z dominance based on direct access to session material were in agreement with ratings based on the analyst's impressions in 12 of the 16 criterial sessions. The four sessions with contrasting ratings demonstrate how the same material may be heard quite differently by the treating analyst who is immersed in the interaction and highly experienced outside observers who listen to or read the session. The design of this study, with its multiple empirical as well as clinical perspectives, provides an opportunity to identify some of the factors associated with such differences.

Phase 3: Specifying changes in functioning within the session. Two sessions, each representing extreme examples of A and Z qualities based on the analyst's impressions, were selected for detailed examination of the event structure, moment by moment. Working by consensus, the analyst–consultants listened to the sessions the way a supervisor might, on the alert for new material and crucial events. Every time a shift, a new development, or some other crucial event took place, a marker was inserted. The units of analysis were then defined by these markers. The consulting clinicians then defined the features of each unit, for the patient and for the analyst.

- *For the patient:* These will be features such as changes in reflective functioning; shifts in the level of anxiety, and other aspects of tension and affect regulation; changes in the representation of objects, in the past or the here-and-now; shifts in the transference, and shifts in level of consciousness, between surface and depth.
- *For the analyst:* The consultants note events such as shifts in the timing and appropriateness of interventions and aspects of the

rhythm of speech, including pausing, interruptions, and concurrent speech.

- *For the dyad:* Synchrony and asynchrony of the interaction are noted.

These qualitative observations showed a distinct structure for what are defined as A (working or integrative), in contrast to Z (difficult or regressive or non-integrative) units or sessions.

Phase 4: Application of objective research methods. The fourth phase of the IPTAR Research Program involves application of objective process research methods to the 16 criterial sessions (9 dominantly A and 7 Z) that were selected on the basis of the analyst's impressions. The empirical measures now in use include the measure of Core Conflictual Relationship Theme (CCRT) developed by Luborsky and his colleagues (Luborsky & Crits-Cristoph, 1998); the Defense Mechanism Rating Scales (DMRS) developed by Perry (1990); the Scales of Incremental Symbolization developed by Freedman, Kagan, Russell, Schaffer, and Webster (2001), and computerized measures of the referential process (Bucci, 2002a, 2002b;). These may be applied in both macro-analytic evaluations of sessions as a whole and micro-analytic studies of the moment by moment interactions within sessions.

Measures of the referential process applied to A and Z sessions

Here we focus on the application of measures developed in the context of Bucci's concept of the referential process and compare these to clinical evaluation of sessions based on A–Z qualities. This work has been carried out in collaboration with Bucci's Referential Process Research Group at the Derner Institute of Adelphi University. The referential process, developed within the theoretical framework of multiple code theory (Bucci, 1997, 2002a), concerns the general function of connecting subjective nonverbal experience, including emotional experience, to the shared verbal code. The process plays a central role in psychoanalysis, or any form of psychotherapy, where emotional experience, dominated by somatic and sensory processes, primarily in subsymbolic formats, must be connected to words.

Phases of the referential process

The referential process includes the following major phases, as they may play out in a session:

1. *Arousal:* The process begins with arousal of an emotional schema, which may be activated by the events of the day and also by the playing out of the therapeutic relationship in the treatment context. The schema as initially aroused is likely to be dominated by sensory and somatic experience dissociated from objects and events and to be expressed in halting, disfluent language.
2. *Imagery and narrative:* Optimally, the patient will then move into a phase of imagery, which may include retrieval of a dream, a fantasy, or a memory of a recent or more distant event, and will tell this in narrative form. The imagery or episode as told in the narrative represents elements of the maladaptive or conflictual emotion schema that has been activated in the session—now connected to objects and events and thus more capable of being translated into words.
3. *Emotional reflection:* Once the story has been told, patient and analyst can then reflect upon it and begin to understand its emotional meaning, to explicate the wishes, expectations, and beliefs that are expressed, and to identify the objects towards which these are directed.
4. *Process of change:* If the process is working, then the words that are spoken by analyst and patient connect to components of the patient's emotion schema that may previously have been dissociated, leading potentially to the reconstruction of the schema that we characterize as *structural change*; this involves connection or re-connection of subsymbolic sensory or somatic components to symbolic nonverbal and verbal forms.

Iteration of the referential process

The connection to previously dissociated components of the schema may then activate some of the dangers that triggered the initial dissociation, perhaps in attenuated form, but with sufficient power to trigger new arousal and iteration of the referential process with new contents. This iteration of the referential process within sessions and across treatments, with new levels of affect and new objects, is a psychological formulation of the process of *working through.*

Linguistic measures of the referential process

Computerized linguistic indicators have been developed that are associated with each phase of the referential process; these include basic measures of Referential Activity (RA), Affect, Reflectivity, and Disfluency, and a number of derived measures based on these, as represented in both patient and analyst speech (Bucci & Maskit, submitted; Maskit, 2006). Using these measures (referring here to patient speech only), we would expect the arousal phase of the referential process to be characterized by high levels of Disfluency, relatively high levels of Affect, and low levels of RA and Reflectivity. The narrative phase is characterized by high RA, with relatively low levels of Reflection and Disfluency. The patient is immersed in a story and tells this fluently; affect may vary. In the emotional reflection phase, RA is likely to be low and Reflection to rise, also accompanied by some increase in Affect. This phase is also likely to be accompanied by an increase in Disfluency as the patient seeks to express material that may not previously have been formulated.

We expect that an effective session will be characterized by relatively complete playing out of the phases of the process, often repeated several times with different contents. Less effective sessions will show interruption and fragmentation of the process; in some cases some components may not appear. Thus the patient may not move into a full narrative phase or may show an extended period of high and fluent Reflectivity without accompanying Affect, indicating intellectual rather than emotional insight.

Conceptual relationship between A–Z fluctuation and the theory of the referential process

We can now look at the conceptual relationship between the fluctuations associated with the referential process and the rhythmic alternation of A and Z qualities that characterizes productive treatment according to the formulation of the IPTAR group. We can see considerable similarity as well as differences between the two formulations:

one, the IPTAR formulation, rooted in the history of psychoanalytic clinical thought; the other, the theory of the referential process, deriving its theoretical foundation from a general psychological theory, the multiple code theory that is rooted in current work in cognitive psychology and related fields and applied to an understanding of the psychoanalytic process.

Perhaps the major similarity is an emphasis in both approaches on patterns of change among different types of functioning as characterizing effective analytic work, both within sessions and across treatments. In the IPTAR formulation, an effective session is characterized by rhythmic alternation between dominantly A and Z phases; effective treatments are characterized by alternation between phases of dominantly A and Z sessions. The referential process is a characterization of an individual's progression through different phases of organized cognitive and emotional functioning; this progression may be seen within a session and also across phases of the treatment.

A major point of difference is that the IPTAR formulation identifies *two* different modes, characterized as A and Z, and examines *alternation* between them; whereas the theory of the referential process postulates *three* major stages of the associative process, with different features associated with each, and examines an individual's *progression* through these.

The differences between the two formulations emerge from the differences in their roots. The IPTAR formulation, based in psychoanalytic theory, accounts for the alternation in terms of the psychoanalytic view that controlled regression is a crucial condition for the working ego to assimilate previously intolerable tension states. The multiple code theory views each phase of the referential process as representing dominance of different organized processing modalities, with systematic progression from subsymbolic to symbolic phases. In the traditional formulation, the goal of treatment may be characterized as increasing the dominance of the organized (secondary process) over regressed or primitive (primary process) modes: "where id was, there ego shall be". For multiple code theory, the goal of treatment is integration of the different processing systems in pursuit of the individual's overall goals; this involves fuller incorporation of affective and somatic components into the individual's schemas of self and other.

Application of language measures to the IPTAR sessions

The language measures developed by Bucci, Maskit, and their colleagues have been applied to the 16 criterial sessions selected to represent dominant A or Z qualities, using both micro- and macroanalytic evaluations. Based on the comparison of the two theoretical frameworks outlined above, we can make the following specific predictions:

1. The phase of arousal, with its disfluent speech and emphasis on somatic and emotional contents, corresponds in some respects to phases of sessions (or whole sessions) characterized by Z qualities in the IPTAR formulation. Arousal, however, might also be associated with the occurrence of explicit transference and affect communication, characterized as A qualities. In general, we would expect RA to be low and the disfluency and Affect measures to be high in Arousal and in Z phases; other measures may not show such correspondence.
2. The phase of imagery and narrative represents processes of exploration associated with A qualities. This phase is marked by high RA and relatively lower levels of the other linguistic features.
3. Some qualities identified with the A zone by Freedman would also be associated with the emotional reflection phase of the referential process: these include integration, consolidation, reflective functions, and interpretations received. This phase is likely to be marked by high levels of Reflection, and some synchronous movement of Affect with Reflection, indicating emotional insight. However, RA is likely to be relatively low as the patient emphasizes functions of reasoning rather than story-telling or imagery; thus may use language that is relatively more abstract and less vivid and immediate. Disfluency is also likely to rise in this phase as the patient struggles to make new connections and express ideas that have been avoided or not previously formulated.

We can see that there is a partial but not fully clear correspondence between the A vs. Z categorization and the phases of the referential process. Based on the areas of correspondence, we would predict A sessions or phases of sessions to be characterized by higher RA in some phases and higher Reflectivity in others. Both approaches would also predict particular patterns of interaction among the several language variables. The IPTAR group would predict more regular alternation between indicators of A and Z qualities in A sessions. From the perspective of the referential process theory, an effective session would be characterized by the sequential playing-out of the phases of the process leading to developmental progression or change, whereas less effective sessions would be those in which the process is interrupted or fragmented.

Some preliminary results

The results of this study have been presented in detail by Bucci and Maskit (submitted). Overall, in A sessions as defined by the analyst's impressions, patients show higher levels of RA, less disfluency, and more systematic patterning of the measures, as expected. They show a lower correlation between RA and Reflectivity, indicating periods of immersion in a narrative, where the patient is absorbed in reliving the experience, without examining its meaning explicitly; and higher correlation between Reflectivity and Disfluency, indicating exploration into new emotional territory. The A and Z sessions show different patterns of fluctuation in RA within the sessions, as well as different overall session scores.

The linguistic analysis also enables examination of features of the patient–therapist interaction. On an overall level, the patient is significantly higher than the analyst in average level of Referential Activity, and this applies for both A and Z sessions ($p < 0.01$ for each set of sessions) . This is characteristic of psychodynamic treatments, seen in all patient–analyst pairs examined thus far. The patient is the main story-teller; deviation from this in a session is noteworthy. In contrast, the analyst is higher than the patient in Reflectivity. This difference is significant ($p < 0.05$) in Z sessions but is less marked ($p < 0.10$) for the A sessions. The patient and analyst were essentially equal in Disfluency in the A sessions, but the patient was significantly higher in Disfluency than the analyst in the Z sessions ($p < 0.05$). The difference occurred primarily through the analyst showing less Disfluency (speaking more fluently) in the Z than in the A sessions. The differences in the Reflection and Disfluency patterns seem to carry similar implications. The analyst is more fluent and shows higher levels of reflectivity than does the patient in Z sessions; we may speculate that the work is more collaborative and shared in the A sessions. Whether the differences in the analyst speech occurred in response to changes in the patient or for other reasons remains to be explored.

The clinician–researcher partnership

The features of this study that cause it to be designated as "third generation" rest primarily on the multiple perspectives that are included: the perspective of the treating analyst; the evaluation by consultants examining the session transcripts or tapes; and the research perspectives provided by the objective measures. The design of the study permits use of each perspective to inform the other. The feedback from research can contribute to developing the clinical and theoretical perspectives that are represented in the definitions of the A and Z dimensions, just as the clinical observations can be used to examine the validity of the research measures. In future work we also expect to examine specific differential predictions of the Freudian model and the theory of the referential process, using both objective measures and clinical observation. In these and other respects, this design potentially places process researchers in a partnership with clinicians, as a source of new discoveries, not only as providing evidence for what clinicians "already know".

A unique opportunity for the evaluation of multiple perspectives on the treatment process is provided by the sessions where the A–Z ratings as reported by the treating analyst differed from the evaluations of the clinical consultants. Here empirical process measures can be used to examine ways in which these 4 cases differed from the other 12, enabling us to identify aspects of the session that influenced the analyst who was immersed in the interaction, and distinguish these from factors influencing the consultants who viewed the session from a neutral stance (Bucci & Maskit, submitted) . With its multiple perspectives, this study has the potential to address what is perhaps the thorniest epistemological question in psychoanalytic research—to disentangle the roles of the analyst as participant and as observer; on the one hand as part of the data to be studied, on the other hand as the unique repository of the subjective experience of the interaction.

The Buenos Aires study: the role of supervision and participation of the analyst

The second study in this third generation addresses similar questions. This study is also an ongoing project, currently being developed by two collaborating research groups, one from the Asociación Psicoanalítica Argentina and the other from the Universidad de Belgrano, both in Buenos Aires (López Moreno, Dorfman Lerner, Schalayeff, & Roussos, 1999). The research investigates indicators of psychic change in six long-term psychodynamic treatments.

Patients are six young women between the ages of 20 and 30, seen once or twice a week at the Racker Centre of the APA, which provides reduced-fee psychoanalytic therapy. *Therapists* are candidates at the Asociación Psicoanalítica Argentina, who had previously been in supervision with senior analysts, the directors of this project, and who agreed to work on this empirical research. Therapists receive free supervision for the cases treated at the Centre.

The therapists were actively involved in the research process; they informed patients about the research, obtained their informed consent, introduced the recording device in the sessions, administered the self-report questionnaires, participated in the clinical meetings, and filled out the diagnostic evaluation described below. The study included effectiveness measures, verbatim session recording, and application of process measures to session transcripts, and also introduced a new approach to use of research measures in the supervision context.

The analysis of the therapeutic process was carried out using two perspectives:

1. the psychoanalytic approach, using therapist notes, supervision, and group meetings to analyse the material in relation to the clinical diagnosis;
2. empirical research methods, including: the SCL-90-R for symptom assessment (Derogatis, 1993); a new diagnostic tool, the DEPD (Differential Elements for Psychodynamic Diagnosis of patients in supervision) developed by members of the Buenos Aires clinical group; the CCRT (Luborsky & Crits-Cristoph, 1998); and a preliminary version of a computerized Spanish RA measure (SRA) developed by Roussos.

Patients were given the SCL-90-R and DEPD prior to beginning treatment and at intervals throughout treatment. The DEPD was developed as a link between the clinical and empirical methods, designed from a psychoanalytic rather than standard diagnostic perspective and aiming at a systematic structural characterization of the patient. The instrument has two modules, one covering patient features such as manifest behaviours, interpersonal relationships, symptoms, conflicts, ego-synthetic functions, and prevailing affects; the second covers the supervisory work, including the evaluation of transferential and countertransferential relationships and impressions of the supervision. Both modules are filled out by both therapist and supervisor and provide independent bases for comparison of their views of the patient and the treatment.

Sessions are transcribed for application of process measures. Thus far, the CCRT and preliminary SRA measures have been applied to the session material.

Participation of the therapist and relationship between research and supervision

There are two major original aspects of this project that address, in different ways, the inclusion of the subjective experience of the therapist as a component of the research, in interaction with other observations. One concerns the use of the DEPD in both supervision and research; the second concerns the use of objective research data in the supervision.

The DEPD was developed as a research measure, but the fact that it is filled out by both therapist and supervisor makes it an aspect of the supervisory relationship. Thus, for example, there might be instances in which the supervisor would confess her difficulties in understanding the patient, while the supervisee could say that the supervision had not been useful to her, and these comments could then be explored further by both participants. While the therapists found the form extremely difficult at first, they also found it valuable in helping them to organize their concepts of the case. As they did the questionnaire repeatedly, they were able to express their feelings and ideas more fluidly and spontaneously, and these advances also held for the clinical meetings.

In general, the researchers–supervisors felt that the use of this research instrument facilitated the transmission and training of psychoanalytic techniques in direct and indirect ways, allowed expression of emotions related to the supervision, and enabled greater internalization of the new information and more useful feedback to the supervisees.

Use of objective process measures in supervision

In one example of the direct use of research measures in supervision, the measures of the referential process as outlined earlier were applied by the researchers to verbatim transcripts of sessions being discussed in supervision. Graphs showing fluctuation of the measures in the course of a session were then discussed by supervisor and therapist. In one session being discussed in supervision, the graph showed several instances where the therapist intervened at a point of relatively high and increasing RA. In one of these, the patient was speaking about her conflictual relationship with her father, generally described as a negative character, and the therapist intervened to rescue the positive aspects of the father. The patient rejected this, beginning to be elusive and vague, saying "yes" but rejecting the therapist's interpretation.

In previous research, reported by Bucci (2002a, 2002b) we have found, in many sessions and many treatments, that it is unusual for a therapist to intervene when referential activity is high or increasing, when the patient is speaking as if well connected to her own explorations—at a moment when, for example, Frau Emmy von N might have said to Freud, "Be quiet and let me talk". Therapists generally listen silently to a narrative that is high in referential activity; then are more likely to intervene as it ends.

Using this research knowledge, the supervisor questioned the therapist about her experience of this point of the session. The therapist did not recognize as hers the type of intervention she had made; she said that it was not her usual interpretive style. On reliving her thoughts of this moment in the supervision, she remembers having said to herself: "but it is a fact that her father was a good person"; then continues: "I am rescuing my father again". As this instance illustrates, the research measures in the supervision were not used as evaluative indicators, but as highlighting possibly significant moments, to stimulate exploration of feelings that might not otherwise have been explicitly noted by therapist or supervisor.

Both the IPTAR and Buenos Aires studies provide, in different ways, models for meaningful process research studies that can be carried out within psychoanalytic institutes. We may note that effective implementation of both projects depended on active collaboration between clinicians in the psychoanalytic institutes and researchers using empirical measures and working in university settings.

Conclusions, questions, moving towards a fourth generation of process research

I have described two ongoing process research studies that meet the criteria of the IPA position outlined by the Committee on Specificity in different ways and that provide the opportunity for developing the type of evidence concerning psychoanalytic theory that was called for by Bernardi's challenge:

1. They work within the framework of psychoanalytic clinical thought.
2. They incorporate the subjective and intuitive judgement of the engaged and experiencing therapist.
3. The evaluation is corroborated by other clinicians viewing the material.
4. These essentially clinical procedures also receive external validation through the application of empirical research measures to recorded texts.

The two studies differ in how they address each of these aspects of the research. The IPTAR study focuses on a single case; the treatment is an analysis; the therapist is a senior analyst in private practice. She does not participate in the research other than to obtain informed consent from the patient and provide her impressions on a tape recording; the other clinicians are senior analysts viewing the material as peer-consultants. The Buenos Aires study follows multiple patients in psychoanalytic psychotherapy; the therapists are candidates in supervision, seeing patients at the reduced-fee clinic of the training institute, and are fully involved in the research; the consultants are senior analysts and supervisors. The Buenos Aires study also incorporates a new and innovative measure of structural change, the DEPD.

Both studies include the impressions of the treating analyst, in different ways. Both include observations of clinical observers—consultants listening to the case material in the IPTAR study and supervisors working with the therapists in the Buenos Aires studies. Both use reliable and valid empirical process measures applied to verbatim session material; in the Buenos Aires study clinical and research measures are used in the supervision; no feedback occurs from the research assessment to the analyst in the IPTAR study.

Both studies have moved us beyond the design of the first- and second-generation process studies to a third generation; what are some of the problems that remain? What is left for new generations of process research?

Goals for a new generation of process research

Based on what we have learned from the research covered in Wallerstein's review and from the two new studies covered here, let me briefly suggest a set of goals that would constitute a *fourth generation* of process research and also address some problems associated with these:

1. *Inclusion of outcome measures*

Fully recorded analytic treatments are needed that meet the criteria of the third-generation *outcome* studies: prospective design, with systematic and objective pre- and post-treatment assessment, and including separate longitudinal follow-up. These provide a framework to examine and distinguish process in more or less successful treatments. Projects by Hilsenroth, Jones, and their colleagues (Ablon & Jones, 1998; Hilsenroth et al., 2003; Jones, 2000) have demonstrated effects of specific aspects of therapeutic process, rated from transcripts and audio- and video-recording, on outcome in short-term psychodynamic therapies.

Here a major question concerns how outcome should be defined—in terms of criteria based on symptoms and behaviours, using standard measures such as the SCL-90 or GAF; or in terms of analytic criteria based on structural change, using measures such as the SPC as developed by Wallerstein, with colleagues including—as described in this volume—DeWitt in San Francisco (chapter 8), Huber and Klug in Munich (chapter 10), and Leuzinger-Bohleber and Fischmann in Hamburg (chapter 9), or the DEPD, developed in the Buenos Aires study described above. It seems clear that an optimal study should include assessment of outcome based on both perspectives: how the patient has fared in terms of criteria of emotional and physical health, including relational, social, and occupational functioning, and evaluation of the internal psychic changes that have occurred. Here we also confront the issue of how long to extend the post-treatment follow-up, and in what form. For example, to examine the hypothesis that a specific outcome of analytic treatment is the development of a stance of self-examination that continues through life, one might wish to examine the relationship between different degrees of structural change measured at termination and further structural change that may occur during extended post-treatment periods.

2. *Multiple perspectives*

Both of the "third-generation" studies that have been described here incorporate multiple clinical and empirical perspectives, including the subjective experience of the treating analyst, along with views of observers who examine verbatim records of the session material. The recognition of the need for multiple points of view and the development of researcher–clinician partnerships may be seen as the crucial contributions of this new wave of research; these advances need to be retained and expanded in subsequent work.

The new approach recognizes the analyst's subjective experience of the session as a *necessary* but not *sufficient* data source. It is precisely because of the reality of subjectivity, because perception and memory are active and constructive processes rather than passive and reproductive ones, that multiple perspectives on the treatment process are necessary. Just as there are gaps in the patient's report of his or her emotional experience, so there may be gaps or distortions in the treating analyst's report of the therapeutic interactions. These may reflect the narrowing vision of the analyst's theoretical orientation or may arise from the analyst's emotional responses to the patient, including experience that has been warded off. The reader of the analyst's notes or reports may seek to make inferences from apparent gaps or inconsistencies in the manifest contents of the analyst's impressions to underlying aspects of the analyst's experience, or to hidden aspects of the therapeutic interactions, just as, in the analytic method, the analyst makes inference to the patient's unconscious experience from gaps in his associations but is hampered in such inference by having access only to what the analyst is able—or chooses—to report. Verbatim recordings of the session are needed to make possible the multiple perspectives that are required.

As a corollary of this point, we may note that the patient's subjective experience is presented in the analyst's impressions only as filtered through the analyst's subjectivity. Should not the patient speak also for himself? The verbatim material provides the reader—or the researcher—with the opportunity to make inferences as to the patient's subjective experience on the basis of the patient's own material, including experience of which the analyst as well as the patient may be unaware.

In addition to the clinical evaluations by external observers, a broad range of reliable and valid empirical process measures should be applied to the session material, as in the second-generation process research studies. These will include measures to be applied to the verbatim transcripts and also measures applied to tape-recordings that examine the nonverbal aspects of the clinical interaction, including emotive and other paralinguistic vocalizations, pausing, vocal tone and modulation. The objective measures may potentially be used to mediate between divergent clinical views. In developing the fourth-generation designs, we also need to address methodological and conceptual problems that have emerged in previous attempts to integrate research measures using different procedures, as in the CAMP studies, and that have not yet been resolved; some of these are reviewed by Bucci (2005).

3. *Development of treatment archives*

As all these data are developed, a crucial problem for the coming generation concerns the need for psychoanalytic archives that will enable sharing of such data and coordination of research results, while maintaining the highest level of safeguards for the confidentiality of the material. Various institutional and technical aspects of this central issue, and some possible solutions, are discussed in depth in this volume by Roussos, Bucci, and Maskit (chapter 12), Klumpner (chapter 11), and Wallerstein (chapter 4).

4. *Building the institute–university interface*

Robert Wallerstein has devoted his career to the integration of clinical work and empirical research in psychoanalysis. The dissociation between clinical and research perspectives that continues to mark the field reflects, in part, the organization of training in psychoanalysis. Since Freud's time, clinical psychoanalysis has been taught in institutes separate from the universities, with little if any research training or training in any areas of academic psychology. Within the universities, there is essentially no presence of psychoanalysis in academic psychology; psychoanalysis may be taught in the humanities but not in the sciences. Most psychoanalytic psychotherapy research is carried out in universities with dynamically oriented clinical psychology programmes; however, the number of such programmes in the United States is diminishing, while the number of behavioural programmes with a substantial research presence is increasing. The two third-generation process research projects that have been described above have been successful in part because they incorporate active collaboration between clinicians from the psychoanalytic institutes and researchers from university psychology departments. To carry forward the legacy of Robert Wallerstein, such collaboration needs to be further developed, so that: (1) the questions that are studied in psychotherapy research are those with which psychoanalysts are concerned; (2) the theoretical issues of psychoanalysis may be seen in relation to new knowledge in related fields such as cognitive psychology, emotion theory, developmental theory, and neuroscience; and (3) advances in research methods appropriate to the study of psychoanalysis may be applied and new methods developed.

5. *Framework of a living theory*

A central conceptual issue, which is perhaps even more difficult and intricate than those outlined above, concerns the theoretical framework within which the measures are defined and the research is carried out. Here we return, from a different perspective, to both of the questions that constituted the framework for this chapter. If we agree that psychoanalytic research must be carried out within the framework of psychoanalytic thought, as postulated by the Committee on Specificity, then the field is faced with a difficult and interesting challenge that needs to be acknowledged—the challenge of developing such a theoretical framework, in which the terms of the theory are clear and well defined and which is also open to revision based on new observations. The Committee was able to agree on the following processes as specific to psychoanalysis: transference, transference regression, interpretation, the recognition of the symbolic, and the judicious use of countertransference as specific to psychoanalysis; but the definitions of these processes, their role in treatment, and the nature of the evidence that would be acceptable to demonstrate their operation are far from clear and vary widely according to theoretical orientation.

A coherent theoretical framework, including a limited number of concepts, defined systematically in terms of one another and in terms of observable events, is necessary for research in psychoanalysis, and also for clinical work. Without such a conceptual framework researchers are limited to quantification of observations; only within a reasonably well-defined network is it possible to make inferences from observations to the inner emotional events with which psychoanalysis is concerned. For collaborative research, such a framework is necessary to determine the degree to which individual measures may be expected to converge or diverge—to know, for example, the extent to which the concepts of transference or structural change as measured by the different research procedures described above correspond to one another, or to the concepts that clinicians understand and use. An example of the need for a coherent and shared theoretical framework may be seen in the attempt to examine the correspondence between the measures of the referential process, developed in the context of a general psychological theory and the IPTAR formulations that are rooted in a Freudian model.

Similar issues arise within the clinical field. Many controversies concerning theory and technique reflect vague and shifting definitions of theoretical terms rather than actual differences in how to work with patients. Concepts such as unconscious communication, projective identification, two-person psychologies, and intersubjectivity provide examples of such misunderstanding (see Bucci, 2001a). Bernardi (2003) points to the difficulty in finding shared criteria of evidence in clinical debates and calls for "at least a minimally neutral arena" (p. 126) for such discussions.

Thus I would argue that the new generation of process research needs to do something that may appear radical: open the questioning as to what is specific to psychoanalytic theory and technique, recognize the theoretical vacuum that still exists in psychoanalysis, to which Thomä and Kächele (1987), Holt (1985), and others have referred, and work through its implications. The theory that is needed must not only be coherent, but also open to revision based on new observations. We cannot have a living theory if our goal remains to *demonstrate* the validity of the concepts of the metapsychology essentially as defined a century ago; the goal must be to *examine and evaluate* their validity and to revise these concepts as new knowledge emerges.

I would argue that it is deeply and centrally psychoanalytic in the best sense to work towards such revision. In his discussion of the Freudian legacy, Gedo (2001) discusses the "yield from invalid first thoughts" as generative of advance in theory. The fact that certain major concepts (such as, for example, regression, resistance, repression, and the primary and secondary processes of thought) played a crucial role in the development of psychoanalytic theory does not place these concepts beyond examination and revision in the context of psychological knowledge today.

I would also argue that the general theory that is needed must be a psychological theory, not limited to psychoanalytic concepts, and not a neurological theory. The psychological level is needed to provide a shareable structure for diverse clinical ideas, and also to provide an interface between psychoanalytic concepts and neurological ones, as neuroscientists also argue (Panksepp, 1999). The multiple code theory provides one such psychological framework; alternative theories need to be developed.

Conclusions

The mission of psychoanalytic treatment research is to build a knowledge base for psychoanalysis; this includes the development of sources of evidence that clinicians will see as relevant to changes in theory and technique. To carry out this mission, to support and assess the continuing innovation that is going on in clinical psychoanalysis, and to develop more effective techniques for a broader range of patients, including those who are at present not well served by psychoanalytic techniques, we need to develop multifaceted sources of evidence, including the subjective experience of the treating clinicians, along with judgements of other clinicians, and also including objective measures.

Such evidence needs to be considered in the context of a psychoanalytic theory that is itself subject to re-examination and reconstruction. I have suggested that a shared psychological model can provide a common framework within which the concept of psychoanalytic process can be systematically formulated and evidence as to whether such a process is going forward in a session and a treatment can be examined. The development of such theoretical common ground provides one type of response to the challenge of "the one and the many"—welcoming innovation and diversity while retaining psychoanalytic identity—that has constituted a central theme of Wallerstein's work.

NOTES

1. Based on a paper presented at the Rapaport–Klein Study Group at Austen Riggs Center, Stockbridge, MA, June 1999.

EPILOGUE
The Wallerstein summary

14

The vision of CAMP and the future of psychoanalytic therapy research

Robert S. Wallerstein

In the last paragraph of their introductory chapter to this volume, Bert Freedman and Wilma Bucci point to the reputation I have acquired over my professional lifetime of a "capacity to digest, filter, and organize the papers presented at a long conference and to produce. . . a summary. . . that unified them into an overall vision, while consistently reflecting what the contributors were trying to say"—something also referred to by Peter Fonagy (chapter 3) and by Dorothea Huber and Guenther Klug (chapter 8)—and on that basis they asked me to write a summarizing chapter and critique in this instance as well. I did agree to the request, but with trepidation, because the day-long symposium out of which this monograph has been organized was a meeting marking the relinquishing of my role as the organizer of and, for more than a decade, my chairmanship of CAMP, the Collaborative Analytic Multi-site Program of the American Psychoanalytic Association (APsaA), dedicated to the promotion of psychoanalytic therapy research within the APsaA and, by extension, within the worldwide psychoanalytic community.

Under the circumstances, some of the contributions were more personal, remarks on my professional lifetime activities in this research arena rather than properly scientific. In my own (professionally) autobiographic chapter, entitled "My Life as a Psychoanalytic

Therapy Researcher and in CAMP" (chapter 4), I describe in detail the trajectory of my own career in psychotherapy research, as well as the organizational role that I was privileged to play from within the establishment, both within the APsaA and, starting somewhat later, within the International Psychoanalytical Association, in promoting psychoanalytic research as a vital and essential component of psychoanalysis as a discipline with claims to credibility within the scientific and intellectual surround of disciplines dedicated to the knowledge of human behaviour (and with its own therapeutic focus on ameliorating the disorders of human behaviour)—and of course, within this framework, the special focus on the vision that guided the creation of CAMP and its accomplishments over that first decade.

I will therefore not essay to describe or to summarize the contributions in the first two parts of this volume. Part I comprises three brief perspectives upon the nature of my organizational and scientific contributions to the field of psychoanalytic research and my own considerably longer personal chapter. Chapter 1 is by Daniel Widlöcher, former president of the IPA, long-time close friend and colleague, as a psychoanalytic researcher and as a partner in the administrative life of the IPA. Chapter 2 is by Dick Fox, then President of the APsaA, also a good friend and a co-worker in the furtherance of the research activity within the APsaA. And chapter 3 is by Peter Fonagy, truly a comrade-in-arms in his fierce dedication to both his own stellar career as a psychoanalytic researcher and in shared and tireless devotion to the worldwide promotion of psychoanalytic research activity. And, parenthetically, I am happy to add my pleasure in Peter's inclusion in his remarks of a tribute to our mutual close friend and collaborator, Joseph Sandler—a man to whom we both owe much, personally and professionally, not the least to his equally vital role as a psychoanalytic researcher and a promoter of the psychoanalytic research enterprise. It is my real regret, and I am confident that Peter shares this, that Joe himself did not live to share this celebratory occasion, not just for me personally, but for the shared research endeavour to which we were indissolubly jointly committed.

The three chapters in Part II, longer and more substantive, are by three close friends with whom I have shared intense working relationships over my research years. Chapter 5, by Otto Kernberg, whom I feel extraordinarily fortunate in having been able to recruit to Topeka and to our Psychotherapy Research Project (PRP) of the

Menninger Foundation in 1961, from his home then as a European Hitler refugee in Chile (and with the essential help of Karl Menninger and his friend, then Senator Frank Carlson from Kansas, in bypassing restrictive immigration procedures). I recruited him to a central role in our project, from which he succeeded me in the project leadership in its final period of data-gathering and task completion when I left Topeka for San Francisco in 1966. In this role he developed the beginnings of his own extremely productive lifetime contributions to the understanding and treatment of the borderline personality organization—work that began with his own intensive studies of the same 42 PRP patients whom I describe in my own book, *Forty-Two Lives in Treatment* (Wallerstein, 1986).

Chapter 6 is by Hartvig Dahl, who started his psychiatric career together with me as fellow residents in the Menninger School of Psychiatry.[1] We both arrived in Topeka as of 1 July 1949. As Hartvig describes his own hegira, our paths there were quite different; we knew each other as fellows in the same programme but, in those days, not well. Our research paths converged much more in later years with a shared involvement in the same field of therapy research, though we had come from very different vantage points: his a microanalytic focus based on the recording and computer technology gradually becoming available, on the moment-to-moment verbatim interactions of the audio-recorded psychoanalytic encounter. His path led to the development (with Virginia Teller) of FRAMES—narrative accounts by patients of Fundamental Repetitive and Maladaptive Emotion Structures, which characteristically encapsulate and express the neurotic difficulties that bring individuals to seek psychotherapeutic help. With the creation of CAMP, Hartvig became a regular participant and contributor, and I have learned much from his presentations, which have always been to me a most formidable and uniquely individually tailored perspective on the analytic process and guide to therapeutic intervention.

Chapter 7 is by Lester Luborsky, who preceded me in Topeka. He was a member of the first group there interested in creating a psychotherapy research programme, engaged in creating what was to become the HSRS, the Health–Sickness Rating Scale; this, in turn, became an integral aspect of the Psychotherapy Research Project (PRP). Lester himself was one of the key members of the initial planning group that I brought together to create PRP. After his many years in a central role in PRP, which also fostered a close personal and family friendship between us, Lester went to the University of Pennsylvania in Philadelphia as a psychotherapy researcher. There, together with numerous colleagues, he created the CCRT, the Core Conflictual Relationship Theme, in an effort to operationalize transference–countertransference interactions as a key process measure in empirical psychotherapy research. The CCRT has, of course, developed into a major worldwide "research industry", with many hundreds of investigators across the globe using it as a central measure in both psychoanalytically informed and also even non-psychoanalytically informed psychotherapy research; and it is from this platform that Lester participated with me, and made presentations, at meetings of CAMP.

To all three of these friends and collaborators in psychoanalytic therapy research I express my deepest thanks for what they say here of my role in relation to their own very impressive, albeit quite different, psychoanalytic therapy research careers. I do appreciate very much what they, and the three who preceded them in their contributions to the conference upon which this volume is based, an array of esteemed colleagues, each an important contributor to the development of psychoanalysis, and all working comrades and friends, have said about me, with my gratitude hopefully admixed with an appropriately realistic mixture of humility over what they have described as my role in the development of research within psychoanalysis, and my influence in helping shape their own development. I add only one final note here, a generational note about the transmission of influence. I want to acknowledge here what I stated more fully and substantively in my own chapter in this volume, my own indebtedness in my chosen career direction to Merton Gill, whom I always saw as mentor, albeit exercised over a distance, as well as comrade and friend in pursuit of shared goals.

To turn now to substantive research. Part III is devoted to studies centred around the development and application of the Scales of Psychological Capacities (SPC)—scales developed by our research group in San Francisco[2] as a successor project—Psychotherapy Research Project II (PRP-II)—to the original Psychotherapy Research Project (PRP) of the Menninger Foundation. In my book of final clinical accounting of the 30-year-long PRP, *Forty-Two Lives in Treatment* (Wallerstein, 1986), the summary of the findings and conclusions emphasized that, contrary to our expectations, not only could clear structural changes in personality organization be demonstrated in those who did well in their treatments in the half of the patient cohort taken into psychoanalysis, but comparable structural changes, indistinguishable in nature, could also be demonstrated in some half of those who did well in various combinations of expressive and supportive psychoanalytic psychotherapies. These structural changes seemed to be based more on various supportive interventions that were not explicitly directly interpretive or aimed at the acquisition of insight.

This major finding, at variance with the conventional wisdom concerning the change mechanisms in psychoanalytically conceptualized therapies, was based, however, on the summarizing judgements of senior seasoned clinicians, not on an empirical and objective change measure with established psychometric properties. To remedy that research weakness, our research group (PRP-II) was established in San Francisco in the late 1980s to create that metric—a scale that could reliably and validly measure "structural change" in underlying personality functioning beyond the already existing measures of symptom change and change in manifest behaviour patterns that assess the kinds of changes brought about in non-interpretive, non-insight-aiming therapies but theoretically do not measure the kinds of changes reached in expressive psychoanalytic therapies.

The rationale and the labours of construction of our SPC that would reflect, within a psychoanalytic conceptual framework, underlying changes in the structure of the personality in a way that adherents of the different theoretical perspectives within psychoanalysis (our pluralism of metapsychologies) could all agree upon has been described in a sequence of articles from our group (DeWitt, Milbrath, & Wallerstein, 1999; DeWitt et al., 1991; Wallerstein, 1988a; Zilberg et al., 1991). This work is summarized and further extended in Chapter 8, Kathryn DeWitt's contribution to this volume. She describes the history of our own unfolding and the conceptual development of the SPC; she also discusses the genesis of the semi-structured interview, with probe questions designed to supplement the usual clinical psychodynamic assessment process in order to fill in the requirement needs of the SPC when they have not emerged in the original diagnostic interviews, as well as a content validity study, two interrater reliability studies, a concurrent validity study, and a test–retest reliability (stability) study.

DeWitt also indicates the wider deployment of our Scales within the psychoanalytic psychotherapy research world, both in the United

States and around the world, including translations into Finnish, French, German, Italian, and Swedish.

What I should add is that we have an authenticated back translation in German carried out between our group and the group headed by Dorothea Huber and Guenther Klug in Munich, Germany—two colleagues initially trained in the use of SPC in a two-week training programme in San Francisco in 1999. A back translation is a two-step process: The initial translation of our English-language original version into German was followed by a translation from German back into English, carried out by another translator who had not seen the original English language text. Subtle, and at times not so subtle, alterations in meaning during the successive translations can then be readily detected, as well as alterations arising from simple misunderstandings of idiomatic expressions unique to a particular language. All such alterations were rectified by suitable changes in the German text, so that now we can be sure that subjects of the PRP in both English and German are being assessed by the same standards and can thus be considered together in cross-national samples. This has not yet been done for translations into other languages, but of course it should be done, and indeed with all translations of research instruments across languages.

Towards the end of her chapter DeWitt also mentions (though not exhaustively) the variety of other instruments developed during the same time period as the SPC, or later, also designed as measures of underlying dynamic, or structural, change in personality organization. Almost all have been developed without knowledge of the parallel efforts of the other groups, and there have been at times startling concordances, like that between the SPC and the Karolinska Psychodynamic Profile (KAPP) (Weinryb, Rössel, & Asberg, 1991) developed in Sweden, each with the identical number of dimensions of personality functioning (17), and with many of them identical in conception and almost in language. Our own group only became aware of the KAPP when we had completed our task of scale construction, and there is no reference to the SPC in the original descriptive write-ups of the KAPP.

A task for future psychotherapy research—in part already partially under way—is to deploy these various structural change outcome measures on the same database of therapies studied, in order to identify convergences and divergences in the assessments, leading possibly in the end to one amalgamated super-instrument or set of scales deployed across the world by concerned psychotherapy researchers, or at least a smaller set of instruments deployed in tandem for their complementary usefulness. Perhaps too Utopian a vision?

The other two chapters in Part III represent work with the SPC by two groups in Germany.

The one group, that of Dorothea Huber and Guenther Klug in Munich (chapter 10)—the investigators trained in the use of the SPC in San Francisco and also responsible for the translation of the scales into German, with back translation—has been the one most methodical and rigorous in elaborating and strengthening the SPC's psychometric properties, working out new conceptual indices along the way and then demonstrating the scales' sensitivity to change in before-and-after studies of changes brought about in psychoanalytic therapy.

To follow sequentially the group's work with the SPC within their Munich Psychotherapy Study: after training a group of German raters, they first undertook an interrater reliability study with a patient sample of 38 depressed patients and concluded with Intra-Class Correlation Coefficients (ICC) ranging from 0.54 to 0.89, with a mean of 0.82, and only 4 of the 35 subdimensions with a reliability score under 0.70. This first pass at working with the SPC was succeeded by a test–retest reliability (or stability) study using 20 patients waiting for psychotherapy placement, done after a two- or three-month interval (and with different raters), with similar results (0.88 stability of the total score, mean of the 35 subdimensions). From there, they undertook a discriminant validity study (with the depressed sample), demonstrating independence of SPC scores from measures of symptom change (construct-distant measures) and a convergent validity study demonstrating some partial correlations with measures of interpersonal problems and of quality of life (construct-near measures) that they also deployed. These validity studies were then replicated, to the same end-result, with a larger sample (47) of depressed patients.

From here, these investigators went on to study construct validity by investigating the SPC's ability to discriminate different diagnostic groups (what they call the "known-groups approach")—in this case cohorts of depressive patients, borderline personality organization patients, and a non-clinical control population. Here, too, they demonstrated predicted discriminations between the three groups that were in each instance in accord with the assumptions of psychoanalytic theory concerning the expected characteristics of the three differing populations. It is here that Huber and Klug introduced a new conceptualization that they dubbed a "splitting index"—that is, the tendency, especially within the borderline group, to deviate from the norm in both subdimensions of a particular capacity, in the directions at different moments both of exaggerated expression and inhibition of the same capacity and characteristically expressed in an ego-syntonic way without anxiety or any sense of conflict or puzzlement. This "splitting index" they operationalized. Here I would interpolate a caveat: one should not assume that this "splitting index" discerned in the borderline group encompasses the totality of the meaning of splitting as a defence mechanism especially characteristic of the borderline disorder.

Lastly, Huber and Klug's group of investigators went on to what they call a "sensitivity to change" study: "the degree to which a measure is likely to reflect changes that actually occur following participation in therapy". They compared the change in SPC scores consequent on therapy with the independent "expert ratings" of experienced psychoanalysts using retrospective judgements made after follow-up interviews, on a 7-point Likert scale, which they call, pejoratively, our "pseudo gold standard". And here they could demonstrate standardized effect sizes (SES) for the SPC of 1.84—far in excess of the usual values in the research literature measuring outcomes in psychotherapy research. Huber and Klug have clearly demonstrated in this coordinated sequence of studies that there is no real change in SPC configurations prior to therapy or outside therapy (the test–retest stability study), but very significant change consequent on successful psychoanalytic therapy, and with a very substantial effect size.

All this, of course, is what it was the original intent of SPC to measure: significant changes in SPC configurations in the direction of more normal or optimal functioning following psychoanalytic therapy and clearly discriminable from measures of symptom- or just manifest behavioural change (the discriminant validity study). It clearly places the SPC at the threshold of being able to pursue the central issue that motivated the establishment of the Scales in the first place—namely, can we determine whether structural changes in personality functioning can be brought about in non-interpretive, non-insight-aiming, supportive therapeutic modes? (and if so—through concomitant micro-analytic study of the therapeutic *process*, using the variety of process measures created in the past few decades—then how?) This alongside the structural changes traditionally thought to come about only in fully interpretive therapies, uncovering unconscious intrapsychic conflicts with continuing working through (and in that case, also—as discerned by process measures—how?).

This is all one way to state the central question that has guided psychoanalytic therapy research, both process and outcome, since its very inception (Wallerstein, 2001b); and Huber and Klug have done more to bring us to that point than any other team. As a last parenthetical note: it is a commonplace when dealing with an abundance of co-determining variables (like the 35 SPC subdimensions) to do a factor-analytic study in order to winnow this large array down to but a few factors with a possible dominant single largest factor. These investigators did essay a factor analysis and found neither a general factor nor a few relevant factors. To explain 80% of the variance, they needed 16 factors. So for now, at least, and until a far larger sample of uses has been carried out and can be summated, the SPC will need to be deployed in its total array of 35 subdimensions.

The other major German research group making significant use of the SPC, the group headed by Marianne Leuzinger-Bohleber of Frankfurt, has worked with them differently. Taking their psychometric properties, as established by our PRP-II group in San Francisco and carried a good deal further by Huber and Klug in Munich, as a base, Leuzinger-Bohleber and her many colleagues have incorporated the SPC as a central instrument in their long-term very comprehensive retrospective study of the courses and outcomes of the analyses of 401 patients treated by the members of the German Psychoanalytic Association (DPV), whose treatments finished between the years 1990 and 1993. In chapter 9 Marianne Leuzinger-Bohleber and Tamara Fischmann describe in detail the structure of her research programme, which comprised intensive interviews with 194 former patients carried out by her analyst colleague research team members—in each case a team member unknown to the former patient and someone from a different city.

There were two taped interviews with the patient, meetings of the interviewer with a (research) supervisor, interviews (by a different interviewer) with the former analyst, and discussion meetings with the local research group, all focused on understanding the course and outcome of each therapy and the nature of changes achieved. In the course of each such study, SPC forms were filled out by the interviewing analyst; after thorough discussion within the research group in an effort to achieve a consensually shared understanding of the case, SPC forms were filled out independently by the research group members.

Embedded within the research programme in this way, Leuzinger-Bohleber indicated three ramifying uses of the SPC: (1) as a retrospectively assessed outcome measure in our originally conceptualized way, albeit in the absence of a research evaluation before the onset of the treatments, changes in SPC patterning over the course of the therapy could not be documented; (2) as a screening instrument filled out by the interviewing analyst between the two interviews with the former patient and thus used to detect areas of missing information to be elicited in the following interview; and (3) even as a diagnostic instrument—for example, using evidences of contradictory functioning and of difficulties in making reasonably confident assessments as examples of unintegrated and borderline psychic functioning. Three detailed case vignettes (one of a successful outcome, one of only a mixed outcome, and one with a clearly negative outcome) are included in the chapter, the last of these indicating how the SPC data contributed to the diagnostic formulation.

At this point, the members of this DPV research programme studying therapeutic courses and outcomes seem firmly committed to using the SPC as a major exploratory and assessment tool within their total programme. I would hope that as the scope of their already very ambitious programme enlarges to include new cases starting in psychoanalytic therapy, they will also include assessments prior to the start of the treatments in order to maximize the research values to be realized from before-and-after comparisons, especially if linked to information gathered during the course of the study concerning the conduct of the therapy and the nature of the research interventions. To the members of the DPV study, the SPC have come to epitomize the combination of conceptual, clinical, and empirical research study within a psychoanalytic framework that has from the start been their central avowed aim.

The first three parts of this volume are a look at the past: my own research past in my role in the development and conduct of our original 30-year-long Psychotherapy Research Project (PRP) of the Menninger Foundation and its successor, the Psychotherapy Research Project (PRP-II) in San Francisco, which created the SPC in the effort to further the findings and conclusions of the earlier project, and also my role through organizational activities within both the APsaA and the IPA to foster psychoanalytic research both in the United States and worldwide, focused of course on the creation of CAMP and my stewardship of its first decade. This has thus included the history of CAMP up to the point at which I relinquished its chairmanship and also of the—to me very gratifying—deployment of the SPC far beyond the confines of our initiating group, to the point where it has achieved a secure place in the panoply of useful outcome measures of the kinds of structural change that have been supposed to be the hallmark of the therapeutic changes brought about within expressive–interpretive psychoanalytic therapies.

The three chapters in Part IV represent the turn-around—the look to the future. Given how far we have come to this point in the shared psychoanalytic therapy research endeavour, what can we foretell about the future, or at least the near future? And within that frame, what can we project as the specific place of CAMP, now RAAPA (Research Associates of the American Psychoanalytic Association)–CAMP? Chapter 12, by Andrés Roussos, Wilma Bucci, and Bernard Maskit, squarely addresses this last question. The question that CAMP was specifically created to address is posed as the specific focus of the chapter: "The lack of a shared database is a major obstacle to the development of psychoanalytic research." I would only add that at this point it may well be *the* major obstacle. In the paragraph prior to that statement, the authors indicate some of the basis for their stand: "Recorded clinical and quasi-clinical material exists in many different sites, with different owners, different formats, and different technologies. Scientific goals and administration of the sites vary widely, with no generally accepted standards for organizing and preserving the data or monitoring their use . . ." and so on. And in the paragraph following their statement, they indicate the consequences of this state of affairs. In the IPA *Open Door Review* (Fonagy, et al., 1999, 2002), a worldwide survey of process and outcome studies of psychoanalytic therapies, "there is, however, no discussion of interaction among the various approaches, no indicators of the extent to which different groups used the same source material or how one study might relate to another *so as to build a coherent field*" (ital. added) . . . and so on.

This, of course, is precisely the problem that CAMP was created to address in bringing together initially the 16 different process-and-outcome psychoanalytic therapy research study groups with whose work I was acquainted at the time (1989–90) in an effort to focus the deployment of their concepts and instruments on the same shared database so that convergences and divergences could be contrasted and compared—and with the hope of a consensual, complementary coming-together. How and why CAMP could never assemble the resources to try to carry out this overarching task is recounted in my own autobiographic presentation in this volume (chapter 4).

The task today is a quantum leap more daunting. There has been not only an explosion of therapy research groups around the world (documented quite thoroughly in the *Open Door Review*) and a proliferation of separate process measures to be encompassed within such a comparative study programme, but also, as I have stated, eight distinct outcome measures that I know of (devised in both the United States and in Europe), all geared to the assessment of structural change beyond the large array of the earlier measures of symptom change and change in manifest behaviour patterns.

What Roussos and his colleagues add, importantly, to these considerations is the most thorough overview and detailing. The task they set—what they modestly call "housekeeping issues"—is the creation of a system with the capacity to include and interconnect clinical and quasi-clinical data sources while building in mechanisms and standards for protecting the privacy of all participants, including patients and therapists, as well as protecting the intellectual property of collaborating researchers. I have elsewhere called that the creation of the "infrastructure" for research, intrinsically unexciting in itself, as the authors say, but essential to the advance of the field and something that no one else will do, but only the analytic research community itself.

Roussos, Bucci, and Maskit do survey some of the major efforts in this direction to date, omitting only, from my perspective, the mention of the indefatigable efforts of Merton Gill, over his entire research lifetime, to bring about precisely what this chapter is all about (including Merton's participation in CAMP from the start as one of its most vociferous advocates), and they end their survey with the very sobering but all too true statement that "There is essentially no systematic way for researchers to know to what extent they are duplicating (on the same sample) or replicating (on different samples) work already done; and no systematic way to identify the gaps where new research can contribute most effectively."

What Roussos, Bucci, and Maskit propose in order to remedy this distressing situation is the creation of what they call "a clinical research library"—either a virtual library, meaning a centralized catalogue of what exists and where, with designated procedures and conditions for access, or, better yet, but all too Utopian perhaps, an actual physical library containing all the original source material—or perhaps a functional clinical research library that could incorporate both as much as possible. The authors then list the many issues that would need to be dealt with in order to bring such a library into being. There are the organizational and administrative issues, of locale, of institutional support, whether within the structure of psychoanalysis, the IPA, or a major university base, or some cooperative arrangement between such different entities; and the assemblage of the requisite financial resources that could guarantee to sustain this expensive effort with the need for librarians, data bank managers, and so on.

Then there are the methodological and technical issues involved in creating the database and platform for electronic cataloguing, the various kinds of formatting involved, including now obsolete systems like reel-to-reel tapes, the needs to reformat periodically, not only to get out of no longer usable systems but to guard against deterioration of data—really, the need for different computers, different platforms, and different word processing programs, and of course the need to maintain separate master copies.

Finally, there are the legal and ethical issues involved in maintaining access to these data files by qualified researchers while at the same time safeguarding the confidentiality and privacy of the therapy participants, creating uniform standards for informed consent, procedures for evaluating the credentials of research applicants, safeguarding email transmissions, perhaps with code encryption, protection of intellectual rights, and legal consultation over setting up issues of ownership, access, rights to privacy—and all of this complicated by the fact that data originate in different national jurisdictions, with different governing laws.

Clearly, all of this is a most formidable and sobering array of tasks that Roussos and his colleagues have spelled out in such detail. They say that now, however, *is* the time to carry forward the vision that they say I articulated in establishing the CAMP framework—though none of us involved in the creation of CAMP foresaw at all the magnitude of this undertaking, so vital to the advance of psychoanalytic therapy research, a magnitude now multiplied several fold because of the transnational nature of the proposed edifice—due, as they say, because we are, "now at a time of a new and expanding generation of clinical research, providing the basic data, the recognition of professional responsibility, and the impetus for new generations in scientific methods to meet the goals of the field". May we collectively be up to this task, which our collective labours to this point now make incumbent upon us.

George Klumpner, in chapter 11, prepared with technical help from his grandson Thomas, presents yet another avenue of psychoanalytic therapy research study. George has over several decades been an active participant and contributor to the ongoing dialogue in the American Psychoanalytic Association's Committee on Scientific Activities, its Fund for Psychoanalytic Research, and then CAMP. From that vantage point, and as a solitary investigator in the fashion that was so characteristic of natural science research before the advent of modern-day complex technology, multidisciplinary teams, and generous public and private funding, George has, over the years, with the possibilities of computer programming, gradually created what he calls the Open Access Project (chapter 11). In his words, it provides for "quantitative studies of psychoanalytic transcripts using data that can be safely shared and processed with a personal computer".

Basically, this project consists of three computer programs: (1) the Data Extractor, which extracts counts of words or phrases from the verbalizations of the patient, the therapist, and various combinations or interactions of the two; (2) the Data Explorer, which creates spreadsheets that can focus on frequencies of specific words or phrases, and their various alternations or interactions; and (3) the Data Analyser, which can regroup, re-sort, and summarize data by any variable in the spreadsheets. Klumpner gives a detailed exposition of just how all this works, the kinds of findings that can be derived, and the kinds of research questions that can be pursued either within this instrument or in other contexts. Added to the armamentarium of already existing process-and-outcome measures, this Open Access Project introduces a new instrument, a new perspective for the pursuit of research questions, either by itself or as an adjunct to other methods of inquiry, either as a component of other studies or as a source of questions that can be then explored in other ways.

From Klumpner's perspective this Open Access Project provides a way to locate where, and how frequently, words and word sequences are used, and then to generate psychoanalytically interesting hypotheses that can be tested both inside and outside the system, all of it in a way that can be safely shared and widely distributed for study because absolutely no personal identification is possible, and all of this using a database—extracted from transcripts of therapy sessions—that can be easily manipulated and studied by anyone using a personal computer. As such, it presents an additional tool for psychoanalytic therapy research, the potential usefulness of which has yet to be explored.

Finally chapter 13, by Wilma Bucci, is a very comprehensive overview of psychoanalytic therapy research work to date and her ambitious but rigorously thought-out projections to advance these endeavours into their logical future.

Bucci's retrospective discussion is built around the structure of my own review of the historical unfolding of psychoanalytic therapy research under the title, "The Generations of Psychotherapy Research" (Wallerstein, 2001b). In that article I identified four generations, both in terms of their temporal onset and also in terms of degree of conceptual and methodological sophistication: (1) the first generation, dating as far back as 1917 and actually extending for a half-century to 1968, consists of retrospective studies, basically simple counts by treating clinicians (or clinics) of percentages of completed cases, improved or not, according to (usually) unspecified criteria, and without individual clinical detail or supporting evidence; (2) the second generation, starting in the 1950s, includes prospective studies carried out by research teams independent of the treating clinicians, according to consensually agreed assessment criteria, and, in some cases, with testable predictions to expectable outcomes; (3) the third generation, starting during the same period as the second generation, adds in efforts to delineate therapeutic process measures (as they were available during that time period) that could begin to illuminate how the achieved outcome changes were brought about; and (4) the fourth generation, actually the original CAMP agenda, which integrates process-and-outcome studies employing the instruments in each category created by the different active psychoanalytic therapy research groups around the country (and even around the world) on a shared database of audiotaped and transcribed therapeutic sessions—to be studied comparatively for convergences and divergences in their assessments of the identical clinical material. This fourth generation was, at the time of my article, still a plan and not yet an actuality.

Bucci's review of these four generations adds in the placement of additional studies in these several categories beyond those that were available to me at the time. The only alteration I would suggest is in the categorization of our own Psychotherapy Research Project (PRP) of the Menninger Foundation (which I had placed into the third generation). One can emphasize different aspects of the findings and conclusions of PRP. From one perspective they could be seen, as Bucci does, as "essentially null with respect to *specificity* of psychoanalytic technique and outcome" (italics added). From our side, what we emphasized was that deep-seated structural change in personality organization, as we assessed it, came about not only in the successful expressive–interpretive psychoanalytic therapies, in accordance with our expectations, but also in about half of the successful non-interpretive, non-insight-aiming, more supportive psychoanalytically conceptualized therapies, where according to the conventional wisdom it had decidedly not been expected. To us, this opened up both the need to replicate this important finding with a better-defined metric for structural change (the SPC, which we created in PRP-II), but also the opportunity to determine the concomitant therapeutic processes that bring about structural changes in non-interpretive therapies not geared to the uncovering of intrapsychic conflict. This we would see as a probe aimed directly at the specificity issue raised by Bucci.

However, the main thrust of Bucci's chapter takes things beyond what *was* done in the past to what *can*, and *should*, be done in the future. She notes properly that my description of the four generations of psychotherapy research is focused primarily on outcome research, which does indeed have a history going back in embryonic form to the second decade of the last century and basically includes—in the third generation—only process research studies created in an era prior to the acceptance of audiotaped sessions as a permissible accompaniment to psychoanalytic treatments (see Wallerstein & Sampson, 1971, for a detailed discussion of this issue) and before the development of computer programs equipped for the micro-analytic study of audiotaped and transcribed verbatim therapeutic sessions.

It is here, then, that Bucci creates her complementary framework, spelling out in detail what she calls four generations of process research: (1) the first generation: the development of a range of objective process measures and establishment of their reliability and validity, mostly accomplished in the decade of the 1970s; (2) the second generation: the application of some of these measures to shared data sets, both in the July 1985 Workshop on Empirical Research in Ulm, Germany (Dahl, Kächele, & Thomä, 1988), a meeting of American and German psychotherapy researchers, each applying their own conceptual frame and their own instruments to a shared database, and also, to a partial extent, in the regular CAMP meetings, as described in chapter 4; (3) the third generation, now emerging, that integrates therapy research with clinical perspectives, described in detail around two currently ongoing projects, that of the Institute for Psychoanalytic Training and research (IPTAR) in New York, headed by Norbert Freedman, and that of the Argentine Psychoanalytic Association (APA), in collaboration with the Universidad de Belgrano, both in Buenos Aires, headed by Clara Maria López Moreno; and (4) the projected fourth generation, the inclusion of psychoanalytically conceived outcome measures that assess structural changes in the ego, of which the SPC, around which so much of the material in this volume is based, is but one exemplar.

In fulfilment, then, of the kind of psychoanalytic therapy research plan towards which this entire volume is pointing, this new fourth-generation research as projected in Bucci's chapter, would comprise the following elements: (1) an array of both micro-analytic (computer-assisted) process measures *and* structural change outcome measures—hopefully after time each set of measures amalgamated down to a smaller complementary group; (2) coordination with psychoanalytically informed clinical perspectives, including those of the therapist, the research group, and even the patient, either directly or as inferred from the text material—that is, multiple complementary perspectives; (3) ideally, within the framework of a psychoanalytic society–university collaboration, where the knowledge base and techniques of cognate disciplines of human intelligence and behaviour ranging from neuroscience to philosophy would interface with psychoanalytic perspectives and hypotheses; and (4) even beyond ideally, in a Panglossian Utopian world with the kind of centralized virtual or actually physical psychoanalytic research library outlined in chapter 12, as the repository for accumulating data and findings, which can then truly serve incrementally towards the continuing growth of psychoanalysis as a science as well as an art.

If this volume can serve as a guidepost to that vision, then its importance will far transcend its marking the life and work of one individual who has played his part in bringing that possibility to this present point.

Notes

1. During the copy-editing stage for this volume I learned, sadly, of Hartvig Dahl's death. The paragraph becomes then, unhappily, a tribute to a lost colleague.

2. Apart from myself, the group originally comprised Kathryn N. DeWitt, Dianna E. Hartley, Saul E. Rosenberg, and Nathan J. Zilberg and, later, Daniel Weiss and then Constance Milbrath. It is now headed by Constance Milbrath and Kathryn N. DeWitt.

SCIENTIFIC BIBLIOGRAPHY

Robert S. Wallerstein

1946

1. The possible relationship of the pleuropneumonia-like organisms to Reiter's disease, rheumatoid arthritis and ulcerative colitis (with Bert Vallee & Louis Turner). *Journal of Infectious Disease, 79,* 134–140, 1946.

1949

2. Longevity of Schistosoma Mansoni: Observations based on a case. *American Journal of Tropical Medicine, 29,* 717–722, 1949.
3. Polymyxin effective in the treatment of Pyocyaneus Sepsis: Report of a case (with Emanuel B. Schoenbach). *Journal of Mt. Sinai Hospital, 16,* 190–196, 1949.
4. Hepatosplenomegaly and liver damage in Graves' disease (with Weldon J. Walker). *Annals of Internal Medicine, 31,* 904–912, 1949.

1950

5. Infectious mononucleosis: With hepatic dysfunction, thrombocytopenic purpura, and isolated peripheral nerve palsy (with Leonard Madison). *American Practitioner, 1,* 624–629, 1950.

6. The role of antibodies in insulin resistance: Report of a case (with Robert M. Berne). *Journal of Mt. Sinai Hospital, 17,* 102–111, 1950.
7. Thrombophlebitis secondary to acute respiratory infection. *Journal of Mt. Sinai Hospital, 17,* 176–182, 1950.

1951

8. Multiple myeloma without demonstrable bone lesions. *American Journal of Medicine, 10,* 325–333, 1951.
9. Treatment of the psychosis of general paresis with combined sodium amytal and psychotherapy: Report of a case. *Psychiatry, 14,* 307–317, 1951. Reprinted in: Louis Diamant (Ed.), *Case Studies in Psychopathology* (pp. 34–49). Columbus, OH: Charles E. Merrill, 1971.

1954

10. Some psychosomatic considerations in Addison's disease: Report of a case (with Richard L. Sutherland & Joseph Lyons). *Psychosomatic Medicine, 16,* 67–76, 1954.
11. Some psychosomatic considerations in dystrophia myotonica: Report of a case (with Sidney Rubin). *Journal of Nervous and Mental Disease, 120,* 277–281, 1954.
12. Unusual wheal reaction in a tattoo: Psychosomatic aspects (with Norman I. Graff). *Psychosomatic Medicine, 16,* 505–515, 1954.
13. Perspectives of the Research Department of The Menninger Foundation (with Gardner Murphy). *Bulletin of the Menninger Clinic, 18,* 223–231, 1954.

1956

14. Comparative study of treatment methods for chronic alcoholism: The Alcoholism Research Project at Winter VA Hospital. *American Journal of Psychiatry, 113,* 228–233, 1956.
15. The Psychotherapy Research Project of The Menninger Foundation (with Lewis L. Robbins, Helen D. Sargent, & Lester Luborsky). *Bulletin of the Menninger Clinic, 20,* 221–278, 1956.

1957

16. *Hospital Treatment of Alcoholism: A Comparative Experimental Study* (with John W. Chotlos, & Merrill B. Friend, Donald W. Hammersley, Ellis A. Perlswig, & G. M. Winship). Menninger Monograph Series, No. 11. New York: Basic Books, 1957.

1958

17. *The Teaching and Learning of Psychotherapy* (with Rudolf Ekstein). New York: Basic Books, 1958. Revised and reprinted, New York: International Universities Press, 1972.
18. Psychologic factors in chronic alcoholism. *Annals of Internal Medicine, 48,* 114–122, 1958.
19. The Psychotherapy Research Project of The Menninger Foundation: Second report. Further notes on design and concepts (with Lewis L. Robbins). *Bulletin of the Menninger Clinic, 22,* 117–125, 1958.
20. Pain, fear and anxiety: A study of their interrelationships (with Ishak Ramzy). *Psychoanalytic Study of the Child, 13,* 147–189, 1958.

1959

21. The research strategy and tactics of the Psychotherapy Research Project of The Menninger Foundation and the problems of controls (with Lewis L. Robbins). In: Eli A. Rubinstein & Morris B. Parloff (Eds.), *Research in Psychotherapy* (pp. 27–43). Washington, DC: American Psychological Association, 1959.
22. *GAP Report #42.* Some observations on controls in psychiatric research. Formulated by the Committee on Research (Dr. Wallerstein, Member), 533–623, 1959.

1960

23. The Psychotherapy Research Project of The Menninger Foundation: Third report. Helen D. Sargent & the Psychotherapy Research Project. *Bulletin of the Menninger Clinic, 24,* 159–163, 1960.
24. The Psychotherapy Research Project of The Menninger Foundation: Third report. Initial studies (with Lewis L. Robbins). *Bulletin of the Menninger Clinic, 24,* 164–189, 1960.
25. The Psychotherapy Research Project of The Menninger Foundation: Third report. Termination studies (with Bernard H. Hall). *Bulletin of the Menninger Clinic, 24,* 190–214, 1960.

1961

26. Report of the Psychotherapy Research Project of The Menninger Foundation, January 1954–July 1961. *International Mental Health Research Newsletter, 3* (December), 12–15, 1961.
27. A estrategia e a tatica de investigacao o projeto de pesquisa em psicoterapia da Menninger Foundation e o problema de controles (with Lewis L. Robbins). *Arquivos da Clinica Pinel, 1,* 166–186, 1961 [Portuguese].

1963

28. The problem of the assessment of change in psychotherapy. *International Journal of Psychoanalysis, 44,* 31–41, 1963.

1964

29. Therapist and patient (with Rudolf Ekstein). In: Mary R. Haworth (Ed.), *Child Psychotherapy* (pp. 437–445). New York: Basic Books, 1964. Reprinted from: *The Teaching and Learning of Psychotherapy*. New York: Basic Books, 1958.
30. The role of prediction in theory building in psychoanalysis. *Journal of the American Psychoanalytic Association, 12,* 675–691, 1964.

1965

31. The goals of psychoanalysis: A survey of analytic viewpoints. *Journal of the American Psychoanalytic Association, 13,* 748–770, 1965.
32. Thyroid "hot spots": A psychophysiological study (with Philip S. Holzman, Harold M. Voth, & Nathaniel Uhr). *Psychosomatic Medicine, 27,* 508–523, 1965.

1966

33. The Psychotherapy Research Project of The Menninger Foundation: An overview at the midway point. In: Louis A. Gottschalk & Arthur H. Auerbach (Eds.), *Methods of Research in Psychotherapy* (pp. 500–516). New York: Appleton-Century-Crofts, 1966.
34. The current state of psychotherapy: Theory, practice, research. *Journal of the American Psychoanalytic Association, 14,* 183–225, 1966.
35. *GAP Report #63.* Psychiatric research and the assessment of change. Formulated by the Committee on Research (Dr. Wallerstein, Chairman), pp. 347–479, 1966.
36. Book review of *Mind and Destiny: A Social Approach to Psychoanalytic Theory,* by Robert Seidenberg & Hortense S. Cochrane. *Psychoanalytic Quarterly, 35,* 437–441, 1966.

1967

37. Development and metapsychology of the defense organization of the ego: Panel Report. *Journal of the American Psychoanalytic Association, 15,* 130–149, 1967.
38. An approach to quantitative problems of psychoanalytic research (with Helen D. Sargent, Lolafaye Coyne, & Wayne H. Holtzman). *Journal of*

Clinical Psychology, 23, 243–291, 1967. (Also published as a separate *Monograph Supplement, No. 23,* July 1967.)

39. Reconstruction and mastery in the transference psychosis. *Journal of the American Psychoanalytic Association, 15,* 551–583, 1967 (pp. 242–255). Reprinted in condensed form in: Albert C. Cain (Ed.), *Survivors of Suicide.* Springfield, IL: Charles C Thomas, 1972.
40. Report of Ad Hoc Committee on Central Fact-Gathering Data of the American Psychoanalytic Association (with David A. Hamburg, Grete L. Bibring, Charles Fisher, Alfred H. Stanton, Harry I. Weinstock, & Ernest Haggard). *Journal of the American Psychoanalytic Association, 15,* 841–861, 1967.
41. Terapeuta e paziente: Probleme di apprendimento (with Rudolf Ekstein). In: Mary R. Haworth (Ed.), *Psicoterapia Infantile* (pp. 559–571). Roma: Armando Armando Editore, 1967 [Italian].

1968

42. Prediction in psychotherapy research: A method for the transformation of clinical judgments into testable hypotheses (with Helen D. Sargent, Leonard Horwitz, & Ann Appelbaum). *Psychological Issues, Monograph No. 21, Vol. 6,* 1–146, 1968.
43. The challenge of the Community Mental Health Movement to psychoanalysis. *American Journal of Psychiatry, 124,* 1049–1056, 1968.
44. A talk about the Psychotherapy Research Project of The Menninger Foundation. *Nederlands Nijdschrift voor de Psychologie en haar Grensgebieden, 23,* 137–164, 1968.
45. The Psychotherapy Research Project of The Menninger Foundation: A semi-final view. In: John M. Shlien (Ed.), *Research in Psychotherapy,* Vol. 3 (pp. 584–605). Washington, DC, American Psychological Association, 1968.
46. Alcoholism: Symptom or disease? Discussion of "A multidisciplinary approach to the treatment of alcoholism", by Ruth Fox. *International Journal of Psychiatry, 5,* 59–65, 1968.
47. Discussion of "Some obstacles to the development of research in psychoanalysis", by George Engel. *Journal of the American Psychoanalytic Association, 16,* 215–222, 1968.
48. Discussion of "On affect control", by Andrew Peto. *International Journal of Psychoanalysis, 49,* 474–476, 1968.

1969

49. Introduction to Panel on Psychoanalysis and Psychotherapy: The relationship of psychoanalysis to psychotherapy—Current issues. *International Journal of Psychoanalysis, 50,* 117–126, 1969.

50. Psychoanalysis and sociology: Articulations and applications (with Neil J. Smelser). *International Journal of Psychoanalysis, 59,* 693–710, 1969. Reprinted in: Neil J. Smelser, *The Social Edges of Psychoanalysis* (pp. 3–35). Berkeley, Los Angeles, & London: University of California Press, 1998.
51. Introduzione al "Panel" su psicoanalisi e psicoterapia: Rapporti fra psicoanálisis e psicoterapia: Probleme attuali. *Rivista di Psicoanalisi, 15,* 213–230, 1969 [Italian].

1970

52. Thyroid "hot spots": Their relationship to life stress (with Harold M. Voth, Philip S. Holzman, & Jerome B. Katz). *Psychosomatic Medicine, 32,* 561–568, 1970.

1971

53. Issues in research in the psychoanalytic process (with Harold Sampson). *International Journal of Psychoanalysis, 52,* 11–50, 1971. Reprinted in: J. Matarazzo, A. Bergin, J. Frank, P. J. Lang, I. M. Marks, H. Strupp (Eds.), *Psychotherapy* (pp. 26–63). Chicago–New York: Aldine–Atherton, 1972. Also reprinted in: Stefan de Schill & Serge Lebovici (Eds.), *The Challenge to Psychoanalysis and Psychotherapy* (pp. 154–178). London & Philadelphia: Jessica Kingsley, 1999.
54. The role of research training: How much, what kind, how? In: Robert R. Holt (Ed.), *New Horizon for Psychotherapy: Autonomy as a Profession* (pp. 241–260). New York: International Universities Press, 1971.
55. Issues in research in the psychoanalytic process (condensation) (with Harold Sampson). In: Irwin M. Marcus (Ed.), *Currents in Psychoanalysis* (pp. 265–302). New York: International Universities Press, 1971.
56. Introduccion a la mesa redonda sobre psicoanálisis y psicoterapia. La relacion entre el psicoanálisis y la psicoterapia. Problemas actuales. *Revista de Psicoanálisis, 28,* 25–49, 1971 [Spanish].

1972

57. Transactional psychotherapy. In: Daniel Offer & Daniel X. Freedman (Eds.), *Modern Psychiatry and Clinical Research* (pp. 120–135). New York: Basic Books, 1972.
58. The futures of psychoanalytic education. *Journal of the American Psychoanalytic Association, 20,* 591–606, 1972.
59. Discussion (with Harold Sampson) of "Some empirical and conceptual bases for coordinated research in psychotherapy." In: Allen E.

Bergin & Hans H. Strupp (Eds.), *Changing Frontiers in the Science of Psychotherapy* (pp. 292–300, 444–446). Chicago: Aldine–Atherton, 1972.

60. Preface to "Psychotherapy and psychoanalysis: Final report of The Menninger Foundation's Psychotherapy Research Project", by Otto F. Kernberg, Esther D. Burstein, Lolafaye Coyne, Ann Appelbaum, Leonard Horwitz, & Harold Voth. *Bulletin of the Menninger Clinic, 36,* Nos. 1/2, vii–x, 1972.
61. Discussion of "Radical and militant youth: A study of Columbia undergraduates", by Robert S. Liebert. *Psychoanalytic Forum, 4,* 52–58, 1972.
62. Discussion of "Supervision by tape: A new method of case supervision", by John A. Lindon. *Psychoanalytic Forum, 4,* 436–442, 1972.
63. *Las Nuevas Dirrecciones de la Psicoterapia. Teoria, Practica, Investigacion.* Buenos Aires: Paidos, 1972 [Spanish].

1973

64. Psychoanalytic perspectives on the problem of reality. *Journal of the American Psychoanalytic Association, 21,* 5–33, 1973.
65. Discussion of "On being sane in insane places", by David L. Rosenhan. *Bulletin of the Menninger Clinic, 37,* 526–530, 1973. Reprinted in: H. H. Strupp, A. E. Bergin, P. J. Lang, I. M. Marks, J. D. Matarazzo, & G. R. Patterson (Eds.), *Psychotherapy and Behavior Change* (pp. 48–52). Chicago: Aldine Publ. Co., 1974.
66. Discussion of "Psychoanalytic implications of reactions of soldiers to the Six-Day War", by Ruth Jaffe. In: Heinrich Z. Winnik, Rafael Moses, & Mortimer Ostow (Eds.), *Psychological Bases of War* (pp. 103–110). New York: Quadrangle Books, & Jerusalem: Jerusalem Academic Press, 1973.
67. *Insegnamento e Apprendimento della Psicoterapia* (with Rudolf Ekstein). Presentazione de Enzo Codignola. Turin: Editore Boringhieri, 1973 [Italian].

1974

68. Herbert S. Gaskill and the history of American psychoanalysis in American psychiatry. *The Denver Psychoanalytic Society Newsletter, 1* (No. 3), December, 1–9, 1974.
69. Foreword to: David W. Allen, *The Fear of Looking: Or Scopophilic–Exhibitionistic Conflicts* (pp. vii–viii). Charlottesville, VA: University Press of Virginia, 1974.
70. Foreword to: Leonard Horwitz, *Clinical Prediction in Psychotherapy* (pp. xiii–xviii). New York: Jason Aronson, 1974.
71. Perspectivas psicoanaliticas quanti ao problema da realidade. *Revista Brasileira de Psicanalise, 8,* 223–253, 1974 [Portuguese].

1975

72. *Psychotherapy and Psychoanalysis: Theory, Practice, Research.* New York: International Universities Press, 1975.
73. Shirley Cooper, M.S., President, American Orthopsychiatric Association. *American Journal of Orthopsychiatry, 45,* 324–327, 1975.

1976

74. Psychoanalysis as a science: Its present status and its future tasks. In: Merton M. Gill & Philip S. Holzman (Eds.), *Psychology versus Metapsychology: Psychoanalytic Essays in Memory of George S. Klein. Psychological Issues, Monograph No. 36, Vol. 9* (pp. 198–228), 1976.
75. Summary of the Sixth Pre-Congress Conference on Training: The contribution of child analysis to the training in adult analysis. *International Journal of Psychoanalysis, 57,* 198–205, 1976.
76. Introduction to Symposium on "Ethics, moral values and psychological interventions." *International Review of Psycho-Analysis, 3,* 369–372, 1976.
77. Foreword to: Mardi J. Horowitz, *Stress Response Syndromes* (pp. xiii–xvi). New York: Jason Aronson, 1976.

1977

78. Psychoanalysis as a profession and psychoanalysis as a science: A stocktaking. In: Stanley Goodman (Ed.), *Psychoanalytic Education and Research: The Current Situation and Future Possibilities* (pp. 307–326). New York: International Universities Press, 1977.
79. Psychic energy reconsidered: Introduction. *Journal of the American Psychoanalytic Association, 25,* 529–535, 1977.
80. Psychotherapy research: One paradigm. In: Peter Ostwald (Ed.), *Communication and Social Interaction* (pp. 189–202). New York: Grune & Stratton, 1977.
81. Foreword (with Herbert S. Gaskill) to: *Psychoanalytic Education and Research: The Current Situation and Future Possibilities* (pp. ix–xvi). New York: International Universities Press, 1977.
82. *Handledning och utbildning i psykoterapi* (with Rudolf Ekstein). Svensk upplaga Bokforlaget Natur och Kultur. Centraltrycheriet AB, Boras, 1977 [Swedish].
83. A contribucao de analise de criencas para o treino de analise de adultos. *Revista Brasileira de Psicanalise, 11,* 225–242, 1977 [Portuguese].

1978

84. Perspectives on psychoanalytic training around the world. *International Journal of Psychoanalysis, 59,* 477–503, 1978.
85. The mental health professions: Conceptualization and reconceptualization of a new discipline. *International Review of Psycho-Analysis, 5,* 377–392, 1978.

1979

86. Book review of *Toward the Validation of Dynamic Psychotherapy,* by David H. Malan. *Journal of the American Psychoanalytic Association, 27,* 276–279, 1979.
87. Réflexions sur le Symposium. In: Edward D. Joseph & Daniel Widlöcher (Eds.), *L'identité du psychoanalyste* (pp. 273–284). Paris: Presses Universitaires de France, 1979 [French].

1980

88. Psychoanalysis and academic psychiatry: Bridges. *Psychoanalytic Study of the Child, 35,* 419–448, 1980.
89. International Scientific Colloquium on the Significance of Insight in Psychoanalytic Theory and Practice. *Bulletin of the Hampstead Clinic, 3,* 153–156, 181–183, 186–187, 192–193, 1980.
90. Foreword to: Donald P. Spence, *Narrative Truth and Historical Truth: Meaning and Interpretation in Psychoanalysis* (pp. 9–14). New York: Norton, 1980.
91. Doctorat en santé mentale: Une création de l'Université de Californie. *Psychoanalyse à l'Université, 5* (No. 18), 343–364, 1980 [French].
92. Diagnosis revisited (and revisited): The case of hysteria and the hysterical personality. *International Journal of Psychoanalytic Psychotherapy, 8,* 533–547, 1980–81.

1981

93. *Becoming a Psychoanalyst: A Study of Psychoanalytic Supervision* (Editor) New York: International Universities Press, 1981.
94. The bipolar self: Discussion of alternative perspectives. *Journal of the American Psychoanalytic Association, 29,* 377–394, 1981.
95. The psychoanalyst's life: Expectations, vicissitudes, and reflections. *International Review of Psycho-Analysis, 8,* 285–298, 1981.
96. International Scientific Colloquium on the Superego: Its Early Roots and the Road from Outer to Inner Conflict as Seen in Psychoanalysis. *Bulletin of the Hampstead Clinic, 4,* 99–101, 108–110, 1981.

97. L'étude psychoanalytique de la réalité. In: *Dix Ans de Psychoanalyse en Amerique (Anthologie du Journal of the American Psychoanalytic Association)* (pp. 263–286). Paris: Presses Universitaires de France, 1981 [French].

1982

98. *Psychotherapy: Impact on Psychoanalytic Training* (Editor, with Edward D. Joseph). New York: International Universities Press, 1982.
99. Analyse d'enfants et analyse d'adultes: Possibilités d'intégration. In: Serge Lebovici & Albert Solnit (Eds.), *La formation du psychoanalyste* (pp. 239–245). Paris: Presses Universitaires de France, 1982 [French].
100. Book review of *The Psychoanalytic Vision: A Controversial Reappraisal of the Freudian Revolution*, by Reuben Fine. *International Review of Psycho-Analysis, 9*, 360–363, 1982.
101. Report of the fund for psychoanalytic research's first five years: Accomplishments, problems and prospects. *Journal of the American Psychoanalytic Association, 30*, 539–549, 1982.

1983

102. Reality and its attributes as psychoanalytic concepts: An historical overview. *International Review of Psycho-Analysis, 10*, 125–144, 1983.
103. Self psychology and "classical" psychoanalytic psychology: The nature of their relationship. In: Arnold Goldberg (Ed.), *The Future of Psychoanalysis* (pp. 19–63). New York: International Universities Press, 1983. Reprinted in: *Psychoanalysis and Contemporary Thought, 6*, 553–595, 1983.
104. Some thoughts about insight and psychoanalysis. *Israel Journal of Psychiatry and Allied Professions, 20*, 33–43, 1983.
105. The Topeka Institute and the future of psychoanalysis. *Bulletin of the Menninger Clinic, 47*, 497–518, 1983.
106. Self psychology and "classical" psychoanalytic psychology—The nature of their relationship: A review and overview (condensation). In: Joseph D. Lichtenberg & Samuel Kaplan (Eds.), *Reflections on Self Psychology* (pp. 313–337). Hillsdale, NJ: Analytic Press, 1983.
107. Defenses, defense mechanisms and the structure of the mind. *Journal of the American Psychoanalytic Association, Supplement 31*, 201–225, 1983. Reprinted in: Harold P. Blum (Ed.), *Defense and Resistance: Historical Perspective and Current Concepts* (pp. 201–225). New York: International Universities Press, 1985.
108. Reflections on the identity of the psychoanalyst. In: Edward D. Joseph & Daniel Widlöcher (Eds.), *The Identity of the Psychoanalyst* (pp. 265–276). New York: International Universities Press, 1983.
109. Book review of *Basic Principles and Techniques in Short-Term Dynamic Psy-*

chotherapy, ed. by Habib Davanloo. *Journal of the American Psychoanalytic Association, 31,* 780–784, 1983.

110. Personal tribute to Anna Freud. *Bulletin of the Hampstead Clinic, 6,* 95–98, 1983.
111. Historical perspective. In: Lydia Temoshok, Craig Van Dyke, & Leonard S. Zegans (Eds.), *Emotions in Health and Illness: Theoretical and Research Foundations* (pp. 3–5). New York: Grune & Stratton, 1983.
112. Tribute to Selma Fraiberg. *Dialogue: A Journal of Psychoanalytic Perspectives, 6,* 5, 1983.
113. International Scientific Colloquium on Fantasy and Reality in the Organisation of the Oedipal Situation. *Bulletin of the Hampstead Clinic, 6,* 147, 148, 154–6, 160, 164, 166, 167–168, 177–178, 179, 181, 183, 184, 185, 186, 187, 189, 191, 192, 194, 196, 205, 206–212, 217–218, 1983.

1984

114. *Personality and Brief Psychotherapy* (with Mardi Horowitz, Charles Marmar, Janice Krupnick, Nancy Wilner, & Nancy Kaltreider). New York: Basic Books, 1984.
115. Psychoanalysis and long-term dynamic psychotherapy. In: Howard H. Goldman (Ed.), *Review of General Psychiatry* (pp. 514–522). Los Altos, CA: Lange Medical Publications, 1984. Reprinted in: Howard H. Goldman (Ed.), *Review of General Psychiatry* (pp. 514–522). Singapore: Lange Medical Publications, Maruzen Asian Edition, 1984.
116. Anna Freud: Radical innovator and staunch conservative. *Psychoanalytic Study of the Child, 39,* 65–80, 1984.
117. The analysis of transference: A matter of emphasis or of theory reformulation? *Psychoanalytic Inquiry, 4,* 325–354, 1984.
118. Book review of *The Standing of Psychoanalysis,* by Brian A. Farrell. *NOUS, 18,* 534–541, 1984.
119. International Scientific Colloquium on the Role of Fantasy in the Adaptive Process. *Bulletin of the Hampstead Clinic, 7,* 166, 186, 189, 190, 192, 194, 195, 197, 198, 200, 204–211, 1984.

1985

120. The concept of psychic reality: Its meaning and value. *Journal of the American Psychoanalytic Association, 33,* 555–569, 1985.
121. *Changes in Analysts and in Their Training* (Editor). International Psychoanalytical Association, Monograph Series No. 4, 1985.
122. How does self psychology differ in practice. *International Journal of Psychoanalysis, 66,* 391–404, 1985. Reprinted in: Arnold Goldberg (Ed.), *Progress in Self Psychology, Vol. 2* (pp. 63–83). New York: Guilford Press, 1986.

123. Book review of *Mind, Brain, Body: Toward a Convergence of Psychoanalysis and Neurobiology*, by Morton F. Reiser. *International Journal of Psychoanalysis, 66*, 518–521, 1985.
124. The role of transference in the doctor–patient relationship. *Western Journal of Medicine, 142*, 681–682, 1985.
125. International Scientific Colloquium on Fantasy and Body Representation in Physical Disturbances. *Bulletin of the Anna Freud Centre, 8*, 111, 113, 114, 115, 117, 120, 122–123, 128–129, 130, 131, 134–135, 135–143, 143–144, 144, 148, 149, 1985.
126. Change and integration in psychoanalysis as a profession: Discussion. In: Calvin F. Settlage & Reed Brockbank (Eds.), *New Ideas in Psychoanalysis: The Process of Change in a Humanistic Science* (pp. 167–176). Hillsdale, NJ: Analytic Press, 1985.
127. Les changements intervenus chez les analystes et dans leur formation (Editor). *Association Psychanalytique Internationale.* Serie de Monographies, Numéro 4, 1985 [French].
128. Cambios en los analistas y en su formacion (Editor). *Asociacion Psicoanalitica Internacional.* Coleccion de Monografias, Numero 4, 1985 [Spanish].
129. Veränderungen bei Analytikern und in der Analytikerausbildung (Editor). *Internationalen Psychoanalytischen Vereinigung, 4*, 1985 [German].

1986

130. *Forty-Two Lives in Treatment: A Study of Psychoanalysis and Psychotherapy.* New York: Guilford Press, 1986.
131. Psychoanalysis as a science: A response to the new challenges. *Psychoanalytic Quarterly, 55*, 414–451, 1986.
132. The termination of the training analysis: The Institute's view. In: Arnold M. Cooper (Ed.), *The Termination of the Training Analysis: Process, Expectations, Achievements* (pp. 35–52). International Psychoanalytical Association, Monograph Series, No. 5, 1986.
133. The transformation of thought that the nuclear age requires: Can we achieve it? *Psychoanalytic Inquiry, 6*, 303–312, 1986.
134. Book review of *Psychoanalysis and Its Discontents*, by John E. Gedo. *Psychoanalytic Quarterly, 55*, 323–334, 1986.
135. Book review of *Severe Personality Disorders: Psychotherapeutic Strategies*, by Otto F. Kernberg. *Journal of the American Psychoanalytic Association, 34*, 711–722, 1986.
136. International Scientific Colloquium on Repeating, Reenactment and Verbalization in Different Stages of Development. *Bulletin of the Anna Freud Centre, 9*, 119, 121, 124, 126, 128, 130, 133, 134, 135–136, 137, 139, 140, 142–152, 1986.

137. La fin de l'analyse didactique: Le point de vue de l'Institut. In: Arnold M. Cooper (Ed.), *La Fin de l'Analyse Didactique: Le Processus. Les Prévisions. Les Réalisations* (pp. 37–56). Association Psychanalytique Internationale. Serie de Monographies, Numéro 5, 1986 [French].
138. La terminacion del analisis didactico: El punto de vista del Instituto. In: Arnold M. Cooper (Ed.), *La Terminacion del Analisis Didactico: El Proceso, Las Expectativas, Los Logros* (pp. 39–58). Asociacion Psicoanalitica Internacional. Coleccion de Monografias, Numero 5, 1986 [Spanish].
139. Die Beendigung der Lehranalyse: Die Sicht des Instituts. In: Arnold M. Cooper (Ed.), *Die Beendigung der Lehranalyse: Prozess, Erwartungen, was erreicht wurde* (pp. 36–53). Internationalen Psychoanalytischen Vereinigung, Vol. 5, 1986 [German].

1987

140. Maintenance of the psychoanalytic identity and functioning in a world in flux: The terms of the dialectic. In: Janine Chasseguet-Smirgel (Ed.), *Maintenance of the Psychoanalytic Identity and Functioning in a World in Flux* (pp. 21–61). International Psychoanalytical Association, Monograph Series, No. 6, 1987.
141. The assessment of analyzability and of analytic outcomes. In: Robert Langs & Editorial Board (Eds.), *The Yearbook of Psychoanalysis and Psychotherapy. Vol. 2* (pp. 416–426). New York: Gardner Press, 1987.
142. Book review of *The Psychoanalytic Process: Theory, Clinical Observation, and Empirical Research,* by Joseph Weiss, Harold Sampson, & the Mount Zion Psychotherapy Research Group. *International Journal of Psychoanalysis, 68,* 565–567, 1987.
143. Foreword to: Stanley S. Weiss, *The Teaching and Learning of Psychoanalysis: Selected Papers of Joan Fleming M.D.* (pp. vii–xii). New York: Guilford Press, 1987.
144. Foreword to: Helmut Thomä & Horst Kächele, *Psychoanalytic Practice I. Principles* (pp. v–viii). New York: Springer Verlag, 1987.
145. Foreword to: Joseph Sandler, *From Safety to Superego* (pp. x–xiv). New York: Guilford Press, 1987.
146. International Scientific Colloquium on Sexual and Gender Identity in Childhood, Adolescence and Adulthood. *Bulletin of the Anna Freud Centre, 10,* 215, 218, 221, 224, 227–228, 230–241, 1987.
147. El psicoanálisis como ciencia: Una respuesta a las nuevas criticas. *Revista de Psicoanálisis, 44,* 9–40, 1987 [Spanish].

1988

148. Psychoanalysis, psychoanalytic science, and psychoanalytic research: 1986. *Journal of the American Psychoanalytic Association, 36,* 3–30, 1988. Reprinted in: *Medelelingenblad, Nederlandse Vereniging voor psychoanalyse* (pp. 11–26), January 1987.
149. One psychoanalysis or many? *International Journal of Psychoanalysis, 69,* 5–21, 1988.
150. Commentary on "Psychoanalytic models of history: Freud and after". In: William McKinley Runyan (Ed.), *Psychology and Historical Interpretation* (pp. 157–165). New York & Oxford: Oxford University Press, 1988.
151. The continuum of reality, inner and outer. In: Harold P. Blum, Yale Kramer, Arlene K. Richards, & Arnold D. Richards (Eds.), *Fantasy. Myth, and Reality: Essays in Honor of Jacob A. Arlow, M.D.* (pp. 305–321). Madison, CT: International Universities Press, 1988.
152. Psychoanalysis in Nazi Germany: Historical and psychoanalytic lessons. *Psychoanalysis & Contemporary Thought, 11,* 351–370, 1988.
153. Psychoanalysis and psychotherapy: Relative roles reconsidered. *Annual of Psychoanalysis, 16,* 129–151, 1988.
154. Assessment of structural change in psychoanalytic therapy and research. *Journal of the American Psychoanalytic Association, Supplement 36,* 241–261, 1988. Reprinted in: Theodore Shapiro (Ed.), *The Concept of Structure in Psychoanalysis* (pp. 241–261). Madison, CT: International Universities Press, 1991.
155. International Scientific Colloquium on Playing: Its Role in Child and Adult Psychoanalysis. *Bulletin of the Anna Freud Centre, 11,* 168–182, 1988.
156. Une psychanalyse ou plusieurs? (compte rendu de l'exposé de Robert S. Wallerstein). *Revue Française de Psychanalyse, 52,* 1035–1039, 1988 [French].
157. Matter over mind (with David W. Allen & Irving Philips). *San Francisco Medicine.* December, 1988, 24–25.

1989

158. The Psychotherapy Research Project of The Menninger Foundation: An overview. *Journal of Consulting & Clinical Psychology, 57,* 195–205, 1989.
159. The future of psychoanalysis (with Edward M. Weinshel.) *Psychoanalytic Quarterly, 58,* 341–373, 1989.
160. Psychoanalysis and psychotherapy: An historical perspective (condensed version). In: Harold P. Blum, Edward M. Weinshel, & F. Robert Rodman (Eds.), *The Psychoanalytic Core: Essays in Honor of Leo Rangell.*

M.D. (pp. 109–146). Madison, CT: International Universities Press, 1989.

161. Psychoanalysis and psychotherapy: An historical perspective. *International Journal of Psychoanalysis, 70,* 563–591, 1989.
162. Follow-up in psychoanalysis: Clinical and research values. *Journal of the American Psychoanalytic Association, 37,* 921–942, 1989.
163. Book review of *Psychoanalysis: A Theory in Crisis* (condensed version), by Marshall Edelson. *New York Times Book Review Section.* Sunday, Feb. 26, p. 36, 1989.
164. Preface and greetings from the International Psychoanalytical Association. In: Arnaldo Novelletto (Ed.), *Italy in Psychoanalysis.* Institute of the Enciclopedia Italiana, 11–13, 1989.
165. International Scientific Colloquium on Self-Esteem and Shame: A Psychoanalytic Approach. *Bulletin of the Anna Freud Centre, 12,* 226, 228, 230, 232, 237, 241, 242, 245–259, 1989.
166. Foreword to: Lawrence H. Rockland, *Supportive Therapy: A Psychodynamic Approach* (pp. vii–x). New York: Basic Books, 1989.
167. Un psicoanálisis o muchos? *Libro Anual de Psicoanálisis 1988, 1–15,* 1989 [Spanish].
168. Introduzione e saluto della Associazione Psicoanalitica Internazionale. In: Arnaldo Novelletto (Ed.), *L'Italia Nella Psicoanalisi.* Istituto della Enciclopedia Italiana, 11–13, 1989 [Italian].
169. Eine Psychoanalyse oder viele? *Zeitschrift für psychoanalytische Theorie und Praxis.* Jahrgang, 4, 126–153, 1989 [German].
170. El self bipolar: Un examen de perspectivas alternativas. *Psico-analisis: Revista de la Asociacion Psicoanalitica de Buenos Aires, 11,* 219–234, 1989 [Spanish].
171. Uno o molte psicoanalisi. *Gli Argonauti, 43,* 253–277, 1989 [Italian].
172. Psychoanalysis and psychotherapy: An historical perspective. *The Japanese Journal of Psycho-Analysis, 33,* 71–86, 1989 [Japanese].
173. Psychoanalysis and psychotherapy: Relative roles reconsidered. *The Japanese Journal of Psycho-Analysis, 33,* 141–153, 1989 [Japanese].

1990

174. Psychoanalysis: The common ground. *International Journal of Psychoanalysis, 71,* 3–20, 1990.
175. The corrective emotional experience: Is reconsideration due? *Psychoanalytic Inquiry, 10,* 288–324, 1990.
176. Karl Menninger and Arthur Marshall: Comments on the early years of the Menninger School of Psychiatry. *The Psychohistory Review, 19,* 123–135, 1990.
177. Book review of *Freud Reappraised: A Fresh Look at Psychoanalytic Theory,*

by Robert R. Holt. *Journal of the American Psychoanalytic Association, 38,* 836–839, 1990.

178. Book review of *The Anatomy of Psychotherapy,* by Lawrence Friedman. *International Review of Psycho-Analysis, 17,* 510–513, 1990.
179. Foreword to: Lester Luborsky & Paul Crits-Christoph, *Understanding Transference: The CCRT Method* (pp. vii–x). New York: Basic Books, 1990.
180. Foreword to: Glen O. Gabbard, *Psychodynamic Psychiatry in Clinical Practice* (pp. ix–xi). Washington, DC: American Psychiatric Press, 1990.
181. International Scientific Colloquium on The Impact of Developmental Considerations on the Aims of Child and Adult Psychoanalysis. *Bulletin of the Anna Freud Centre, 13,* 123, 132, 136–137, 144–162, 1990.
182. Foreword to: Patrick Casement, *Learning from the Patient* (pp. xi–xiv). New York: Guilford Press, 1990.
183. Foreword to: Phyllis Tyson & Robert L. Tyson, *Psychoanalytic Theories of Development: An Integration* (pp. ix–xiv). New Haven, CT, & London: Yale University Press, 1990.
184. Zum Verhältnis von Psychoanalyse und Psychotherapie. Wiederaufnahme einer Diskussion. *Psyche, 44,* 967–994, 1990 [German].

1991

185. *The Doctorate in Mental Health: An Experiment in Mental Health Professional Education* (Editor). Lanham (MD), New York, & London: University Press of America, 1991.
186. Psychoanalytic education and research: A transformative proposal. *Psychoanalytic Inquiry, 11,* 196–226, 1991.
187. A conceptual analysis and strategy for assessing structural change (with Nathan J. Zilberg, Kathryn N. DeWitt, Dianna E. Hartley & Saul E. Rosenberg). *Psychoanalysis & Contemporary Thought, 14,* 317–342, 1991.
188. Scales of psychological capacities: Development of an assessment approach (with Kathryn N. DeWitt, Dianna E. Hartley, Saul E. Rosenberg, & Nathan J. Zilberg). *Psychoanalysis & Contemporary Thought, 14,* 343–361, 1991.
189. Psychoanalytic psychotherapies. In: *Encyclopedia of Human Biology, Vol. 6* (pp. 293–303). San Diego, CA: Academic Press, 1991.
190. The future of psychotherapy. *Bull. Menninger Clin., 55,* 421–443, 1991. Reprinted in: Stefan de Schill & Serge Lebovici (Eds.), *The Challenge to Psychoanalysis and Psychotherapy* (pp. 69–86). London & Philadelphia: Jessica Kingsley, 1991.
191. Book review of *Psychoanalysis: A Theory in Crisis,* by Marshall Edelson. *Journal of the American Psychoanalytic Association, 39,* 810–814, 1991.

192. Psychiatry, psychoanalysis and psychotherapy. *The Psychodynamic Newsletter: Master Clinician Series, 1*, 3–7, 1991.

193. Foreword to: Horacio Etchegoyen, *The Fundamentals of Psychoanalytic Technique* (pp. xxvii–xxxii). London & New York: Karnac, 1991.

194. International Scientific Colloquium on Maturational and Experiential Components in Character Formation. *Bulletin of the Anna Freud Centre, 14*, 213, 218, 223, 228, 231, 233–250, 1991

195. Observations on the personal myth and on theoretical perspectives in psychoanalysis. In: Peter Hartocollis & Ian Davidson Graham (Eds.), *The Personal Myth in Psychoanalysis* (pp. 357–372). Madison, CT: International Universities Press, 1991.

196. Letters to Editor, Psychoanalysis and psychotherapy (exchange with Merton Gill). *International Journal of Psychoanalysis, 72*, 161–164, 165–166, 1991.

197. Letter to Editor, Psychoanalysis: The common ground (exchange with Sidney & Esther Fine). *International Journal of Psychoanalysis, 72*, 166–167, 1991.

1992

198. *The Common Ground of Psychoanalysis* (Editor). Northvale, NJ, London: Jason Aronson, 1992.

199. The goals of psychoanalysis reconsidered. In: Alan Sugarman, Robert A. Nemiroff, & Daniel P. Greenson (Eds.), *The Technique and Practice of Psychoanalysis, 2, A Memorial Volume to Ralph R. Greenson* (pp. 63–90). Madison, CT: International Universities Press, 1992.

200. Comments on psychoanalysis, pure and applied. *International Review of Psycho-Analysis, 19* (Special), 1–6, 1992.

201. The Menninger Project. In: Donald K. Freedheim (Ed.), *History of Psychology: A Century of Change* (pp. 401–408). Washington, DC: American Psychological Association, 1992.

202. International Scientific Colloquium on Therapeutic Process in Child and Adult Psychoanalysis. *Bulletin of the Anna Freud Centre, 15*, 173–182, 1992.

203. Los tratamientos psicoanalitocos: Una perspectiva historica. *Hogar del Libro:* Colecion–PDU/13: Barcelona, 1992 [Spanish].

204. Follow-up in psychoanalysis: What happens to treatment gains? *Journal of the American Psychoanalytic Association, 40*, 665–690, 1992.

205. Foreword to: Eugenio Gaddini, *A Psychoanalytic Theory of Infantile Experience: Conceptual and Clinical Reflections* (ed. Adam Limentani) (pp. vii–x). London & New York: Tavistock/Routledge, 1992.

206. Psychoanalytic research. *Newsletter of the International Psycho-Analytic Association*, Summer Issue, 20–21, 1992.

207. Psychoanalytic research. *Newsletter of the International Psycho-Analytic Association,* Winter Issue, 29–31, 1992.

1993

208. Manutencao da identidade psicanalitica e functionamento num mundo em mutacao: Os termos da dialetica. *Boletim Informativo: Publicacao da Associacao Brasileira de Psicoanalise, 2,* 65–90, 1993 [Portuguese].
209. Foreword to: Veikko Tahka, *Mind and Its Treatment: A Psychoanalytic Approach* (pp. xiii–xix). Madison, CT: International Universities Press, 1993.
210. Between chaos and petrification: A summary of the Fifth IPA Conference of Training Analysts. *International Journal of Psychoanalysis, 74,* 165–178, 1993.
211. On transference love: Revisiting Freud. In: Ethel Spector Person, Aiban Hagelin, & Peter Fonagy (Eds.), *On Freud's "Observations on Transference Love"* (pp. 57–74). International Psychoanalytical Association Monograph Series, No. 3, New Haven, CT, & London: Yale University Press, 1993.
212. *Psicoanalisi e Psicoterapia* (ed. Margherita Lang). Milan: FrancoAngeli, 240 pp., 1993 [Italian].
213. International Scientific Colloquium on Regression and Progression in Adult and Child Psychoanalysis. *Bulletin of the Anna Freud Centre, 16,* 254–264, 1993.
214. Psychoanalysis as science: Challenge to the data of psychoanalytic research. In: Nancy E. Miller, Lester Luborsky, Jacques B. Barber, & John P. Docherty (Eds.), *Psychodynamic Treatment Research: A Handbook for Clinical Practice* (pp. 96–106). New York: Basic Books, 1993.
215. *Vyucba a Vycvik v Psychoterapii* (with Rudolf Ekstein). Veda Vydavatelstvo Slovenskej Akademie Vied, Bratislava, Slovakia, 1993 [Slovak].
216. The effectiveness of psychotherapy and psychoanalysis: Conceptual issues and empirical work. *Journal of the American Psychoanalytic Association, 41* (*Suppl.*), 299–312, 1993. Reprinted in: Theodore Shapiro & Robert N. Emde (Eds.), *Research in Psychoanalysis: Process, Development, Outcome* (pp. 299–312). Madison, CT: International Universities Press, 1995.
217. Psychoanalytic research. *Newsletter of the International Psycho-Analytic Association, 2* (No. 1), 30–31, 1993.
218. The history of lay analysis in the United States. *Newsletter of the International Psycho-Analytic Association, 2* (No. 2), 19–21, 1993.
219. Psychoanalytic research. *Newsletter of the International Psycho-Analytic Association, 2* (No. 2), 35–36, 1993.

1994

220. Psicoanálisis y psicoterapia dinamica prolongada. In: Howard H. Goldman (Ed.), *Psychiatria General* (pp. 503–513). Mexico City: El Manual Moderno, SA de CV, 1994 [Spanish].
221. International Scientific Colloquium on Aims and Criteria for Termination of Adult and Child Psychoanalysis. *Bulletin of the Anna Freud Centre, 17*, 173–182, 1994.
222. Borderline disorders: Report on the Fourth IPA Research Conference. *International Journal of Psychoanalysis, 75*, 763–774, 1994.
223. Psychotherapy research and its implications for a theory of therapeutic change: A forty-year overview. *Psychoanalytic Study of the Child, 49*, 120–141, 1994. Reprinted in: *Samiksa (Journal of the Indian Psychoanalytic Society) 49*, 13–32, 1995.
224. The ambivalence about research. *Newsletter of the International Psycho-Analytic Association, 3* (No. 2), 45–46, 1994.
225. Sull'amore di transfert. Freud rivisitato. In: Ethel Spector Person, Aiban Hagelin, & Peter Fonagy (Eds.), *Studi Critici su L'Amore Di Transfort* (pp. 41–58). Milan: Raffaello Cortina Editore, 1994 [Italian].

1995

226. Obituary: Erik Erikson (1902–1994). *International Journal of Psychoanalysis, 76*, 173–175, 1995.
227. Obituary: Merton Max Gill (1914–1994). *International Journal of Psychoanalysis, 76*, 399–402, 1995. Reprinted in: *Annual of Psychoanalysis, 24*, 13–17, 1996.
228. Research in psychodynamic therapy. In: Harvey J. Schwartz, Efrain Bleiberg, & Sidney H. Weissman (Eds.), *Psychodynamic Concepts in General Psychiatry* (pp. 431–456. Washington, DC, & London: American Psychiatric Press, 1995.
229. *The Talking Cures: The Psychoanalyses and the Psychotherapies*. New Haven, CT, & London: Yale University Press, 1995.
230. Book review of *Psychoanalysis in Transition: A Personal View*, by Merton M. Gill. *Journal of the American Psychoanalytic Association*, 595–600, 1995.
231. Reality. In: Burness E. Moore & Bernard D. Fine (Eds.), *Psychoanalysis: The Major Concepts* (293–305). New Haven, CT, & London: Yale University Press, 1995.
232. Locating Erikson in contemporary psychoanalysis, *Psychoanalytic Dialogues, 5*, 567–577, 1995.
233. The relation of theory to technique. *Journal of Clinical Psychoanalysis, 4*, 527–542, 1995.

234. Entre el caos y la petrificacion: Resumen de la Quinta Conferencia de Analistas Didacticas de API. *Libro Anual de Psicoanálisis IX* (1993), 239–251, 1995 [Spanish].
235. Psychoanalytic research. *Newsletter of the International Psycho-Analytic Association, 4* (No. 2), 34–35, 1995.

1996

236. Outcomes of psychoanalysis and psychotherapy at termination and at follow-up. In: Edward Nersessian & Richard G. Kopff, Jr. (Eds.), *Textbook of Psychoanalysis* (pp. 531–573). Washington, DC, & London: American Psychiatric Press, 1996.
237. Continuation of Limentani history of the IPA. *International Journal of Psychoanalysis, 77,* 156–158, 1996.
238. Ideas and identities: The life and work of Erik Erikson (Editor). *Psychoanalysis & Contemporary Thought, 19,* 161–365, 1996.
239. Commentary: Common ground or not? In: Daniel Hill & Carole Grand (Eds.), *The British Schools of Psychoanalysis: Pluralism and Convergence in the Clinical Setting* (pp. 91–114). Northvale, NJ, & London: Jason Aronson, 1996.
240. Research in psychodynamic psychotherapy. *The Mt. Sinai Journal of Medicine, 63,* 167–177, 1996.
241. The relation of theory to therapy: An alternative vision. *Psychoanalytic Inquiry, 16,* 491–507, 1996.
242. The Psychotherapy Research Project of The Menninger Foundation: An Overview. In: *Foreign Psychology,* Institute of Psychology, Russian Academy of Sciences 6, 44–53, 1996 [Russian, reprinted from: *Journal of Consulting & Clinical Psychology, 57,* 195–205, 1989].
243. The identity of psychoanalysis: The question of lay analysis. *Bulletin of the Menninger Clinic, 60,* 514–535, 1996.
244. Book review of *The Supervisory Encounter: A Guide for Teachers of Psychodynamic Psychotherapy and Psychoanalysis,* by Daniel Jacobs, Paul David, & Donald Jay Meyer. *Bulletin of the Menninger Clinic, 60,* 548–551, 1996.
245. Psychoanalysis and psychotherapy: An historical perspective (with summaries in Portuguese & Spanish). *Arquivos de Psiquiatria. Psicoterapia e Psicanalise, 3,* 123–158, 1996 [reprinted from: *International Journal of Psychoanalysis, 70,* 563–591, 1989].
246. Psychoanalytic research: Where do we disagree? *Newsletter of the International Psycho-Analytic Association, 5* (No. 1), 15–17, 1996.

1997

247. Merton Gill, Psychotherapy and Psychoanalysis: A Personal Dialogue. *Journal of the American Psychoanalytic Association, 45,* 233–256, 1997.

248. Commentary on Samuel Arbiser's "Psychoanalysis in Argentina." *Fort Da* (Journal of the Northern California Society of Psychoanalytic Psychology), *3*, 10–12, 1997.

249. Die Zukunft der Psychotherapie. In: Stefan de Schill, Serge Lebovici, & Horst Kächele (Eds.), *Psychoanalyse und Psychotherapie: Herausforderung und Lösungen für die Zukunft* (pp. 48–63). Stuttgart & New York: Georg Thieme Verlag, 1997 [German, translated from: *Bulletin of the Menninger Clinic*, *55*, 421–443, 1991].

250. Wichtige Fragen der Psychoanalytischen Prozessforschung (with Harold Sampson). In: Stefan de Schill, Serge Lebovici, & Horst Kächele (Eds.), *Psychoanalyse und Psychotherapie: Herausforderung und Lösungen für die Zukunft* (pp. 132–154). Stuttgart & New York: Georg Thieme Verlag, 1997 [German, translated from *International Journal of Psychoanalysis*, *52*, 11–50, 1971].

251. El psicoanálisis como ciencia: Una respuesta a los nuevos desafios. In: Alejandro M. Wagner (Ed.), *Psicoanálisis v Ciencia* (pp. 45–79). Buenos Aires, Ediciones Dunken, 1997 [Spanish, translated from *Psychoanalytic Quarterly*, *55*, 414–451, 1986].

252. Resultados del psicoanálisis y de la psicoterapia en la terminacion y en el desarrollo. In: Alejandro M. Wagner (Ed.), *Psicoanálisis v Ciencia* (pp. 85–124). Buenos Aires: Ediciones Dunken, 23, 1997 [Spanish, translated from *Textbook of Psychoanalysis* (pp. 531–573). Edward Nersessian & Richard G. Kopff, Jr., eds., 1996].

253. Foreword to: Joseph Sandler, Alex Holder, Christopher Dare, & Anna Ursula Dreher, *Freud's Models of the Mind: An Introduction* (pp. xiii–xvi). London: Karnac, 1997.

254. Foreword to: Brian Martindale, Margarete Morner, Maria Eugenia Cid Rodriguez, & Jean-Pierre Videt (Eds.), *Supervision and Its Vicissitudes* (pp. xiii–xviii). London: Karnac, 1997.

255. Intervention modes in psychoanalysis and in psychotherapies: A revised classification (with Kathryn N. DeWitt). In: Jorge Ahumada, Jorge Olagaray, Arlene Kramer Richards, & Arnold D. Richards (Eds.), *The Perverse Transference and Other Matters: Essays in Honor of R. Horacio Etchegoyen* (pp. 87–114). Northvale, NJ *&* London: Jason Aronson, 1997. Reprinted in: *Journal of Psychotherapy Integration*, *7*, 129–150, 1997.

256. Katamnesen in der Psychoanalyse: Zu ihrem klinischen und empirischen Wert. In: Marianne Leuzinger-Bohleber & Ulrich Stuhr (Eds.), *Psychoanalysen im Rückblick* (pp. 46–60). Psychosozial-Verlag, 1997 [German, translated from *Journal of the American Psychoanalytic Association*, *37*, 921–942, 1989].

257. La ricerca psicoanalitica: Su cosa non siamo d'accordo? *Richard e Piggle*, *5*, 296–298, 1997 [Italian].

1998

258. Erikson's concept of ego identity reconsidered. *Journal of the American Psychoanalytic Association, 46,* 229–247, 1998.
259. *Ideas and Identities: The Life and Work of Erik Erikson* (Editor, with Leo Goldberger). Madison, CT: International Universities Press, 1998.
260. *A Cura Pela Fala: As Psicanalises e as Psicoterapias* [*The Talking Cures*, translated by Maria Adriana Verissima Veronese]. Porto Alegre, Brasil, Artmed, 1998 [Portuguese].
261. The IPA and the American Psychoanalytic Association: A perspective on the Regional Association Agreement. *International Journal of Psychoanalysis, 79,* 553–564. 1998.
262. Psychoanalysis: The future of an illusion? *Newsletter of the International Psycho-Analytic Association, 7* (No. 1), 43–45, 1998.
263. *Lay Analysis: Life Inside the Controversy.* Hillsdale, NJ, & London: Analytic Press, 1998.
264. The new American Psychoanalysis: A commentary. *Journal of the American Psychoanalytic Association, 46,* 1021–1043, 1998.
265. Sobre el amor de transferencia: Consideraciones sobre Freud. In: Ethel Spector Person, Aiban Hagelin & Peter Fonagy (Eds.), *En Torno a Freud: "Observaciones Sobre el Amor de Transferencia"* (pp. 35–51). Madrid: Biblioteca Nueva, 1998 [Spanish].

1999

266. Discussion of Peter Hildebrand's article: "The Cabernite Affair". *Bulletin of the British Psychoanalytic Society, 35* (No. 1), 35–39, 1999.
267. Psychoanalytic research and the IPA: History, present status and future potential (with Peter Fonagy). *International Journal of Psychoanalysis, 80,* 91–109, 1999.
268. "The Cabernite affair." *Bulletin of the British Psychoanalytic Society, 35* (3), 22–24, 1999.
269. A half-century perspective on psychoanalysis and psychotherapy: The historical context of Joseph Sandler's contributions In: Peter Fonagy, Arnold M. Cooper, & Robert S. Wallerstein (Eds.), *Psychoanalysis on the Move: The Work of Joseph Sandler* (pp. 30–50). London & New York: Routledge, 1999.
270. *Psychoanalysis: Clinical and Theoretical.* Madison, CT: International Universities Press, 1999.
271. Freud and culture in our fin de siècle revisited. In: Nancy Ginsburg & Roy Ginsburg (Eds.), *Psychoanalysis & Culture at the Millenium* (pp. 355–379). New Haven, CT, & London: Yale University Press, 1999.
272. Obituary: Joseph J. Sandler (1927–1998). *Newsletter of the International Psycho-Analytic Association, 8* (No. 1), 44–45, 1999.

273. Diagnosi riveduta (e ancora riveduta): Il caso dell'isteria e la personalita isterica. In: Franco Scalzone & Gemma Zontini (Eds.), *Perche L'Isteria? Attualita di una Malattia Ontologica* (pp. 177–193). Naples, Liguori Editori, 1999 [Italian, reprinted from: *International Journal of Psychoanalytic Psychotherapy, 8,* 533–547, 1980–81].
274. L'avenir de la psychothérapie. In: Stephan de Schill & Serge Lebovici (Eds.), *A la Recherche de l'Avenir* (pp. 11–148). Paris, Presses Universitaires de France (PUF), 1999 [French, translated from *Bulletin of the Menninger Clinic, 55,* 421–443, 1991].
275. La recherche dans le domaine du processus psychoanalytique: Questions. In: Stephan de Schill & Serge Lebovici (Eds.), *A la Recherche de l'Avenir* (pp. 291–337). Paris, Presses Universitaires de France (PUF). 1999 [French, translated from *International Journal of Psychoanalysis, 52,* 11–50, 1971].
276. La identidad del psicoanálisis. *Imagen Psicoanalitica, 7,* 33–59, 1999 [Spanish, translated from *Bulletin of the Menninger Clinic, 60,* 514–535, 1996].
277. Commentary on "Making the case for psychoanalytic therapies in the current psychiatric environment" by John G. Gunderson & Glen O. Gabbard. *Journal of the American Psychoanalytic Association, 47,* 728–735, 1999.
278. Commentary on book review by Janine Puget of *Psychoanalysis, Dictatorship, and Torture: Don't Talk About It,* by Helena Besserman Vianna. *Journal of the American Psychoanalytic Association, 47,* 965–973, 1999.
279. Scales of psychological capacities: Support for a measure of structural change (with Kathryn N. DeWitt & Constance Milbrath). *Psychoanalysis & Contemporary Thought, 22,* 453–480, 1999.
280. La psicologia del self y la psicologia psicoanalitica "clasica": La naturaleza de su relacion. In: Guillermo Lancelle (Ed.), *El self en la Teoria y en la Practica* (pp. 115–164). Buenos Aires, Paidos, 1999 [Spanish].

2000

281. Response to Young-Bruehl (1999). *Psychoanalytic Psychology, 17,* 160–163, 2000.
282. The question of lay analysis. *The Affiliate Council Newsletter, 2* (No. 1), 10–11, 2000.
283. Psychoanalysis and long-term dynamic psychotherapy (with Mitchell D. Wilson). *Review of General Psychiatry* (5th edition, pp. 453–462). New York: Lange Medical Books/McGraw-Hill, 2000.
284. *Forty-Two Lives in Treatment: A Study of Psychoanalysis and Psychotherapy* (paperback edition). New York: Other Press, 2000.
285. Where have all the patients gone? They're still here. *Psychoanalytic Inquiry, 20,* 503–526, 2000.

286. Book review of *Does Psychoanalysis Work?*, by Robert M. Galatzer-Levy, Henry Bachrach, Alan Skolnikoff, & Sherwood Waldron, Jr. *Journal of the American Medical Association, 284*, 1712–1713, 2000.
287. Psychoanalytic research: Where do we disagree? In: André Green & Daniel Stern, *Clinical and Observational Psychoanalytic Research: Roots of a Controversy* (pp. 27–31). London: Karnac, 2000.
288. Introduction to the Proceedings of the First Latin American Conference on Psychoanalytic Research [Introduccion a los Procidimientos de la Primera Conferencia Latino Americana de Investigacion Psicoanalitica]. In: *First Latin American Research Conference on Psychoanalysis [Primera Conferencia Latino Americana de Investigacion en Psicoanálisis]* (English: pp. 411–416; Spanish: pp. 417–423). London: International Psychoanalytical Association, 2000.
289. Letters: The Lobo-Cabernite affair. *Journal of the American Psychoanalytic Association, 48*, 1030–1036, 2000.
290. Merton Max Gill, M.D., and Merton Gill, Psychotherapy and Psychoanalysis: A Personal Dialogue. In: Doris K. Silverman & David L. Wolitzky, *Changing Conceptions of Psychoanalysis: The Legacy of Merton M. Gill* (pp. 15–19, 198–219). Hillsdale, NJ, & London: Analytic Press, 2000.
291. Ko-Refarat: Discussion of Ronald Britton's "A post-Kleinian approach to the ego". In: Gabriele Weidenfeller (Ed.), *Das Ich: Eine vernachlassigte Instanz* (pp. 38–48). Frankfurt/M.: Deutsche Psychoanalytische Vereinigung (DPV), 2000.
292. Die Entwicklung und moderne Umgestaltung der (Amerikanischen) Ich-Psychologie [condensed version]. In: Gabriele Weidenfeller (Ed.), *Das Ich: Eine vernachlassigte Instanz* (pp. 49–74). Frankfurt/M.: Deutsche Psychoanalytische Vereinigung (DPV), 2000 [German].
293. The trajectory of psychoanalysis: Past and future. *Samiksa, 54*, 17–28, 2000.
294. Modos de interpretacion en psicoanálisis y en psicoterapias psicoanaliticas: Una clasificacion revisada (with Kathryn N. DeWitt). In: J. Ahumada, J. Olagaray, A. Kramer Richards, & A. David Richards (Eds.), *Las Tareas del psicoanálisis. Ensayos en honor R. Horacio Etchegoyen* (pp. 114–143). Buenos Aires: Polemos, 2000 [Spanish].

2001

295. Die Generationen der Psychotherapieforschung: Ein Überblick. In: Ulrich Stuhr, Marianne Leuzinger-Bohleber & Manfred Beutel (Eds.), *Langzeit-Psychotherapie: Perspektiven für Therapeuten und Wissenschaftler* (pp. 38–60). Stuttgart: Verlag W. Kohlhammer, 2001 [German].
296. Book review of *Countertransference and Regression*, by L. Bryce Boyer.

Newsletter of San Francisco Psychoanalytic Institute and Society (pp. 3–4). March, 2001.

297. The generations of psychotherapy research: An overview. *Psychoanalytic Psychology, 18,* 243–267, 2001.
298. Foreword to: Serge Frisch (Ed.), *Psychoanalysis and Psychotherapy: The Controversies and the Future* (pp. xiii–xix). London: Karnac, 2001.
299. Entwicklung und moderne Transformation der (Amerikanischen) Ich-Psychologie. *Psyche, 55,* 649–684, 2001 (German).
300. La trajectoire de la psychanalyse: Ou en somme-nous aujourd'hui? *Revue Française de Psychanalyse* (Numéro hors-serie), 81–92, 2001 (French). Erratum: Vol. 66, p. 679, 2002.
301. Psychotherapy research and psychoanalytic practice: Commentary on papers by Lester Luborsky & Hans H. Strupp. *Psychoanalytic Dialogues, 11,* 621–634, 2001.
302. Book review of *Cassandra's Daughter: A History of Psychoanalysis,* by Joseph Schwartz. *American Imago, 58,* 723–737, 2001.
303. Letter to the Editor. *Contemporary Psychoanalysis, 37,* 505–509, 2001.
304. Zur Übertragungsliebe: Wiederbegegnung mit Freud. In: Ethel Person, Aiban Hagelin, & Peter Fonagy (Eds.), *Über Freud's "Bemerkungen über die Übertragungsliebe"* (pp. 73–94). Stuttgart: Frommann-Holzboog Verlag, 2001 [German].
305. Transference in psychoanalysis. In: Neil Smelser & Paul Baltes (Eds.), *International Encyclopedia of the Social and Behavioral Sciences, Vol. 23* (pp. 15851–15856). Oxford: Elsevier, 2001.

2002

306. The generations of psychotherapy research: An overview. In: Marianne Leuzinger-Bohleber & Mary Target (Eds.), *Outcomes of Psychoanalytic Treatment: Perspectives for Therapists and Researchers* (pp. 30–52). London: Whurr Publishers, 2002.
307. Association Psychoanalytique Internationale. In: Alain de Mijolla (Ed.), *Dictionnaire International de la Psychoanalyse* (pp. 140–147). Paris: Calmann-Levy, 2002 [French].
308. Psychoanalytic therapy research: An overview. *The American Psychoanalyst, 36* (No. 1), 10, 13, 2002.
309. Obituary: William Gillespie (1905–2001). *International Journal of Psychoanalysis, 83,* 277–281, 2002.
310. APsaA–IPA history: Determinants of the certification and training analyst issues. *The American Psychoanalyst, 36* (No. 2), 14, 2002.
311. The growth and transformation of American ego psychology. *Journal of the American Psychoanalytic Association, 50,* 135–169, 2002.
312. The common ground. *The Affiliate Council Newsletter, 4* (No. 1), 1, 6–7, 2002.

313. Psychoanalytic treatments within psychiatry: An expanded view. *Archives of General Psychiatry, 59,* 499–500, 2002.
314. The organizational maturation of the IPA. *Newsletter of the International Psycho-Analytic Association, 11* (No. 1), 24–26, 2002.
315. Psychotherapy research: The issue of structural change. *Newsletter of the San Francisco Psychoanalytic Institute & Society* (Sept.), p. 8, 2002.
316. Letter to the Editor. Wallerstein on lay analysis and the lawsuit. *Journal of the American Psychoanalytic Association, 50,* 639–642, 2002.
317. La ricerca psicoanalitica: Su cosa non siamo d'accordo? In: Vincenzo Bonaminio & Paolo Fabozzi (Eds.), *Quale Ricerca per la Psicoanalisi?* (pp. 36–38). Milan: FrancoAngeli, 2002 [Italian].
318. Le questioni della ricerca nel processo psicoanalitico (with Harold Sampson). In: Vincenzo Bonaminio & Paolo Fabozzi (Eds.), *Quale Ricerca per la Psicoanalisi?* (pp. 168–231). Milan: FrancoAngeli, 2002 [Italian].
319. Le questioni della ricerca psicoanalitica: Aggiornamenti. In: Vincenzo Bonaminio & Paolo Fabozzi (Eds.), *Quale Ricerca per la Psicoanalisi?* (pp. 232–241). Milan: FrancoAngeli, 2002 [Italian].
320. The trajectory of psychoanalysis: A prognostication. *International Journal of Psychoanalysis, 83,* 1247–1267, 2002.
321. The IPA and psychoanalytic research. *International Psychoanalysis: News Magazine of the International Psychoanalytical Association, 11* (No. 2), 39, 2002.
322. Reconsidering an analytic outcome: Success or failure. In: Joseph Reppen & Martin A. Schulman (Eds.), *Failures in Psychoanalytic Treatment* (pp. 121–151). Madison, CT: International Universities Press, 2002.
323. Norbert Freedman: Psychoanalytic therapy researcher. In: Richard Lasky (Ed.), *Symbolization and Desymbolization: Essays in Honor of Norbert Freedman* (pp. 30–49). New York & London: Other Press, 2002.
324. Discussion of Brenner: Reflections on psychoanalysis: A critique. *Journal of Clinical Psychoanalysis, 11,* 133–143, 2002.
325. The Menninger Clinic and Topeka as I experienced them: 1949–1966. *Bulletin of the Menninger Clinic, 66,* 320–326, 2002.
326. Erikson's concept of ego identity reconsidered. *Samiksa, 56,* 1–14, 2002. [Reprinted from: *Journal of the American Psychoanalytic Association, 46,* 229–247, 1998.]

2003

327. *Commitment and Compassion in Psychoanalysis: Selected Papers of Edward M. Weinshel* (Editor), Hillsdale, NJ, & London: Analytic Press, 2003.
328. Psychoanalytic therapy research: Its coming of age. *Psychoanalytic Inquiry, 23,* 375–404, 2003.

329. The intertwining of politics and science in psychoanalytic history. *Journal of the American Psychoanalytic Association, 51* (*Suppl.*), 7–21, 2003.
330. The history of lay analysis: Emendations. *Journal of the American Psychoanalytic Association, 51* (*Suppl.*), 273–282, 2003.

2004

331. *Psychoanalysis: Education, Research, Science, and Profession.* Madison, CT: International Universities Press, 2004.
332. In Memoriam: Alec Skolnick, M.D. 1914–2004. *Newsletter. San Francisco Psychoanalytic Institute and Society* (March), p. 8, 2004.
333. Psychoanalytic understanding and psychoanalytic therapy: Veikko Tahka's Contributions. In: Aira Laine (Ed.), *Power of Understanding: Essays in Honour of Veikko Tahka* (pp. 1–28). London: Karnac, 2004.
334. From dissidence to pluralism in psychoanalysis—And onto what? In: Martin S. Bergmann (Ed.), *Understanding Dissidence & Controversy in the History of Psychoanalysis* (pp. 201–228). New York: Other Press, 2004.
335. A response to the Symposium "Understanding Dissidence": After the fact. In: Martin S. Bergmann (Ed.), *Understanding Dissidence & Controversy in the History of Psychoanalysis* (pp. 361–370). New York: Other Press, 2004.
336. Introducción a la mesa redonda sobre psicoanálisis y psicoterapia. La relación entre el psicoanálisis y la psicoterapia. Problemas actuales. *Revista Lacaniana de Psicoanálisis. 2*, 167–180, 2004. [Spanish]

2005

337. Psicanalisa e psicoterapia de orientacao analitica: Raizes historicas e situacao atual. In: Cláudio L. Eizirik, Rogerio W. Aguiar, & Sidnei S. Schetatsky (Eds.), *Psicoterapia de Orientacao Analitica: Fundamentos Teoricos e Clinicas* (pp. 43–57). Porto Alegre: Artmed Editora, 2005 [Portuguese].
338. Outcome research. In: Ethel S. Person, Arnold M. Cooper, & Glen O. Gabbard (Eds.), *Textbook of Psychoanalysis* (pp. 301–315). Washington, DC, & London: American Psychiatric Publishing, 2005.
339. Foreword to: Jozef Corveleyn, Patrick Luyten, & Sidney J. Blatt (Eds.), *The Theory and Treatment of Depression* (pp. 1–4). Leuven, Belgium: Leuven University Press; Mahwah, NJ: Lawrence Erlbaum Associates, 2005.
340. Psychoanalysis, the relational turn, and philosophy. In: Jon Mills (Ed.), *Relational and Intersubjective Perspectives in Psychoanalysis: A Critique* (pp. 311–343). Lanham, MD: Jason Aronson, 2005.

341. Will psychoanalytic pluralism be an enduring state of our discipline? *International Journal of Psychoanalysis, 86,* 623–626, 2005.
342. Dialogue or illusion? How do we go from here? Response to André Green. *International Journal of Psychoanalysis, 86,* 633–638, 2005.
343. Book review of *Experiences of Depression: Theoretical, Clinical & Research Perspectives,* by Sidney J. Blatt. *Journal of the American Psychoanalytic Association, 53,* 644–650, 2005.
344. International Psychoanalytical Association. In: Alain de Mijolla (Ed.), *International Dictionary of Psychoanalysis, Vol. 2* (pp. 854–860). Farmington Hills, MI: Macmillan Reference, Thomson-Gale, Publisher, 2005.
345. San Francisco Psychoanalytic Society and Institute. In: Alain de Mijolla (Ed.), *International Dictionary of Psychoanalysis, Vol. 3* (pp. 1529–1532). Farmington Hills, MI: Macmillan Reference, Thomson-Gale, Publisher, 2005.
346. Response to Dr. Epstein. *International Journal of Psychoanalysis, 86,* 1714, 2005.
347. The Lobo–Cabernite affair revisited: And commentary on articles by Villela and Rubin. *Psychoanalytic Review, 92,* 839–856, 2005.

2006

348. The Psychodynamic Diagnostic Manual: An overview (with Stanley L. Greenspan & Nancy McWilliams). *Psychologist–Psychoanalyst, 26* (No. 1), 10–12. (Also in: *The American Psychoanalyst, 39* (No. 4), 14, 19, Fall/ Winter 2005.)
349. Faculty of Medicine: Memorial Minutes (to Margaret Brenman-Gibson, with seven others). *Harvard University Gazette* (April 20), 2006.
350. Response to Luyten, Blatt, and Corveleyn, *International Journal of Psychoanalysis, 87,* 580–581, 2006.
351. Freud and his legacy. Letter to Editor, *The New York Times,* May 14, Section 4, p. 11, 2006.
352. One psychoanalysis or many? Reprinted in: *Contemporary Psychoanalysis in America: Leading Analysts Present their Work* (Arnold M. Cooper, ed.) (pp. 691–720). Washington, DC: American Psychiatric Publishing, Inc., 2006.
353. The Relevance of Freud's Psychoanalysis in the 21st Century: Its Science and its Research. *Psychoanalytic Psychology, 23,* 302–326, 2006.
354. *PDM Task Force (2006). Psychodynamic Diagnostic Manual.* Silver Springs, MD: Alliance of Psychoanalytic Organizations. (Associate Chair), 2006.
355. Psychoanalytically based nosology: Historic origins. In: *PDM Task Force: Psychodynamic Diagnostic Manual* (pp. 385–402). Silver Springs, MD: Alliance of Psychoanalytic Organizations, 2006.

356. Psychoanalytic therapy research: Its history, present status, and projected future. In: *PDM Task Force: Psychodynamic Diagnostic Manual* (pp. 511–535). Silver Springs, MD: Alliance of Psychoanalytic Organizations, 2006.
357. Outcome Studies (Adult). In: *The Edinburgh International Encyclopedia of Psychoanalysis* (Ross M. Skelton, General Editor) (pp. 343–346). Edinburgh: Edinburgh University Press, 2006.
358. Entwicklungslinien der Psychoanalyse seit Freud: Divergenzen und Konvergenzen einer Wissenschaft im steten Wandel [Sigmund Freud at 150 and the trajectory of psychoanalysis, his enduring creation]. *Psyche, 60*, 798–828, 2006 [German].
359. In Memoriam: Milton Lozoff, M.D. 1914–2006. *Newsletter, San Francisco Psychoanalytic Institute & Society* (October), 8–9, 2006.
360. Book review of "*The Quiet Revolution in American Psychoanalysis: Selected Papers of Arnold Cooper*", edited by Elizabeth L. Auchincloss. *American Journal of Psychiatry, 163*, 2021 [correction, p. 2199], 2006.
361. *Skalen Psychischer Kompetenzen (SPK): Ein Messinstrument für therapeutische Veränderung in der psychischen Struktur* (with Dorothea Huber & Guenther Klug). Stuttgart: Kohlhammer, 2006 [German].

2007

362. Karl A. Menninger: A personal perspective. Publication pending, *American Imago*, 2007.
363. Leo Rangell and I: Where do we differ? Publication pending, *Psychoanalytic Psychology*, 2007.
364. Reply to Leo Rangell. Publication pending, *Psychoanalytic Psychology*.
365. The optimal structure for psychoanalytic education today: A feasible proposal? Publication pending, *Journal of the American Psychoanalytic Association*, 2007.

REFERENCES AND BIBLIOGRAPHY

**Entries with an aterisk represent additional important sources not cited in the text.*

Ablon, J. S., & Jones, E. E. (1998). How expert clinicians' prototypes of an ideal treatment correlate with outcome in psychodynamic and cognitive-behavioral therapy. *Psychotherapy Research, 8* (1): 71–83.

Alexander, F. (1937). *Five-Year Report of the Chicago Institute for Psychoanalysis: 1932–1937.* Chicago, IL: Chicago Institute for Psychoanalysis.

Alexander, F., & French, T. M. (1946). *Psychoanalytic Therapy: Principles and Application.* New York: Ronald Press.

APA (1994). *Diagnostic and Statistical Manual of Mental Disorders* (4th edition). Washington, DC: American Psychiatric Association.

*Bachrach, H. M., et al. (1991). On the efficacy of psychoanalysis. *Journal of the American Psychoanalytic Association, 39*: 871–916.

Bachrach, H. M., Weber, J. J., & Solomon, M. (1985). Factors associated with the outcome of psychoanalysis (clinical and methodological considerations): Report of the Columbia Psychoanalytic Center Research Project (IV). *International Review of Psychoanalysis, 12*: 379–388.

Barber, J. P., Crits-Christoph, P., & Luborsky, L. (1990). A guide to the CCRT standard categories and their classification. In: L. Luborsky & P. Crits-Christoph (Eds.), *Understanding Transference: The Core Conflictual Relationship Theme Method* (pp. 37–50). New York: Basic Books.

Bartholomew, K., & Horowitz, L. (1991). Attachment styles among young adults: A test of a four-category model. *Journal of Personality & Social Psychology, 61*: 226–244.

Bateman, A., & Fonagy, P. (2001). Treatment of borderline personality disorder with psychoanalytically oriented partial hospitalization: An 18-month follow-up. *American Journal of Psychiatry, 158* (1): 36–42.

Beck, A. T., Ward, C. H., Mendelson, M., Mock, J., & Erbaugh, J. (1961). An inventory for measuring depression. *Archives of General Psychiatry, 4*: 561–571.

Bellak, L., Hurvich, M., & Gediman, H. K. (1973). *Ego Functions in Schizophrenics, Neurotics and Normals: A Systematic Study of Conceptual, Diagnostic and Therapeutic Aspects.* New York: John Wiley.

Bernardi, R. (1997). Investigación clinica e investigación empiríca sistemática en psicoánalisis [Clinical research and systematic empirical research in psychoanalysis]. *Revista Uruguaya de Psicoanálisis, 84/85*: 53–68.

Bernardi, R. (2002). The need for true controversies in psychoanalysis: The debates on Melanie Klein and Jacques Lacan in the Rio de la Plata. *International Journal of Psychoanalysis, 83*: 851–873.

Bernardi, R. (2003). What kind of evidence makes the analyst change his/her theoretical and technical ideas? In: M. Leuzinger-Bohleber, A. U. Dreher, & J. Canestri (Eds.), *Pluralism and Unity? Methods of Research in Psychoanalysis* (pp. 125–136). London: International Psychoanalytical Association.

*Beutel, M., & Rasting, M. (2001). Langzeittherapien aus der Rückschau ehemaliger Patienten. In: U. Stuhr, M. Leuzinger-Bohleber, & M. Beutel (Eds.), *Langzeit-Psychotherapie. Perspektiven für Therapeuten und Wissenschaftler* (pp. 187–200). Stuttgart: Kohlhammer Verlag.

Bibring, E. (1937). Symposium on the theory of therapeutic results of psychoanalysis. *International Journal of Psychoanalysis, 18*: 7–33.

Blatt, S. J., & Auerback, J. D. (1998). "The Contribution of the Assessment of Mental Representations to Understanding the Therapeutic Process and the Nature of Severe Psychopathology". Paper presented at the Eighth Research Conference of the International Psychoanalytical Association, University College London.

*Bohleber, W., & Drews, S. (Eds.) (2001). *Die Gegenwart der psychoanalyse—die Psychoanalyse der Gegenwart: 100 Jahre psychoanalyse—50 Jahre Deutsche Psychoanalytische Vereinigung.* Stuttgart: Klett-Cotta.

Bucci, W. (1995). The multiple code theory and the psychoanalytic process: A framework for research. *Annual of Psychoanalysis, 22*: 239–259.

Bucci, W. (1997). *Psychoanalysis and Cognitive Science: A Multiple Code Theory.* New York: Guilford Press.

Bucci, W. (2001a). Pathways of emotional communication. *Psychoanalytic Inquiry, 20*: 40–70.

Bucci, W. (2001b). Toward a "psychodynamic science": The state of current research. *Journal of American Psychoanalysis, 49* (1): 57–68.

Bucci, W. (2002a). Multiple code theory and the referential process: Applications to process research. In: P. Fonagy (Ed.), *An Open Door Review of Outcome Studies in Psychoanalysis* (2nd revised edition, pp. 192–195). London: International Psychoanalytical Association.

Bucci, W. (2002b). Referential Activity (RA): Scales and computer procedures. In: P. Fonagy (Ed.), *An Open Door Review of Outcome Studies in Psychoanalysis* (2nd revised edition, pp. 286–288). London: International Psychoanalytical Association.

Bucci, W. (2005). Basic concepts and methods of psychoanalytic process research. In: E. Person, A. Cooper, & G. Gabbard (Eds.), *Textbook of Psychoanalysis* (pp. 339–355). Arlington, VA: American Psychiatric Press.

Bucci, W., & Maskit, B. (submitted). Beneath the surface of the therapeutic interaction: The psychoanalytic method in modern dress. *Journal of the American Psychoanalytic Association* (http://www.referentialprocess.org).

Clarkin, J. F., Caligor, E., Stern, B., & Kernberg, O. F. (2002). *Structured Interview of Personality Organization (STIPO).* Unpublished manuscript, Personality Disorders Institute, New York Presbyterian Hospital, White Plains, NY.

*Clarkin, J. F., Yeomans, F. E., & Kernberg, O. F. (1999). *Psychotherapy for Borderline Personality.* New York: John Wiley.

Cohen, J. (1988). *Statistical Power Analysis for the Behavioral Sciences* (2nd edition). Hillsdale, NJ: Lawrence Erlbaum.

Coriat, I. (1917). Some statistical results of the psychoanalytical treatment of the psychoneuroses. *Psychoanalytic Review, 4*: 209–216.

Dahl, H. (1988). Frames of mind. In: H. Dahl, H. Kächele, & H. Thomä (Eds.), *Psychoanalytic Process Research Strategies* (pp. 51–66). New York: Springer-Verlag.

Dahl, H. (1998). The voyage of el Rubaiyat to the discovery of FRAMES. In: R. Bornstein & J. Masling (Eds.), *Empirical Studies of the Therapeutic Hour* (pp. 179–227). Washington, DC: American Psychological Association.

Dahl, H., Kächele, H., & Thomä, H. (1988). *Psychoanalytic Process Research Strategies.* New York: Springer-Verlag (accessed 13 March 2007 at: http://sip.medizin.uni-ulm.de/abteilung/buecher/pprs.pdf).

Dahl, H., & Teller, V. (1994). The characteristics, identification and applications of FRAMES. *Psychotherapy Research, 4*: 252–274.

Dahl, H., Teller, V., Moss, D., & Trujillo, M. (1978). Countertransference examples of the syntactic communication of warded-off contents. *Psychoanalytic Quarterly, 47*: 339–363.

Derogatis, L. (1993). *Symptom Checklist-90-Revised.* Minneapolis, MN: National Computer Systems.

Derogatis, L. R., Lipman, R. S., & Covi, L. (1973). SCL-90-R: An outpatient psychiatric rating scale. *Psychopharmacology Bulletin, 9*: 13–28.

DeWitt, K. N. (1997). "Inter-Rater Reliability of the Scales of Psychological Capacities Support for a Measure of Structural Change." Paper presented at Seventh IPA Research Conference, London, UCL.

DeWitt, K. N., Hartley, D., Rosenberg, S. E., Zilberg, N. J., & Wallerstein, R. S. (1991). Scales of psychological capacities: Development of an assessment approach. *Psychoanalysis & Contemporary Thought, 14*: 343–361.

DeWitt, K. N., Milbrath, C., & Wallerstein, R. S. (1999). Scales of psychological capacities: Support for a measure of structural change. *Psychoanalysis & Contemporary Thought, 22*: 453–480.

*Dreher, A. U. (1998). *Empirie ohne Konzept? Einführung in die psychoanalytische Konzeptforschung.* Stuttgart: Klett-Cotta.

Dreher, A. U. (2000). *Foundations for Conceptual Research in Psychoanalysis: Psychoanalytic Monograph 4.* London: Karnac.

*Dreher, A. U. (2001). Welche Ziele verfolgen Psychoanalytiker? In: U. Stuhr, M. Leuzinger-Bohleber, & M. Beutel (Eds.), *Langzeit-Psychotherapie. Perspektiven für Therapeuten und Wissenschaftler* (pp. 93–105). Stuttgart: Kohlhammer.

*Dührssen, A., & von Jorswieck, E. (1965). Eine empirisch-Statistische Untersuchung zur Leistungsfähigkeit psychoanalytischer Behandlung. *Der Nervenarzt, 36*: 166–169.

Eisenstein, S., Levy, N. A., & Marmor, J. (1994). *The Dyadic Transaction: An Investigation into the Nature of the Psychotherapeutic Process.* New Brunswick, NJ: Transaction.

Eissler, K. R. (1950). The Chicago Institute of Psychoanalysis and the sixth period of the development of psychoanalytic technique. *Journal of General Psychology*: 103–157.

Erle, J. B. (1979). An approach to the study of analyzability and analysis: The course of forty consecutive cases selected for supervised analysis. *Psychoanalytic Quarterly, 48*: 198–228.

Erle, J. B., & Goldberg, D. A. (1979). Problems in the assessment of analyzability. *Psychoanalytic Quarterly, 48*: 48–84.

Erle, J. B., & Goldberg, D. A. (1984). Observations on assessment of analyzability by experienced analysts. *Journal of the American Psychoanalytic Association, 32*: 715–737.

*Faller, H., & Frommer, J. (Eds.) (1994). *Qualitative Psychotherapieforschung. Grundlagen und Methoden.* Heidelberg: Assanger.

Feldman, F. (1968). Results of psychoanalysis in clinic case assignments. *Journal of the American Psychoanalytic Association, 16*: 274–300.

Fenichel, O. (1930). *Statistischer Bericht über die therapeutische Tätigkeit 1920–1930* (pp. 13–19). Vienna: Internazionale Psychoanalytischer Verlag.

*Fischer, G., & Riedesser, P. (1999). *Lehrbuch der Psychotraumatologie.* Munich: Ernst Reinhardt Verlag.

Fleiss, J. L. (1971). Measuring nominal scale agreement among many raters. *Psychological Bulletin, 76*: 378–382.

Fonagy, P., et al. (Eds.) (1999). *An Open Door Review of Outcome Studies in Psychoanalysis.* London: International Psychoanalytical Association..

Fonagy, P., et al. (Eds.) (2002). *An Open Door Review of Outcome Studies in*

Psychoanalysis (2nd revised edition). London: International Psychoanalytical Association.

Fonagy, P., & Target, M. (1994). The efficacy of psychoanalyses for children with disruptive disorders. *Journal of the American Academy of Child and Adolescent Psychiatry, 33*: 45–55.

Fonagy, P., & Target, M. (1996). Predictors of outcome in child psychoanalysis: A retrospective study of 763 cases at the Anna Freud Centre. *Journal of the American Psychoanalytic Association, 44*: 27–77.

*Franke, G. (1995). *SCL-90-R: Die Symptom-Checkliste von Derogatis: Deutsche Version—Manual.* Göttingen: Beltz Test.

Freedman, N., Hoffenberg, J. D., Vorus, N., & Frosch, A. (1999). The effectiveness of psychoanalytic psychotherapy: The role of treatment duration, frequency of sessions, and the therapeutic relationship. *Journal of the American Psychoanalytic Association, 47*: 741–772.

Freedman, N., Kagan, D., Russell, J., Schaffer, C., & Webster, J. (2001). *Scales of Incremental Symbolization: Manuals 1–4.* New York: Institute for Psychoanalytic Research, Research Division.

Freedman, N., Lasky, R., & Hurvich, M. (2003). Two pathways towards knowing psychoanalytic process. In: M. Leuzinger-Bohleber, A. U. Dreher, & J. Canestri (Eds.), *Pluralism and Unity? Methods of Research in Psychoanalysis* (pp. 207–221). London: International Psychoanalytical Association.

*Friebertshäuser, B., & Prengel, A. (Eds.) (1997). *Handbuch qualitative Forschungsmethoden in der Erziehungswissenschaft.* Munich: Juventa.

Gedo, J. E. (2001). The enduring scientific contributions of Sigmund Freud. *Annual of Psychoanalysis, 29*: 105–115.

*Gerdes, N., & Jäckel, W. H. (1995). Der IRES—Fragebogen für Klinik und Forschung. *Rehabilitation, 34*: 13–24.

Gill, M. M. (1976). Metapsychology is not psychology. In: M. M. Gill & P. S. Holzman (Eds.), *Psychology versus Metapsychology: Psychoanalytic Essays in Memory of George S. Klein* (pp. 71–105). Psychological Issues, Monograph No. 36. New York: International Universities Press.

Gill, M. M., & Hoffman, I. Z. (1982). A method for studying the analysis of aspects of the patient's experience of the relationship in psychoanalysis and psychotherapy. *Journal of the American Psychoanalytic Association, 30*: 137–168.

Gleser, G. C., & Ihilevich, D. (1969). An objective instrument for measuring defense mechanisms. *Journal of Consulting & Clinical Psychology, 33*: 51–60.

Grawe, K., Donati, R., & Bernauer, F. (1994). *Psychotherapie im Wandel. Von der Konfession zur Profession.* Göttingen: Hogrefe.

Green, A. (1996a). What kind of research in psychoanalysis. *International Psychoanalysis: The Newsletter of the IPA, 5* (1): 10.

Green, A. (1996b). Response to Dr. Wallerstein. *International Psychoanalysis: The Newsletter of the IPA, 5* (1): 18–21.

Grenyer, B. F. S. (2002). *Mastering Relationship Conflicts: Discoveries in Theory, Research, and Practice.* Washington, DC: American Psychological Association.

Grenyer, B., & Luborsky, L. (1996). *Mastery of Core Relationships.* Washington, DC: American Psychoanalytic Association.

*Habermas, J. (1968). *Technik und Wissenschaft als Ideologie.* Frankfurt a.M.: Suhrkamp.

Hamburg, D. A., Bibring, G. L., Fisher, C., Stanton, A. H., Wallerstein, R. S., Weinstock, H. I., & Haggard, E. (1967). Report of ad hoc committee on Central Fact-Gathering Data of the American Psychoanalytic Association. *Journal of the American Psychoanalytic Association, 15*: 841–861.

*Hampe, M. (2000). Pluralismus der Erfahrung und die Einheit der Vernunft. In: M. Hampe & M. Lotter (Eds.), *"Die Erfahrungen, die wir machen, sprechen gegen die Erfahrungen, die wir haben." Über Formen der Erfahrung in den Wissenschaften* (pp. 27–41). Berlin: Duncker & Humblot.

Henrich, G., & Herschbach, P. (2000). Questions on Life Satisfaction (FLZ[M]) —A short questionnaire for assessing subjective quality of life. *European Journal for Psychology Assessment, 16*: 150–159.

*Henry, W. P., Strupp, H. H., et al. (1994). Psychodynamic approaches. In: A. Bergin & S. Garfield (Eds.), *Handbook of Psychotherapy and Behavior Change* (pp. 467–508). Oxford: John Wiley.

Hentschel, U., Kießling, M., & Wiemers, M. (1998). *Fragebogen zu Konfliktbewältigungsstrategien (FKBS).* Göttingen: Hogrefe.

Herschbach, P., Henrich, G., & Oberst, U. (1994). Lebensqualität in der Nachsorge. Eine Evaluationsstudie in der Fachklinik für Onkologie und Lymphologie, Bad Wildungen-Reinhardshausen. *Praxis der Klinischen Verhaltensmedizin und Rehabilitation, 28*: 241–251.

Hiller, W., Zaudig, M., & Mombour, W. (1995). *Internationale Diagnosen-Checkliste für ICD-10 und DSM-IV (IDCL).* Göttingen: Hogrefe.

Hilsenroth, M. J., Ackerman, S. J., Blagys, M. D., Baity, M. R., & Mooney, M. A. (2003). Short-term psychodynamic psychotherapy for depression: An examination of statistical, clinically significant, and technique-specific change. *Journal of Nervous and Mental Disease, 191*: 349–357.

Hoffman, I. Z., & Gill, M. M. (1988). A scheme for coding the patient's experience of the relationship with the therapist (PERT): Some applications, extensions, and comparisons. In: H. Dahl, H. Thomä, & H. Kächele (Eds.), *Psychoanalytic Process Research Strategies.* New York: Springer.

Hoglend, P., Bogwald, K.-P., & Amlo, S. (2000). Assessment of change in dynamic psychotherapy. *Journal of the American Psychoanalytic Association, 9* (4): 190–199.

Holt, R. (1985). The current status of psychoanalytic theory. *Psychoanalytic Psychology, 2*: 289–315.

Holt, R., & Luborsky, L. (1958). *Personality Patterns of Psychiatrists: A Study in Selection Techniques, Vol. 1.* New York: Basic Books.

*Holzhey, H. (2001). Flug und Fall der Seele—Philosophische Reflexionen in anthropologischer Absicht. In: U. Stuhr, M. Leuzinger-Bohleber, & M. Beutel (Eds.), *Langzeit-Psychotherapie. Perspektiven für Therapeuten und Wissenschaftler* (pp. 17–37). Stuttgart: Kohlhammer.

Horowitz, L. M., Rosenberg, S. E., Baer, B., Ureno, G., & Vallasenor, V. (1988). Inventory of interpersonal problems: Psychometric properties and clinical application. *Journal of Consulting & Clinical Psychology, 56*: 885–892.

Huber, D., Brandl, T., & Klug, G. (2004). The Scales of Psychological Capacities: Measuring beyond symptoms. *Psychotherapy Research, 14* (1): 89–106.

Huber, D., Henrich, G., & Herschbach, P. (1988). Measuring the quality of life: A comparison between physically and mentally chronically ill patients and healthy persons. *Pharmacopsychiatry, 21*: 453–455

Huber, D., & Klug, G. (2002). The Munich Psychotherapy Depression Study (MPDS): Comparing the effects of psychoanalysis and psychotherapy. In: P. Fonagy (Ed.), *An Open Door Review of Outcome Studies in Psychoanalyis* (2nd revised edition). London: International Psychoanalytical Association).

Huber, D., Klug, G., & von Rad, M. (1997). "How to Measure Structural Change". Paper presented at the 28th Annual Conference of the Society for Psychotherapy Research, Geilo (25–29 June).

*Huber, D., Klug, G., & von Rad, M. (2001). Die Münchener Prozess-Outcome Studie—Ein Vergleich zwischen Psychoanalysen und psychodynamischen Psychotherapien unter besonderer Berücksichtigung therapiespezifischer Ergebnisse. In: U. Stuhr, M. Leuzinger-Bohleber, & M. Beutel (Eds.), *Langzeit-Psychotherapie. Perspektiven für Therapeuten und Wissenschaftler* (pp. 260–270). Stuttgart: Kohlhammer.

Huber, D., Klug, G., & von Rad, M. (2002). The Munich Psychotherapy Study: A process–outcome comparison between psychoanalyses and psychodynamic psychotherapies with regard to mode-specific effects. In: M. Leuzinger-Bohleber & M. Target (Eds.), *Outcomes of Psychoanalytic Treatment: Perspectives for Therapists and Researchers* (pp. 223–234). London: Whurr; New York: Brunner-Routledge.

Jacobson, E. (1971). *Depression: Comparative Studies of Normal, Neurotic, and Psychotic Conditions.* New York: International Universities Press.

Jacobson, N. S., & Truax, P. (1991). Clinical significance: A statistical approach to defining meaningful change in psychotherapy research. *Journal of Consulting & Clinical Psychology, 59*: 12–19.

James, W. (1907). The one and the many (Lecture 4). In: *Pragmatism: A New Name for Some Old Ways of Thinking* (pp. 49–63). New York: Longmans, Green.

Jones, E. (1936). *Decennial Report of the London Clinic of Psychoanalysis, 1926–1937.* London: London Clinic of Psychoanalysis.

Jones, E. E. (2000). *Therapeutic Action: A Guide to Psychoanalytic Therapy.* Northvale, NJ: Jason Aronson.

Jones, E. E. (2001). *Therapeutic Action: A Guide to Psychoanalytic Research.* Northvale, NJ: Jason Aronson.

Jones, E. E., Cumming, J. D., & Horowitz, M. J. (1988). Another look at the nonspecific hypothesis of therapeutic effectiveness. *Journal of Consulting & Clinical Psychology, 56*: 48–55

Kächele, H., & Mergenthaler, E. (1984). Auf dem Wege zur computerunterstutzen Textanalyse in der psychotherapeutischen Prozessforschung. In: U. Baumann (Ed.), *Makro- und Mikroperspektive* (pp. 223–239). Göttingen: Hogrefe.

Kantrowitz, J. L. (1986). The role of the patient–analyst "match" in the outcome of psychoanalysis. *Annual of Psychoanalysis, 14*: 273–297.

*Kantrowitz, J. L. (1995). The beneficial aspects of the patient–analyst match. *International Journal of Psychoanalysis, 76*: 299–313.

Kantrowitz, J. L. (1997a). Ergebnisforschung in der Psychoanalyse. Rückblick und Neubewertung. In: M. Leuzinger-Bohleber & U. Stuhr (Eds.), *Psychoanalysen im Rückblick* (pp. 61–73). Gießen: Psychosozial-Verlag.

Kantrowitz, J. L. (1997b). "The Symmetrical Aspect of the Therapeutic Relationship: It Takes Two to Have a Therapeutic Alliance." Paper presenterd at the 7th IPA Research Conference, London (July 3).

Kantrowitz, J. L. (2004a). Writing about patients I: Analysts' ways of protecting confidentiality and conflictual views about their methods. *Journal of the American Psychoanalytic Association, 52* (1): 69–99.

Kantrowitz, J. L. (2004b). Writing about patients II: Patients' reading about themselves and their analysts' perceptions of its effect. *Journal of the American Psychoanalytic Association, 52* (1): 101–123.

Kantrowitz, J. L., Katz, A. L., & Paolitto, F. (1990b). Follow-up of psychoanalysis five to ten years after termination. II: Development of the self-analytic function. *Journal of the American Psychoanalytic Association, 38* (3): 637–650.

Kantrowitz, J. L., Katz, A. L., & Paolitto, F. (1990c). Follow-up of psychoanalysis five to ten years after termination. III: The relation between the resolution of the transference and the patient–analyst match. *Journal of the American Psychoanalytic Association, 38* (3): 655–678.

Kantrowitz, J. L., Katz, A. L., Paolitto, F., Sashin, J., & Solomon, L. (1987a). Changes in the level and quality of object relations in psychoanalysis: Follow-up of a longitudinal prospective study. *Journal of the American Psychoanalytic Association, 35*: 23–46.

Kantrowitz, J. L., Katz, A. L., Paolitto, F., Sashin, J., & Solomon, L. (1987b). The role of reality testing in psychoanalysis: Follow-up of 22 cases. *Journal of the American Psychoanalytic Association, 35*: 367–385.

Kantrowitz, J. L., Katz, A. L., & Paolitto, F. (1990a). Follow-up of psychoanalysis five to ten years after termination: I: Stability of change. *Journal of the American Psychoanalytic Association, 38* (2): 471–496.

Kantrowitz, J. L., Paolitto, F., Sashin, J., Solomon, L., & Katz, A. L. (1986). Affect availability, tolerance, complexity, and modulation in psychoanalysis: Follow-up of a longitudinal prospective study. *Journal of the American Psychoanalytic Association, 34*: 529–559.

Karush, A., Easser, B. R., Cooper, A. M., & Swerdloff, B. (1964). The evaluation of ego strength: I. A profile of adaptive balance. *Journal of Nervous & Mental Disease, 139*: 332–349.

Kazdin, A. E. (1998). *Research Design in Clinical Psychology* (3rd edition). Boston: Allyn & Bacon.

Kazdin, A. E. (1999). The meanings and measurement of clinical significance. *Journal of Consulting & Clinical Psychology, 67*: 332–339.

*Keller, W., Dilg, R., Westhoff, G., Rohner, R., & Studt, H. (1997). Zur Wirksamkeit ambulanter (jungianischer) Psychoanalysen und Psychotherapien. Eine katamnestische Studie. In: M. Leuzinger-Bohleber & U. Stuhr (Eds.), *Psychoanalysen im Rückblick. Methoden, Ergebnisse und Perspektiven der neueren Katamneseforschung* (pp. 432–453). Gießen: Psychosozial-Verlag.

*Keller, W., Westhoff, G., Dilg, R., Rohner, R., & Studt, H. H. (2001). Wirksamkeit und Kosten—Nutzen—Aspekte ambulanter (jungianischer) Psychoanalysen und Psychotherapien—Eine katamnestische Studie. In: U. Stuhr, M. Leuzinger-Bohleber, & M. Beutel (Eds.), *Langzeit-Psychotherapie. Perspektiven für Therapeuten und Wissenschaftler* (pp. 343–355). Stuttgart: Kohlhammer.

Kernberg, O. (1975). *Borderline Conditions and Pathological Narcissism.* New York: Jason Aronson.

Kernberg, O. (1981). Structural interviewing. *Psychiatric Clinics of North America, 4*: 169–194.

Klumpner, G. (1992). *A Guide to the Language of Psychoanalysis: An Empirical Study of the Relationships among Psychoanalytic Terms and Concepts.* Madison, CT: International Universities Press.

Knapp, P. H., Levin, S., McCarter, R. H., Wermer, H., & Zetzel, E. (1960). Suitability for psychoanalysis: A review of one hundred supervised analytic cases. *Psychoanalytic Quarterly, 29*: 459–477.

Kohut, H. (1970). Scientific activities of the American Psychoanalytic Association: An inquiry. *Journal of the American Psychoanalytic Association, 18*: 462–484.

*Krusche, H. (in press). *"Schade um die schöne Zeit." Zur Erfolgsbeurteilung psychoanalytischer Langzeittherapie bei traumatisierten Patienten.* Kassel: Promotion Universität Kassel.

Lambert, M. J., & Bergin, A. E. (1994). The effectiveness of psychotherapy. In: A. E. Bergin & S. L. Garfield (Eds.), *Handbook of Psychotherapy and Behaviour Change* (pp. 143–189). New York: John Wiley.

Lambert, M. J., & Hill, C. E. (1994). Assessing psychotherapy outcomes and processes. In: A. E. Bergin & S. L. Garfield (Eds.), *Handbook of Psychotherapy and Behaviour Change* (pp. 72–113). New York: John Wiley.

Langer, I., & Schulz von Thun, F. (1974). Messung komplexer Merkmale in Psychologie und Pädagogik. *Erziehung und Psychologie, 68*: 62–95.

*Lear, J. (1997). The Shrink is in. In: M. Leuzinger-Bohleber & U. Stuhr (Eds.), *Psychoanalysen im Rückblick. Methoden, Ergebnisse und Perspektiven der neueren Katamneseforschung* (pp. 92–105). Gießen: Psychosozial-Verlag.

*Leuzinger-Bohleber, M. (1995). Die Einzelfallstudie als psychoanalytisches Forschungsinstrument. *Psyche, 49* (5): 434–481.

Leuzinger-Bohleber, M. (1997). *"... die Fähigkeit zu lieben, zu arbeiten und das Leben zu geniessen." Zu den vielen Facetten psychoanalytischer Katamneseforschung.* Giessen: Psychosozial Verlag.

*Leuzinger-Bohleber, M. (2000). Psychoanalyse—Erfahrungswissenschaft des Unbewußten. In: M. Hampe & M.-S. Lotter (Eds.), *"Die Erfahrungen, die wir machen, sprechen gegen die Erfahrungen, die wir haben." Über Formen der Erfahrung in den Wissenschaften. Series: "Erfahrung und Denken. Schriften zur Förderung der Beziehungen zwischen Philosophie und Einzelwissenschaften," Vol. 86* (pp. 145–167). Berlin: Duncker & Humblot.

*Leuzinger-Bohleber, M. (2001). Katamnesen—ihre klinische relevanz. In: U. Stuhr, M. Leuzinger-Bohleber, & M. Beutel (Eds.), *Langzeit-psychotherapie. Perspektiven für Therapeuten und Wissenschaftler* (pp. 160–186). Stuttgart: Kohlhammer.

*Leuzinger-Bohleber, M. (2002a). A follow-up study—critical inspiration for our clinical practice? In: M. Leuzinger-Bohleber & M. Target (Eds.), *Outcomes of Psychoanalytic Treatment: Perspectives for Therapists and Researchers* (pp. 143–173). London: Whurr; New York: Brunner-Routledge.

*Leuzinger-Bohleber, M. (2002b). Introductory remarks. In: M. Leuzinger-Bohleber & M. Target (Eds.), *Outcomes of Psychoanalytic Treatment: Perspectives for Therapists and Researchers* (pp. 1–13). London: Whurr; New York: Brunner-Routledge.

*Leuzinger-Bohleber, M. (2002c). Quelques remarques critiques illustrées par un suivi représentatif de psychoanalyses et thérapies psychoanalytiques de longue durée. *Bulletin de la Société Psychoanalytiques de Paris, 63*: 157–175.

*Leuzinger-Bohleber, M., Dreher, A. U., & Canestri, J. (2003). *Pluralism and Unity? Methods of Research in Psychoanalysis.* London: International Psychoanalytical Association.

*Leuzinger-Bohleber, M., & Stuhr, U. (Eds.) (1997). *Psychoanalysen im Rückblick. Methoden, Ergebnisse und Perspektiven der neueren Katamneseforschung.* Gießen: Psychosozial-Verlag.

*Leuzinger-Bohleber, M., Stuhr, U., Beutel, M., Rüger, B., & Kächele, H. (2001). Efectos a largo plazo del psicoanálisis y de las terapias psicoanalíticas: un Estudio representativo de seguimiento. In: R. Florenzano, J. P. Jiménez, R. Isla, G. De la Parra, P. Riumalló, & S. Valdivieso (Eds.), *Investigación en psicoanálisis y psicoterapia* (pp. 73–85). Santiago: IPA/SPR.

*Leuzinger-Bohleber, M., Stuhr, U., Rüger, B., & Beutel, M. (2000). "How to Study the Quality of Psychoanalytic Treatments? A Combination of

Qualitative and Quantitative Approaches in a Representative Follow-up Study." Paper presented at the Joseph Sandler Research Conference, London (4 March).

*Leuzinger-Bohleber, M., Stuhr, U., Rüger, B., & Beutel, M. (2001). Langzeitwirkungen von Psychoanalysen und Psychotherapien. Eine multiperspektivische, repräsentative Katamnesestudie. *Psyche, 55* (3): 193–276.

*Leuzinger-Bohleber, M., Stuhr, U., Rüger, B., & Beutel, M. (2002). *Forschen und Heilen in der Psychoanalyse. Berichte und Ergebnisse aus Forschung und Praxis.* Stuttgart: Kohlhammer.

*Leuzinger-Bohleber, M., Stuhr, U., Rüger, B., & Beutel, M. (2002a). Comment évaluer la qualité de traitements psychanalytiques? Une association de méthodes de recherche psychanalytique et non-psychanalytique dans une étude de suivi représentative et multi-perspectiviste de psychanalyses et thérapies psychanalytiques de longue durée. *EPF Bulletin (France).*

*Leuzinger-Bohleber, M., Stuhr, U., Rüger, B., & Beutel, M. (2002b). Psychoanalytic and non-psychoanalytic research methods in a multiperspective, representative follow-up study of psychoanalyses and psychoanalytic long-term therapies. *EPF Bulletin (UK).*

*Leuzinger-Bohleber, M., Stuhr, U., Rüger, B., & Beutel, M. (2004). Psychoanalytische Forschung und die Pluralität der Wissenschaften. Einige kritische Anmerkungen illustriert am Beispiel einer repräsentativen, multiperspektivischen Katamnesestudie von Psychoanalysen und psychoanalytischen Langzeitbehandlungen. *EPF Bulletin (Germany).*

*Leuzinger-Bohleber, M., Stuhr, U., Rüger, B., & Beutel, M. (submitted). How to study the outcome of psychoanalytic treatments? A representative, multiperspective follow-up study of psychoanalyses and psychoanalytic long-term therapies. *International Journal of Psychoanalysis.*

*Leuzinger-Bohleber, M., & Target, M. (Eds.) (2002). *Outcomes of Psychoanalytic Treatment: Perspectives for Therapists and Researchers.* London: Whurr; New York: Brunner-Routledge.

Leuzinger-Bohleber, M., et al. (2002). The psychoanalytic follow-up study (DPV): A representative multicentre study of long-term psychoanalytic therapies. In: M. Leuzinger-Bohleber & M. Target (Eds.), *Outcomes of Psychoanalytic Treatment: Perspectives for Therapists and Researchers.* London: Whurr; New York: Brunner-Routledge.

Library of Congress (1996). *Building Digital Collections: Technical Information and Background Papers.* National Digital Library Program (NDLP) internal documentation (available at: http://memory.loc.gov/ammem/about/techIn.html).

Lienert, G. A., & Raatz, U. (1998). *Testaufbau und Testanalyse* (6th edition). Weinheim: Beltz.

López Moreno, C., Dorfman Lerner, B., Schalayeff, C., & Roussos, A. (1999). Investigación empirica en Psicoanálisis. *Revista de Psicoanálisis, 56* (3): 677–693.

Luborsky, L. (1962). Clinicians' judgments of mental health: A proposed scale. *Archives of General Psychiatry, 7*: 407–417.

Luborsky, L. (1977). Measuring a pervasive psychic structure in psychotherapy: The Core Conflictual Relationship Theme. In: N. Freeman & S. Grand (Eds.), *Communicative Structures and Psychic Structures* (pp. 367–395). New York: Plenum Press.

Luborsky, L., & Crits-Cristoph, P. (1988). The assesment of the transference by the CCRT method. In: H. Dahl, H. Kächele, & H. Thomä (Eds.), *Psychoanalytic Process Research Methods* (pp. 99–108). New York: Springer-Verlag.

Luborsky, L., & Crits-Cristoph, P. (1990). *Understanding Transference: The Core Conflictual Relationship Theme Method.* New York: Basic Books.

Luborsky, L., & Crits-Cristoph, P. (1998). *Understanding Transference: The CCRT Method* (2nd edition). Washington, DC: American Psychological Association Press.

Luborsky, L., Stuart, J., Friedman, S., Diguer, L., Seligman, D., Bucci, W., Pulver, S., Krause, E., Ermold, J., Davison, W., Woody, G., & Mergenthaler, E. (2001). The Penn Psychoanalytic Treatment Collection: A set of complete and recorded psychoanalyses as a research resource. *Journal of American Psychoanalysis, 49* (1): 217–234.

Luder, M., Neukom, M., & Thomann, B. (2000). The JAKOB Database: Psychodynamic psychotherapy research at the University of Zurich. Presentation of the database and research methods in the field of clinical narration under the direction of Prof. Dr. Brigitte Boothe. *Forum Qualitative Social Research (Online Journal), 1* (3) (accessed 13 March 2007 at: http://qualitative-research.net/fqs-texte/3-00/3-00luderetal-e.pdf).

Maskit, B. (2006). "Smoothing Discourse Variables to Capture the Flow of Verbal Interaction." Paper presented at the North American Society for Psychotherapy Research, Burr Oak, Ohio.

Menninger, K. A. (1954). *The Human Mind.* New York: Alfred Knopf (first published 1930).

*Mentzos, S. (2001). Versuch einer klinisch orientierten psychosomatischen Klassifikation von Borderline-zuständen. In: U. Stuhr, M. Leuzinger-Bohleber, & M. Beutel, M. (Eds.), *Langzeit-Psychotherapie. Perspektiven für Therapeuten und Wissenschaftler* (pp. 410–421). Stuttgart: Kohlhammer Verlag.

Mercer, R. C., & Loesch, L. C. (1979). Audiotape ratings: Comments and guidelines. *Psychotherapy: Theory, Research and Practice, 16*: 79–85.

Mergenthaler, E. (1985). *Textbank Systems: Computer Science Applied in the Field of Psychoanalysis.* New York: Springer.

Mergenthaler, E. (1996). Emotion-Abstraction Patterns in verbatim protocols: A new way of describing psychotherapeutic processes. *Journal of Consulting and Clinical Psychology, 64* (6): 1306–1318.

Mergenthaler, E., & Kächele, H. (1988a). The Ulm Text Bank Management System: A new way of describing psychotherapy process. In: H. Dahl, H.

Kächele, & H. Thomä (Eds.), *Psychoanalytic Process Research Strategies* (pp. 195–212). New York: Springer-Verlag.

Mergenthaler, E., & Kächele, H. (1988b). University of Ulm: The Ulm Text Bank Research Program. In: L. Beutler & M. Crago (Eds.), *International Psychotherapy Research Program* (pp. 219–225). New York: Pergamon.

Milrod, B., et al. (2000). Open trial of psychodynamic psychotherapy for panic disorder: A pilot study. *American Journal of Psychiatry, 157* (11): 1878–1880.

Moore, B. E., & Fine, B. D. (Eds.) (1990). *Psychoanalytic Terms and Concepts.* New Haven, CT: American Psychoanalytic Association and Yale University Press.

*Moser, U. (2005). *Psychische Mikrowelten.* Göttingen: Vandenhoeck.

*Namnun, A. (1968). The problem of analyzability and the autonomous ego. *International Journal of Psychoanalysis, 49*: 770–777.

Norman, H. F., Blacker, K. H., Oremland, J. D., & Barrett, W. G. (1976). The fate of the transference neurosis after termination of a satisfactory analysis. *Journal of the American Psychoanalytic Association, 24*: 471–498.

NSF (2003). *Digital Library Initiative Phase II.* National Science Foundation (accessed 27 July 2006 at: http://.dli2.nsf.gov/).

O'Connell, L. (2001). "The Relationship between Psychological Capacities and Adult Attachment Status." PhD Dissertation, California School of Professional Psychology, Alameda, CA.

OPD Task Force (2000). OPD—*Operationalized Psychodynamic Diagnostics: Foundations and Manual.* Seattle/Toronto/Bern/Göttingen: Hogrefe & Huber.

OPD Task Force (2001). *Operationalisierte psychodynamische Diagnostik.* Bern: Huber.

*Oremland, J., Blacker, K., & Haskell, F. (1975). Incompleteness in "successful" psychoanalyses: A follow-up study. *Journal of the American Psychoanalytic Association, 23*: 819–844.

Panksepp, J. (1999). Emotions as viewed by psychoanalysis and neuroscience: An exercise in consilience. *Neuro-Psychoanalysis, 1*: 15–38.

Perneger, T. V. (1998). What's wrong with Bonferroni adjustments. *British Medical Journal, 316*: 1236–1238.

Perry, J. C. (1990). *The Defense Mechanism Rating Scales* (5th edition). Private publication, Cambridge.

Pfeffer, A. Z. (1959). A procedure for evaluating the results of psychoanalysis: A preliminary report. *Journal of the American Psychoanalytic Association, 7*: 418–444.

Pfeffer, A. Z. (1961). Follow-up study of a satisfactory analysis. *Journal of the American Psychoanalytic Association, 9*: 698–718.

Pfeffer, A. Z. (1963). The meaning of the analyst after analysis: A contribution to the theory of therapeutic results. *Journal of the American Psychoanalytic Association, 11*: 229–244.

Pilkonis, P. A., Imber, S. D., Lewis, P., & Rubinsky, P. (1984). A comparative outcome study of individual, group and conjoint psychotherapy. *Archives of General Psychiatry, 41*: 431–437.

Rapaport, D. (1959). The structure of psychoanalytic theory: A systematizing attempt. In: S. Koch (Ed.), *Psychology: A Study of a Science. (Study 1, Conceptual and Systematic). Vol. 3: Formulations of the Person and the Social Context* (pp. 55–183). New York: McGraw-Hill.

Renals, S., De Jong, F., Federico, M., Lamel, L., Sebastiani, F., Wright, R., Goldman, J., Bird, R., Stewart, D., Fleischhauer, C., Kornbluh, M., & Oard, D. (2003). *EU–US Working Group on Spoken-Word Audio Collections.* National Science Foundation (accessed 27 July at: http://www.dli2.nsf.gov/internationalprojects/working_group_reports/spoken_word.html).

Rosenberg, S. E., DeWitt, K. N., & Wallerstein, R. S. (1996). "Initial Data on Inter-rater Reliability of Scales of Psychological Capacities". Unpublished manuscript.

Roth, A., Fonagy, P., Parry, G., Target, M., et al. (1996). *What Works for Whom? A Critical Review of Psychotherapy Research.* New York: Guilford Press.

Roy, C., & Perry, J. C. (2004). Instruments for the assessment of childhood trauma in adults. *Journal of Nervous and Mental Disease, 192* (5): 343–351.

*Rudolf, G., Grande, T., Dilg, R., Jakobsen, T., Keller, W., Oberbracht, C., Pauli-Magnus, C., Stehle, S., & Wilke, S. (2001). Strukturelle Veränderungen in psychoanalytischen Behandlungen—Zur Praxisstudie analytischer Pangzeittherapien (PAL). In: U. Stuhr, M. Leuzinger-Bohleber, & M. Beutel (Eds.), *Langzeit-Psychotherapie. Perspektiven für Therapeuten und Wissenschaftler* (pp. 238–259). Stuttgart: Kohlhammer.

*Rüger, B. (2001). Statistisches Design und Repräsentativität der psychoanalytischen Katamnese-studie (DPV). In: U. Stuhr, M. Leuzinger-Bohleber, & M. Beutel (Eds.), *Langzeit-Psychotherapie. Perspektiven für Therapeuten und Wissenschaftler* (pp. 149–159). Stuttgart: Kohlhammer.

*Sandell, R. (2001). Multimodale analyse von temporären Interaktionen in der Wirksamkeit von psychoanalysen und Langzeit-Psychotherapien. In: U. Stuhr, M. Leuzinger-Bohleber, & M. Beutel (Eds.), *Langzeit-Psychotherapie. Perspektiven für Therapeuten und Wissenschaftler* (pp. 203–214). Stuttgart: Kohlhammer.

Sandell, R., Blomberg, J., Lazar, A., Carlsson, J., Broberg, J., & Schubert, J. (2000). Varieties of long-term outcome among patients in psychoanalysis and long-term psychotherapy: A review of findings in the Stockholm Outcome of Psychoanalysis and Psychotherapy Project (STOPPP). *International Journal of Psychoanalysis, 81* (5): 921–942.

Sandler, J. (1983). Reflections on some relations between psychoanalytic concepts and psychoanalytic practice. *International Journal of Psychoanalysis, 64*: 35–45.

*Sandler, J., & Dreher, A. U. (1996). *What Do Psychoanalysts Want? The Problem of Aims in Psychoanalytic Therapy.* London/New York: Routledge.

Sandler, J., Dreher, A., & Drews, S. (1991). An approach to conceptual research in psychoanalysis illustrated by a consideration of psychic trauma. *International Review of Psychoanalysis, 18* (2): 133–141.

Sashin, J. I., Eldred, S. H., & van Amerongen, S. T. (1975). A search for predictive factors in institute supervised cases: A retrospective study of 183 cases from 1959 to 1966 at the Boston Psychoanalytic Society and Institute. *International Journal of Psychoanalysis, 56*: 343–359.

Schachter, J., & Brauer, L. (2001). The effect of the analyst's gender and other factors on post-termination patient–analyst contact. *International Journal of Psychoanalysis, 82*: 1123–1132

Schepank, H. (1995). *Der Beeinträchtigungs-schwere-score.* Göttingen: Beltz Test.

Schlessinger, N., & Robbins, F. P. (1974). Assessment and follow-up in psychoanalysis. *Journal of the American Psychoanalytic Association, 22*: 542–567.

Schlessinger, N., & Robbins, F. P. (1975). The psychoanalytic process: Recurrent patterns of conflict and changes in ego functions. *Journal of the American Psychoanalytic Association, 23*: 761–782.

*Schlessinger, N., & Robbins, F. P. (1983). *A Developmental View of the Psychoanalytic Process: Follow-up Studies and Their Consequences.* Madison, CT: International Universities Press.

Seligman, M. (1995). The effectiveness of psychotherapy: The Consumer Reports study. *American Psychologist, 50* (12): 965–974.

*Sennett, R. (1998). *Der flexible Mensch.* Berlin: Berlin Verlag.

Shapiro, T. (2002). From monologue to dialogue: A transition in psychoanalytic practice. *Journal of the American Psychoanalytic Association, 50* (1): 199–219.

Shedler, J., & Westen, D. (1998). Refining the measurement of axis II: A *q*-sort procedure for assessing personality pathology. *Assessment, 5*: 335–355.

Silberchatz, G., Curtis, J. T., Fretter, P. B., & Kelly, T. J. (1988). Testing hypotheses of psychotherapeutic change processes. In: H. Dahl, H. Kächele, & H. Thomä (Eds.), *Psychoanalytic Process Research Strategies.* New York: Springer-Verlag.

*Sloane, R. B., Staples, F. R., Cristol, A. H., Yorkston, N. J., & Whipple, K. (1975). Short-term analytically oriented psychotherapy versus behavior therapy. *American Journal of Psychiatry, 132* (4): 373–377.

Smith, M. L., Glass, G. V., & Miller, T. I. (1980). *The Benefits of Psychotherapy.* Baltimore, MD: Johns Hopkins University Press.

Stewart, M. C., & Cervone, H. F. (2003). Building a new infrastructure for digital media: Northwestern University Library. *Information Technology and Libraries, 22* (2).

Strout, P. E., & Fleiss, J. L. (1979). Intraclass correlations: Uses in assessing rater reliability. *Psychological Bulletin, 86*: 420–428.

Strupp, H. H., Horowitz, L. M., & Lambert, M. J. (Eds.) (1997). *Measuring Patient Changes in Mood, Anxiety, and Personality Disorders.* Washington, DC: American Psychological Association.

Strupp, H., Schacht, T., & Henry, W. (1988). Problem–treatment–outcome congruence: A principle whose time has come. In: H. Dahl, H. Kächele, & H. Thomä (Eds.), *Psychoanalytic Process Research Strategies* (pp. 1–14). New York: Springer-Verlag.

*Stuhr, U. (2001). Methodische Überlegungen zur Kombination qualitativer und quantitativer Methoden in der psychoanalytischen Katamneseforschung und Hinweise zu ihrer Integration. In: U. Stuhr, M. Leuzinger-Bohleber, & M. Beutel (Eds.), *Langzeit-Psychotherapie. Perspektiven für Therapeuten und Wissenschaftler* (pp. 133–148). Stuttgart: Kohlhammer.

*Stuhr, U., Leuzinger-Bohleber, M., & Beutel, M. (Eds.) (2001). *Langzeit-Psychotherapie. Perspektiven für Therapeuten und Wissenschaftler.* Stuttgart: Kohlhammer. Verlag.

Sundin, E., Armelius, B., & Nilsson, T. (1994). Reliability studies of scales of psychological capacities: A new method to address psychological change. *Psychoanalysis & Contemporary Thought, 17*: 591–617.

Szecsödy, I., Varvin, S., Amadei, G., Stoker, J., Beenen, F., & Klockars, L. (1997). "The European Multi-Site Collaborative Study of Psychoanalysis (Sweden, Finland, Norway, Holland and Italy)." Paper presented at the Symposium on Outcome Research, IPA Congress, Barcelona, Spain (August).

*Terr, L. C. (1991). Childhood traumas: An outline and overview. *American Journal of Psychiatry, 148*: 10–20.

Terr, L. C. (1994). *Unchained Memories: True Stories of Traumatic Memories, Lost and Found.* New York: Basic Books.

Thomä, H., & Kächele, H. (1987). *Psychoanalytic Practice, Vol. 1: Principles.* New York: Springer-Verlag.

*Tschuschke, V., & Kächele, H. (1998). Was leistet Psychotherapie? Zur Diskussion um differentielle Effekte unterschiedlicher Behandlungskonzepte. In: M. Fäh & G. Fischer (Eds.), *Sinn und Unsinn in der Psychotherapieforschung* (pp. 137–162). Gießen: Psychosozial Verlag.

*Tschuschke, V., Kächele, H., & Hölzer, M. (2000). Gibt es unterschiedlich effektive Formen von Psychotherapie? In: M. Hochgerner, & E. Wildberger (Eds.), *Was heilt in der Psychotherapie?* (pp. 90–127). Vienna: Facultas-Univ. Verlag.

Tuckett, D. (1993). Some thoughts on the presentation and discussion of the clinical material in psychoanalysis. *International Journal of Psychoanalysis, 74*: 1175–1188.

Waldron, S., Scharf, R., Hurst, D., Firestein, S., & Burton, A. (2004). What happens in a psychoanalysis? A view through the lens of the analytic process scales. *International Journal of Psychoanalysis, 85* (2): 443–466.

Wallerstein, R. S. (1986). *Forty-Two Lives in Treatment: A Study of Psychoanalysis and Psychotherapy.* New York: Guilford Press.

Wallerstein, R. S. (1988a). Assessment of structural change in psychoanalytic therapy and research. *Journal of the American Psychoanalytic Association (Suppl.) 36*: 241–261.

Wallerstein, R. S. (1988b). One psychoanalysis or many? *International Journal of Psychoanalysis, 69* (1): 5–21.

Wallerstein, R. S. (1989a). Follow-up in psychoanalysis: Clinical and research values. *Journal of the American Psychoanalytic Association, 37* (4): 921–941.

Wallerstein, R. S. (1989b). The psychotherapy research project of the Menninger Foundation: An overview. *Journal of Consulting and & Clinical Psychology, 57*: 195–205.

Wallerstein, R. S. (1990). Foreword. In: L. Luborsky & P. Crits-Cristoph, *Understanding Transference: The Core Conflictual Relationship Theme Method.* New York: Basic Books.

Wallerstein, R. S. (1991). Assessment of structural change in psychoanalytic therapy and research. *Journal of the American Psychoanalytic Association, 36 (Suppl.)*: 241–261.

Wallerstein, R. S. (1992). Psychoanalysis: The common ground. In: R. Wallerstein (Ed.), *The Common Ground of Psychoanalysis.* (pp. 203–242). Northvale, NJ: Jason Aronson.

Wallerstein, R. S. (1995). *The Talking Cures: The Psychoanalyses and the Psychotherapies.* New Haven, CT: Yale University Press.

Wallerstein, R. S. (1996). Psychoanalytic research: Where do we disagree? *International Psychoanalysis: The Newsletter of the IPA, 5* (1): 15–17.

*Wallerstein, R. S. (1997). Katamnesen in der Psychoanalyse zu ihrem klinischen und empirischen Wert. In: M. Leuzinger-Bohleber & U. Stuhr (Eds.), *Psychoanalysen im Rückblick, Methoden, Ergebnisse und Perspektiven der neueren Katamneseforschung* (pp. 46–60). Gießen: Psychosozial-Verlag.

Wallerstein, R. S. (1998). Psychoanalysis: The future of an illusion? *International Psychoanalysis: The Newsletter of the IPA,* 7 (1) (accessed 17 May 2004 at: http://eseries.ipa.org.uk/prev/newsletter/98–1/wallerst.htm).

*Wallerstein, R. S. (2001a). Die Generationen der Psychotherapieforschung—Ein Überblick. In: U. Stuhr, M. Leuzinger-Bohleber, & M. Beutel (Eds.), *Langzeit-Psychotherapie. Perspektiven für Therapeuten und Wissenschaftler* (pp. 38–60). Stuttgart: Kohlhammer.

Wallerstein, R. S. (2001b). The generations of psychotherapy research: An overview. *Psychoanalytic Psychology, 18*: 243–267.

*Wallerstein, R. S. (2002). The generations of psychotherapy research: An overview. In: M. Leuzinger-Bohleber & M. Target, M. (Eds.), *Outcomes of Psychoanalytic Treatment: Perspectives for Therapists and Researchers* (pp. 30–52). London: Whurr; New York: Brunner-Routledge.

Wallerstein, R. S., & DeWitt, K. N. (1997). Intervention modes in psychoanalysis and in psychoanalytic psychotherapies: A revised classification. In: J. L. Ahumada, J. Olagary, A. K. Richards, & A. D. Richards (Eds.), *The Perverse Transference and Other Matters* (pp. 87–114). New York: Jason Aronson.

Wallerstein, R. S., DeWitt, K. N., Hartley, D., Rosenberg, S. E., & Zilberg, N. J. (1986). *The Scales of Psychological Capacities, version 1.* Unpublished.

Wallerstein, R. S., & Fonagy, P. (1999). Psychoanalytic research and the IPA: History, present status and future potential. *International Journal of Psychoanalysis, 80*: 91–109.

Wallerstein, R. S., Robbins, L., Sargent, H., & Luborsky, L. (1956). The Psychotherapy Research Project of the Menninger Foundation. *Bulletin of the Menninger Clinic, 20*: 221–280.

Wallerstein, R. S., & Sampson, H. (1971). Issues in research in the psychoanalytic process. *International Journal of Psychoanalysis, 52*: 11–51.

Wallerstein, R. S., et al. (1957). *Hospital Treatment of Alcoholism: A Comparative Experimental Study*. Menninger Monograph Series, No. 11. New York: Basic Books.

Wampold, B. (2001). *The Great Psychotherapy Debate: Models, Methods and Findings*. Hillsdale, NJ: Lawrence Erlbaum.

Weinryb, R. M., Rössel, R. J., & Asberg, M. (1991). The Karolinska Psychodynamic Profile: I. Validity and dimensionality. *Acta Psychiatrica Scandinavica, 83*: 64–92.

West, M., & Sheldon-Keller, A. (1994). *Patterns of Relating: An Adult Attachment Perspective*. New York: Guilford Press.

Zilberg, N. J., Wallerstein, R. S., DeWitt, K. N., Hartley, D., & Rosenberg, S. E. (1991). A conceptual analysis and strategy for assessing structural change. *Psychoanalysis & Contemporary Thought, 14*: 317–342.

INDEX